AGAINST THE GRAIN
The Literary Life of a Poet

By Reed Whittemore

Poetry

Heroes & Heroines, 1946
An American Takes a Walk, 1956
The Self-Made Man and Other Poems, 1959
The Boy from Iowa: Poems and Essays, 1962
The Fascination of the Abomination: Poems, Stories, and Essays, 1963
Return, Alpheus: A Poems for the Literary Elders of Phi Beta Kappa, 1964
Poems, New and Selected, 1967
Fifty Poems Fifty, 1970
The Mother's Breast and the Father's House, 1974
The Feel of Rock: Poems of Three Decades, 1982
The Past, the Future, The Present: Poems Selected and New, 1990
Ten from Ten & One More (chapbook), 2007
A Season of Waiting: Selected Poems: 1946-2006 (trans. into Hebrew
   by Moshe Dor), 2007

Other

(Editor) *Robert Browning*, 1960
Little Magazines (pamphlet), 1963
Ways of Misunderstanding Poetry (lecture), 1965
The Little Magazine and Contemporary Literature (with others), 1966
From Zero to the Absolute (essays), 1967
William Carlos Williams: Poet from Jersey, 1975
The Poet as Journalist: Life at The New Republic, 1976
A Whittemore Miscellany (sound recording), 1977
Pure Lives: The Early Biographers, 1988
Whole Lives: Shapers of Modern Biography, 1989
*Six Literary Lives: The Shared Impiety of Adams, London, Sinclair,
   Williams, Dos Passos, and Tate*, 1993

AGAINST THE GRAIN
The Literary Life of a Poet

A Memoir by
Reed Whittemore

Foreword by Garrison Keillor

DRYAD PRESS WASHINGTON, D.C.
In association with the University of Alaska Press

Text and cover design by Sandy Rodgers
Text is typeset in ITC Giovanni Book: 10.5 over 14

The paper used in this publication meets the minimum requirement of American National Standard for Information Sciences — Permanence of paper for Printed Library Materials, ANSIZ39.48

Dryad Press
P.O. Box 11233
Takoma Park, Maryland 20913
www.dryadpress.com; publisher@dryadpress.com

Against the Grain is published in association with the University of Alaska Press (www.uaf.edu/uapress) and is distributed by the Chicago Distribution Center, University of Chicago Press, 800-621-2736, fax: 800-621-8476.

The author is grateful for permission to quote from previously published and unpublished sources:

The letters and excerpts from Ezra Pound copyright ©2007 by the Estates of Mary de Rachewiltz and Omar S. Pound and used by permission of New Directions Publishing Corporation. The letters and poetry from William Carlos Williams are copyright ©2007 by the Estates of William Eric Williams and Paul H. Williams and used by permission of New Directions Publishing Corporation. The correspondence by Arthur Mizener is used by permission of Rosemary Mizener Colt and the correspondence with Howard Nemerov by permission of Margaret Nemerov. The letters from Anne Sexton are reprinted with permission of Sterling Lord Literistic, Inc. The letter from Allen Ginsberg copyright ©2007 by The Allen Ginsberg Estate and used with permission. Kenneth Fearing's "Andy and Jerry and Joe" copyright ©1994 by Jubal Fearing and Phoebe Fearing. A continuation of these acknowledgments will be found in the List of Photographs and Art (p. ix-x) and Acknowledgments (p. 329).

Library of Congress Cataloging-in-Publication Data

Whittemore, Reed, 1919-
    Against the grain : the literary life of a poet : a memoir / by Reed Whittemore ;
        foreword by Garrison Keillor.
        p. cm.
    Includes index.
    ISBN-13: 978-1-928755-09-8 (alk. paper)
        1. Whittemore, Reed, 1919- 2. Poets, American—20th century—Biography.
    I. Title.
    PS3545.H868Z53   2007
    811'.54—dc22   2007029385
    [B]

For Helen

Contents

List of Photographs and Art

Foreword

REED WHITTEMORE owns the only sort of immortality that matters to
a writer, which is to have written things that people remember years later.
There is the perfect imagist poem about the enormous silence that follows
after a high school band finishes practicing on the football field in a small
town and the poem about the man waiting and waiting and waiting for
the woman upstairs to get dressed for the party he sincerely doesn't want
to go to. There is the poem about the French Foreign Legion and the heat
and the gin and the bitters and everyone itching and bitching. There is his
fabulous rant against New York ("Let me not be unfair Lord to New York
that sink that sewer/ Where the best and the worst and the middle/ Of our
land and all others go in their days of hope to be made over/ Into granite
careerists") and his "Psalm" ("The Lord feeds some of His prisoners better than others") and his love song to America—

> Your suitors grow old, old, their lyrics sodden,
> And their passions fizz in the soft westering rhetoric,
> But you, oh Nik Nak Nookie, Dairie Queene,
> From all your Southern Cal to Keep Maine Green....

— which springs from a deep comic fountain, the deep well of American
jitterbug language and spirited jazz, and like so many of the jazz greats,
Reed ("Sweets") Whittemore likes to hang out in professor clothes. Poet
clothes are for tourists. Your real American poet doesn't need to go
around in a serape and sandals, Jim Bob, he goes undercover in a blue suit
and white shirt and you don't know he is a poet unless you read his stuff.

Memorability is no small matter. There are Large Pachyderms in
Poetry World with lists of awards as long as a pool cue, whose names give
off deluxe reverberations of distinguishment and rotundity and luminos-
ity and enchiladatude, and you know them and I know them, and they
come to Your Town to speak and to read, and the literati are in a happy
dither about who will sit next to Whom, and yet if one tries to remember,

say, a particular poem his or her eminence wrote, there is only a series of graynesses and a faint recollection of scattered precipitation. They are like the lady in W's poem "Mrs. Benedict" who is remembered many years later for all her talk but what she said is, alas, beyond recall.

This prospect is so painful to us writers that we can't talk about it. We struggle to put the goods on the page (acid-free so it will last and last) in a durable form and we have our shining moment and then it's gone and the future of our hard work is awful to contemplate. We come upon ourselves in a used bookstore in good condition for 35 cents, we spot ourselves on a library shelf, and the most we can possibly hope for — the most — is that once a year or so, a tall bookish young woman will pull us out and open us up and something, something, will catch her eye to the extent that she will sit down and read. Maybe our friends the English teachers will put us in front of their restless charges but that is not the same as being read as we know who have been English teachers. We are hoping for that tall girl in the khaki shorts who has been striving for success and now she needs friendship and understanding and she turns to books.

And if she gets to W and passes over the two yards of Whitman and pulls out Whittemore's masterful *The Mother's Breast & The Father's House*, she will notice his haiku ("A traditional haiku has seventeen syllables/Hasn't it?") alongside his New York rant and his marvelous fable of marriage ("Well there was the story of the little pig/Who grew up to be an enormous handsome but anal hog/And was always sweeping and dusting the slops/So that the widow Brown thought she was going mad") and she will come upon his little catechism:

> To achieve faith one must suffer for decades
> And to suffer one must get up early and raise a family and go to work
> Suffering is middle class
> It was invented by Benjamin Franklin
> It begins with the search for a loaf of bread and ends with funeral expenses
> It is composed of ten parts body and five parts bank account
> It is caused by God
> Being part of His clumsy plan to extract positive charges from His creation
> In anticipation of something better

It is a sustained, witty, morally serious wham-bam poem that if she were to stand up at the Grand Poetry Slam tonight in front of the young and

restless drinking vodka Mazurkas in the basement of Guy's Lounge and if
she shouted out the whole thing, people would clap and yell for more.
She could holler out the Foreign Legion poem and "The Abominable
Snowman" and she could recite—

In good ole day ze king need no committee.
Was nize,
Him says, them does; him sells, them buys.
Good system.
But then come big push make king one of guys.
So king buy chairs, say me no king me chairman.
So knocked off paradise.

What makes R.W. permanently readable and relevant is his wit and
humor, which is the underground spring that keeps the gardens of
American literature green. Even in Whitman (yes! Those long lists!) and
Dickinson ("Hope is the thing with feathers"), even in Hawthorne and
Melville, Emerson, and on into our own day, and in R.W.'s kin Elizabeth
Bishop and Howard Nemerov and Kenneth Rexroth, the comic muse is
what gives them a voice that sounds contemporary to us decades later. It's
what makes Mark Twain readable. And also Sweets Whittemore.

I did not meet him in a library but in a classroom in Minneapolis in
July, 1964, a movie-star handsome poet and teacher conducting a class in
modern American Lit. I sat in the middle of the room. He paced up and
down the aisles as he talked about literature as the defender of humanity
against the violence of the mass, a noble undertaking but also a job of
work that a man or woman does in the ordinary course of things, just as
you would plant a field or weld a fence. He was an engaging teacher, hungry for a conversation which I could not give him, being too crippled by
self-consciousness, too aware that I went from his class to my job in the
scullery, carrying stacks of steaming-hot dishes to the head of the cafeteria line, but his one line about literature being a job stuck with me and
sticks still. Other teachers dazzled us with how they could reel off erudite
paragraphs — no hands! — about the intellectual cross-currents of the
age in which this poor ignorant writer toiled at his task, but Mr.
Whittemore took a ground view of literature.

I went out and bought with my own money earned in the scullery the
hardcover edition of his *The Fascination of the Abomination* and read it over

and over, as one does if one is broke and invests in a book — for the afflu-
ent, books are shiny beads, and for the poor, books are bread — and I
loved the story of the thirteen-year-old boy riding his bike no-handed for
seventeen miles of paved and unpaved road on Cape Cod for no reason
other than to do an amazing thing and the story of the boy lying in bed
and waiting for 12:29 so he can pull the string he has rigged to turn on
the radio on the bureau in exact time for the tubes to warm up for Sammy
Richey and His Connecticut Smoothies on "Noonday Melodies" on
WTIC. (And now, reading this memoir, I see that those boys were Reed
himself, growing up in New Haven, amusing himself amidst the implaca-
ble troubles of his elders.)

The teacher who paced that classroom was a man who did not find
Hamlet a useful role model and who was not, perhaps, as stunned by
Thoreau as some of us were when we were 17. He came along a little early
to go live in a commune and grow beans and weave his own shirt. World
War II veterans tended not to do that and, having learned how to live with
the Army, tended not to look on all social organizations as corrupt and
worthy of subversion, only as slow, frustrating, worth struggling with,
capable of accomplishing good, and, in the end, much more interesting
than a pond, more worthy of attention. And so Mr. Whittemore left
Minnesota soon after I met him and went off to Washington to become
a laureate, critic, teacher, biographer, and satirist. Politics is in need of
poetry if it will have a humane soul and not be locked up in a professional cabinet, and so he served as a poet of the capital. The idea of a life
of bemused separation seemed unworthy to him. And so he became an
amiable radical, a servant of the greater invisible community, and perhaps
because he considered that that community could use a good rant against
New York, the capital of American Lit, that this would be a useful tonic
against those dreamy photographs of the Chrysler Building at night, he
went to work and did it —

Oh New York let me be fair you hell town
I was born to the north of you have lived to the west of you
I have sneaked up on you by land air and sea and been robbed in your
    clip joints
I have left you hundreds of times in the dream that I could
Leave you
            but always you sit there

Sinking
        my dearest my sweet
Would you buy these woids?

The happy servant of the community walks that no-man's-land between
lyrical and comic poetry where so few poets dare to go —

To pass through the season of loss and emerge with a good suit
Is to thank God
And take inventory

"The poet is somebody who writes poems because he has failed at everything else," wrote R when he was in one of those long moods, but failure
is useful camouflage for a satirist—

I can see no artists at all, but I know that they're out there
Struggling against the heat and the walls to retain their integrity,
Which some of them know and some of them don't know that they can't
    possibly keep.
           But going hard at it anyway, as I am.

As he did, and now, as he rests in his old age, those of us who remember
the high school band, the man pacing downstairs, the New York rant, the
psalm, the Foreign Legion, and much more, are given this feast of a memoir of a man of letters of our time, to rummage in his desk and read his
mail and find out where those poems came from. "Some books are undeservedly forgotten," said W.H. Auden. "None are undeservedly remembered." Mr. Whittemore's are remembered and that is all the reward one
could wish for.

GARRISON KEILLOR

Preface

CALL HIM R. I do in this literary memoir of Reed Whittemore, a now aged poet, essayist, critic, little magazine editor, biographer, teacher. Some years ago I wrote an article about R's literary life for the reference work *Contemporary Authors*. It began in first person, but shifted almost imperceptibly to a third-person narration. I don't remember why exactly — perhaps that *I* seemed too self-serving as it often did for New Englanders of my generation; perhaps referring to R as *he* gave the narration a much-needed relief from the relentless I. . . I. . . I. Though such memoirs are rare, there has been the example of fellow New Englander Henry Adams in *The Education of Henry Adams*, a book that was central to R's thinking about American culture. As he later wrote in a book about the art of biography, "for most of my adult life, I have lived with *The Education*, argued about it, and written about it or near it."

Every life is made up of hundreds of details, much too many for any biographer or autobiographer to accumulate, let alone write down (though the size of some modern tomes indicates those biographers have tried). The author of any life, another's or his own, must select details that can be shaped into a coherent and truthful story. R became preoccupied with such concerns in writing *William Carlos Williams: Poet from Jersey* in the mid-1970s.

Back to the *Education*. Adams placed his third-person self into the midst of American culture and wrote virtually nothing of his personal life. Read the book and you will not hear about his marriage, about his love for Clover, about her suicide, about his grief. Adams chose to exclude all this and dealt primarily with his intellectual life. In *Against the Grain*, while R's wife Helen and their four children make important appearances, the focus is primarily on the literary life.

At the same time, I do not pretend to explore the growth of this poet's mind — there's only limited room at the table for the Wordsworthian sublime; besides, that's not my inclination. Rather, this memoir gives glimpses into R's work over 60 years, his poetic and literary concerns, including numbers of poems that he still cares for, and recollections of friends who have meant a great deal to him and without whom he would likely have traveled a different path. He has probably omitted much that has been important, though not purposely — but only because of his failing memory.

Shelley once wrote, in full rhetorical flight, poets are the "unacknowledged legislators of the world" — though some poets would still like to think so, R long ago left such delusions behind. Still, that doesn't mean he's ever stopped trying to make it so.

AGAINST THE GRAIN
The Literary Life of a Poet

Beginnings

I wish you first to picture this hero at his breakfast sitting in his high chair in the kitchen. His porridge is in the porridge bowl before him. He eats porridge with a little (but highly symbolic) silver spoon, then picks up the bowl, shouts "All gone!" and throws it over his shoulder. Of course the reader may now wonder skeptically if he really remembers these events. The answer is that of course he does because he was there — was he not? — and does not wish his memories to be questioned. After all they are backed up by dozens of snapshots of my small hero. In them he is chubby and round-faced. He is overdressed, and in winter he is invisible behind coats, caps, mittens. There is usually a dog beside him, a white Samoyed, and he seems a tiny personage beside his two large half-brothers, in knickers, with slicked-back hair. Always of course there is Mother near, perhaps holding him and smiling at him while standing beside her Wills Sainte Claire (what a fancy car) with a metal goose flying on the radiator.

But where is little R's father in all this? From the photographic evidence he seems always to have been busy at his office or making house calls (*those* were the days) except once when someone caught him holding little R on his shoulder.

And what of other characters? No pictures remain but they may reveal themselves slowly as this hero grows into his proper geographic, social and historic contexts. Thus geographically he started life in Southern Connecticut, in a town (New Haven) with a large university right in its center. (The university will be of no interest until later.) In R's growing time this center could be reached by taking a "K" trolley down Whitney Avenue past the Peabody Museum (full of dinosaurs) to, perhaps, the corner of Church and Chapel Streets. So when he grew large enough to have money in his pocket he rode that trolley down to that corner in order to buy jazz records at Loomis's music store. Otherwise his growing took place close to home, where he practiced riding his bent Columbia bicycle no-handed on Edgehill Road and St. Ronan Street. Still the trolley remained in memory years later in "The Elm City," a poem of reverie in cold Minnesota.

> The hard yellow reversible wicker seats
> Sit in my mind's warm eye varnished row on row
> In the old yellow childhood trolley
> At the end of the line at Cliff Street where the conductor
> Swings the big wooden knob on the tall control box
> Clangs the dishpan bell and we wander off
>
> To tiptoe on stones and look up at bones in cases
> In the cold old stone and bone of the Peabody Museum
> Where the dinosaur and the mastodon stare us down
> And the Esquimaux and the Indians stare us down
>
> In New Haven
> The Elm City
>
> I left that town long ago for war and folly
> Phylogeny rolled to a stop at the old Peabody
> I still hear the dishpan bell of the yellow trolley

Now, socially. R's family was, on his mother's side (Carr), northern New England though its accents were not as nasal as Calvin Coolidge's (to whom this northern side claimed a most remote connection). The father's side on the other hand was largely local — that is, southern New England but surely not as far south as Bridgeport. Nor was it possessed of ties to the snobbish New York set permeating Greenwich. In other words, this family on both sides was Yankee though not promiscuous about it, being too well bred.

And history? Let me turn to photos again, especially an early shot now hanging on R's closet door that perhaps gives a glimpse of later troubles. In it R is perhaps four. He is wearing a sailor suit and is sitting on a tricycle in the middle of the driveway of an ugly stucco house at 175 East Rock Road, not quite a block from Whitney Avenue. He is holding the handlebars firmly and has his feet firmly on the pedals, but he is not looking firm. Is he or is he not planning to make the machine move? Does he or does he not know that it *can* move? On these points the picture is silent, and while I now shouldn't worry about him — knowing that he did make his tricycles and bicycles move — I do worry a little, seeing an odd passivity there as if....

Yes, for when I move to a later picture hanging right next to the troubled tricycle I seem to see more of the same. In this he is sixteen. He is standing on a dock between his mother and father, with the prow of an oceangoing steamer as background. His mother is wearing a cloche, looking smart and smiling. His suited father is trying to smile though troubled by the wind blowing his hair. But as for R? I am sorry to say that he seems expressionless there too. If I look closely, I can see a very slight smirk lurking in the face, not in the lips so much as the eyes, but since he tended to be scornful of the world at an early age, I may be imposing something that is not there. At any rate, either with or without a smirk the photo blankness is worrisome.

Also worrisome is a photo of R's twin half brothers Frank and Dick, taken perhaps before he was born. They were eleven years older than R, yet more striking than their age difference is the radically different mood or manner the picture itself puts forth. It is a studio portrait as if from a different era and culture, and in it the two little look-alikes, dressed to the teeth, are standing solemnly stiff and determined with a studio rocking horse between them. I'll murmur "daguerreotype" cautiously, for the images are brown-and-white rather than black-and-white. They suggest (to my ignorance) the early days of photography featuring a cumbersome camera perched on a tripod and manned by a busy technician who fusses at getting the boys properly posed, then retreats under his camera blanket and cries out "Hold it! Don't move!"

I find it relevant that R as a child had every reason to think the determined twins lived in a world unrelated to his own. Psychologically he was indeed an only child, and his expressionlessness in the tricycle photo may well have concealed annoyance that in his aloneness he had just been referred to by some adult as Little Reed. "Reed" is a flossy name anyway, but "Little Reed" is flossiness diminished to cuteness. Little R definitely didn't like it. It put him off on an island with "small fry" (his father's phrase). It made him somehow meaningless and disconnected from everybody else, as on his tricycle.

Not that the father liked being called "Big Reed" either — but he didn't complain. He was not a complainer. He was a neat small man with a neat small moustache. He had become a doctor because his father and his father's father had been doctors, successful ones. He (an unsuccessful one) first entered practice with his father, Dr. Frank Hamilton Whittemore, in 1904 and went to his office mechanically for more than thirty years. He played bridge well and built complicated early radios in a basement workshop. He was low on passion except when angry — at FDR, Franklin Delano Roosevelt, for instance or Mrs. FDR — and when angry he said little, preferring to mumble and let his ears grow red. Also, as a New Englander he was reticent about major matters such as (indeed) the tragic death of the twins' mother. Consequently, neither he nor little R's mother ever told little R of the death.

That first wife is a true scholarly problem. R knows little about her even now but the evidence is strong that she was living with Big Reed and their twins in the house of Big Reed's widowed mother (always known to R as Nangma) at No. 193 East Rock Road in New Haven at the time of the tragedy. Yet little R was to become grown, and to be long out of Yale, out of the Air Force, and into the teaching of English in faraway Carleton College — with both Mother and Father long dead — before a Carleton colleague, a former New Havenite, reported that before R was born there had been a neighborhood dinner party several blocks away at which the first wife excused herself and went upstairs. There, with Big Reed in attendance, she died — of ptomaine poisoning. R's informant added that the death had been the talk of the town and she wondered why R had not known about it. So did little R, and so now do I, imagining that after the event the rich and dignified party host and hostess might have at least seen the inside of a courtroom.

But now I'll go back and enlarge upon circumstances leading to little R's move from 175 East Rock Road to Grandmother's house at No. 193. My guess is that R's mother, as a replacement wife, had started at 175 rather than 193 at her own request, she being a little unmonied girl from North Adams, Massachusetts, teaching school in the Palisades when Big Reed found her. So R's father and she, marrying within a year of the poisoning, had moved into a separate establishment. But then Nangma — who was no fool — must have said that she needed to be taken care of and won. And for all of little R's childhood she was his mother's enemy.

R's mother called her, among other things, "Deep-Purple Nangma" because she was often formally dressed with a purple choker around her neck when she stepped forth in the morning from her two-room second-

Big R and Little R

Little R at nine months…

…and at under two

R's mother at 193 East Rock Road

floor quarters to "issue orders" to her "troops." Her troops were Lottie the cook and her husband John, the butler and houseman. Lottie was round and black, dressed in blue with a white apron and black patent-leather shoes with one strap across the instep. John was tall and black in a white coat, often in the pantry cleaning silverware with paste in a copper sink, or he was outside sweeping the front walk, or smoking in the cellar — where he told R about railroads and winning at the numbers.

When Nangma had completed her daily "tour of duty" with them (it is not clear where R's mother picked up this military verbiage), she would return to her chambers for the day, letting Lottie bring her lunch there (her rooms were, except for Lottie, off-limits). She would not come out again until supper time when she would enter the dining room in her somehow ever deeper purple, and would there "preside" even though saying nothing authoritative (with R's Father also saying nothing authoritative) while R's mother sat at the head of the table. It seemed that her chief military job at supper was that of correcting R's table manners and telling him — when he dutifully said after dessert that he had had "a great sufficiency" — that he was excused.

Nangma allowed Mother to order the meals but little else. The dead living room was Nangma's living room, the vast Chinese vase her vase, the excellent house her house. The domain of Mother's became two-and-a-half bedrooms on the second floor — one was R's — plus a small room called the den in the rear on the first floor where bridge was played once or twice a week with just two other couples. When R's father lost his not-vast capital in a radio stock, Nangma knew what to do. She set up a trust for her money that bypassed Father and Mother, leaving — after her own losses in the Crash, and after several years of gifts to the twins Frank and Dick as they finished college (and Frank law school) — a small amount to be divided among them and R. R's mother went to drinking.

Of course it is at this point that R's childish simplicities could use a further explanation describing the mother-Nangma relationship. Naturally R couldn't understand why his mother had it in for Nangma. Nangma never told him — as his mother did — that his little radio was too loud, though Nangma was of course deaf as a post. Nangma never entered R's room except when he was sick — and then she wouldn't complain, just stroke his head. And Nangma let him do pretty much what he wanted in

the house even though it was her house — as R's mother kept mentioning unpleasantly. After all, R had his own fine bedroom there looking out
on East Rock Road, and his own attic playroom with his electric train and
chemistry set, and his own basement workbench.

How old was he when the unpleasantness in the house became
almost physical? I don't know if R can say — it harbored within him for
years and became a poem "When Father Left in the Morning" in the
1970s, when he was experiencing his own difficulties.

When father left in the morning
He had the mark of evening
On him, but at evening the evening
Was wholly evening.
He lay with forever
After supper.

Mother watched him
From the other bed,
Brushing her hair back, looking for slippers,
Smoking.
Somewhere out in the hall
Were the living. She was ill.

The moon revolved
Over East Rock Road.
The Packard sat by the curb.
I lay in my bed in the next room
Listening,
Waiting for news.

But the news in the evening
Was always the same news,
And in the morning
The drift was to evening.
I was grown
Before morning came.

But let unpleasantness be deferred for a while, though the reader should
understand that it existed and that R was not easy with his mother about
it. He found her to be a much better mother when she didn't mention
Nangma at all but busied herself in her own workroom at her many proj-

ects (including pasting pictures on plywood for R to cut up into puzzles). Then she could often be heard softly singing as if all were well in her world, especially singing a song about a Williams man who went far far away. It was mostly when she was in bed at night that R in the next room knew of her anger by overhearing it, that is, by hearing her Nangma-venom aimed at Father, hearing it build slowly as Father was going to sleep, and hearing him mutter at intervals, "Yes dear."

But I'll put aside such evenings and turn to mornings. On a usual school morning at No. 193 R wakes up in his comfortable bed with all his small-fry paraphernalia scattered about. He trots to the bathroom in his pajamas. He pees. He trots into their room and stands at his father's elbow as Father stands at the bedroom's little sink and strops his razor. His father is already dressed except for a starched shirt and its separate stiff collar, which are always temporarily stretched out on his bed, the collar tied to the shirt — at the back only — by a gold collar button. He puts down the razor and asks R what is next. "You lather," R says. "Hundred percent," Father says and picks up his little Yardley soap dish in order to rub his soft lather brush in it. He puts a touch of lather on R's nose, then whizzes the brush all over his own face (but not the mustache) and neck, then says, "Now?" And R says, "Now you do it." And Father says, "Hundred percent."

He is wearing a white undershirt and neatly pressed gray pants, and from their waist his gray suspenders hang down neatly. He is also wearing his black silk socks and his black patent leather shoes. He starts with his right temple, then moves to the left, then creeps down to his difficult chin with a mole on it that has to be skirted, and cuts away at tiny clumps with short jerky movements. Then he moves to his throat and changes his style again. He sticks his tongue out and bites at it (R thinks this is funny) as he executes long dangerous upward sweeps. He is done in no time. He draws back his funny tongue. He rinses the razor and dries it on a paper towel. He says, "That's that." And R says "Hundred per cent."

And Mother from her bed says, "Thank God."

Ah but Father still has to move over to the bed for shirt and collar. He puts them on quickly and buttons all the buttons except at the top where a second gold collar button has to be inserted under his shaved neck. That button has first to be found in a little leather box on his bureau and then attached (1) through the two holes in the shirt, and (2) through the two holes in the collar, the operation stirring up tongue-wiggling. But now he is done. He takes his well-pressed coat from his neat closet, puts the coat on, checks his shaving art again in the mirror, and heads down for breakfast saying, "You get dressed now." And R goes to his room to do so, with Mother saying "Thank God" from her bed again.

There are episodes of R's childhood that remain vivid still. In one, he's alone in the backseat of his mother's Wills Sainte Claire. She is driving and talking with a friend. R is bored, bouncing around on the backseat, fooling with the door handle. And now, surprise, he is out on the dirt road with scuffed knees watching the car drive off without him. He is running after it, crying. Years later, artist daughter Cate memorialized the story in a triptych of paintings.

⸺

Though R's memory has been getting poorer, it is likely that soon after a shaving session he is driven down Whitney Avenue to perhaps Edwards Street in an unmemorable car by his mother (she would not have her fine late Model A Ford Convertible until later) to be educated at a little private school, Mrs. Weiss's. He soon falls down the school's front steps, breaking his right wrist, and no further learning takes place there. Then he changes schools and is to be found walking several blocks down Whitney Avenue — all by himself — to Canner Street Elementary where again learning is limited to just one lesson though at least *inside* the school. There he is to be found sitting in the back row of a class in Music Appreciation and listening to a French composition by someone French (perhaps the name is San Swan?) that is somehow *about* a swan and that the teacher says *sounds* like a swan. So much for Canner Street Elementary.

And now, with no further education occurring, R has become grown enough to be driven to Hopkins Grammar School across town. And here too the learning seems to have been singular since in three years he reads only *The Vicar of Wakefield*. Decades later I am still wondering how a respectable teacher perversely named Mr. Reid (Vic) at a respectable school — which the sign out front says was founded in 1660 — could have limited R's education not only to one book, but to that book. I recently took *The Vicar* from the library and found it amusing but surely much too archaic a sample of the novel form to appeal to a twelve-year-old. I'll let *The Vicar* go back to the library in peace so that R's real education may proceed at home.

Daughter Cate's series of paintings of Little R, bored, in the backseat of his mother's car, falling out, then running after it (above and opposite page).

I'll add parenthetically that God was not much of a presence in R's young life. "Monk Bede," a poem that he wrote years later, opens with a brief memory of his growing up without much religion.

If as a child I was dropped in a bowl by a bishop,
Or was otherwise handled with thumbs by godly authority,
I don't know it. The best of my memory informs me that my soul suffered
Little from churches and tracts, and grew into puberty
Without any provocation other than reason....

193 East Rock Road was a white building with rhododendrons under the front window and a heavy brass doorknocker that butler and houseman John made shine. Beyond the doorknocker was a front hall with Nang-ma's Chinese vase next to a long dark table containing only a silver tray for visitors to place their cards in. To the right of the hall was the dining room, with a heavy sideboard and another dark table, this one for dining. To the left of the hall was the living room, with a gas-heater fireplace, long bookcases holding uncut books, two stiff couches, and a big blue leather

rocking chair next to a table covered with *Saturday Evening Posts*. In a corner was a grand piano with a player mechanism hidden in a drawer under the keyboard. Next to the piano was a case for piano rolls. "The Blue Danube" had a small, neatly pencilled circle on it, as guide for a pre-reader.

To the rear of the hall the staircase rose to a landing with a grandfather clock. When R climbed the fourteen stairs, passed the slow pendulum, and walked around the landing, he came to his own room, three more steps up, front right. In the hall he did nothing except stroke Cat, who slept on the heat register under the silver tray.

Number 193 had a gravel driveway leading to a backyard where there was space for only one large tree, one broken swing and a graveled turn-around area in front of a single garage door. The door led to a two-car space in the cellar garage containing (by this time) Mother's fine Ford and Father's boring Chrysler coupe. Luckily a good-size vacant field existed beyond No.193's small lot, and it was easily reached through a hole in the fence. There one could (and did) dig a clubhouse. R was the only member of the club and it was admittedly a dull club until a neighbor boy joined in order to help enlarge it so that two could fit. Unfortunately the neighbor boy then bloodied his hand while shoveling and ran home down the middle of Edgehill Road shouting, "What a cut!" and never returned. So the club became boring again since R's other friends (all except Jane and she was a girl, though her back yard abutted on R's) lived far away on St. Ronan Street. R then gave up the clubhouse and moved inside No.193.

Starting in a fine attic playroom, next to the small room occupied by John and Lottie, R's education truly began. He liked to lie down in the dark beside his electric train and watch the engine-light come straight at him. Or he liked to lie there with the engine stopped but its light on so that he could read educational volumes such as *Tom Swift*, the *Rover Boys* and the *Boy Allies*, all having been left behind by the Twins. Oddly the Twins had not left copies of the Horatio Alger books such as *Sink or Swim*, *Do and Dare*, *Strive and Succeed*, but Tom Swift and his friends were good substitutes, being much more readable than *The Vicar of Wakefield*, which…but that subject is off limits for now. R will now move down to the second floor front.

Yes his bedroom looked right out on East Rock Road where at dusk an old man on a bicycle with a long stick came along each night and lit the gas streetlight for pete's sake. ("For pete's sake" was big with R's father.) The bedroom was a fine school for many small-fry matters but its most exciting property was its Japanese "waltzing mice," given to him, possibly to annoy Mother, by his half-brothers. (The Twins were a problem for R's mother when they were present; but that was seldom and R knew them only when they dropped in from school or college at vacation time. Their empty rooms had banners on the walls: Taft, Choate, Lehigh, which were taken down, and replaced by For God, for Country, and for Yale.) The mice lived in a goldfish bowl with a little cardboard-and-cotton house in the middle. They ate seeds and slept all day. They raced around the sides of the bowl all night. And they could be picked up at any time and held in the hand for study, especially for the benefit of R's mother. They also drank water and were clean and white and educational.

As for the first floor, it was there in the living room on dark late afternoons that R learned to play the piano by inserting a roll — preferably "The Blue Danube" — and pushing buttons to slow or speed the waltz. And when he was tired of that, he could go into the kitchen and play checkers with John.

Moving down to the cellar garage he could work at his workbench next to Father's, where he had his own powerful Sears Roebuck jigsaw on which he cut up pictures (those his mother pasted on plywood in her workroom) into hundreds of intricate pieces to make fine jigsaw puzzles. Finally, also in the cellar garage, he taught himself at perhaps age 13 how to drive a car one spring afternoon when he came home from Hopkins Grammar early on the trolley and his mother was out somewhere — though her Model A was in.

And the key was in it. First he made sure the gear was in neutral. Then he started the motor and wiggled the clutch, pushing the clutch down and putting the gear stick into what he knew was first. Then he let out the clutch just a little bit further, even practicing how to put on the brake really quick. Soon he had the car moving nicely forward *and* back, forward *and* back, two or three feet each way, never touching either end of the garage. (The Chrysler was out.) Of course the garage was starting to be smelly and he was thinking he ought to open the garage door — though he wasn't ready to take the car out yet — when his foot slipped off the clutch and he banged hard into the front of the garage, stalling the engine and knocking down a rake and two shovels.

But R's mother was out, and John and Lottie were up in the attic, and deaf Nangma wouldn't have heard the crash if he had gone through the wall. So he was in the clear. He made sure the ignition was off; he pushed the car away from the wall with his own hands; and he put the shovels back. When R's mother came home he was upstairs in his room reading *The Vicar of Wakefield*. Hundred percent.

On Becoming Grown

R now moved forward in his education, from living at home and attending Hopkins Grammar School to facing his first foreign assignment — three years at Andover. He never learned to like the place and when, thirty-five years later, he and his wife Helen sent their first son Ned there, Ned didn't like it either. There seems to be a rule of puberty against liking such prisons. The trapped ones have to be unhappy, have to be lonely, have to suffer insufferable authority. So R — to suffer Andover from 1934 to 1937— began his trials on the third floor of Cheever House, an old yellow wooden building on the Main Street hill leading to downtown. There sociable Johnnie A of Detroit, lonely Dave Jones of Greensboro, and R lived in creaky third floor singles for a year. Johnnie was a bully who liked wrestling R down and sitting on him; but Dave, one of just two blacks in the school then, was like R in being solemn and civilized. So they shared loneliness, talked about Johnnie the bully, about how much they disliked Andover, and about how bad the food in the dining hall was. In the tradition of Andover they also both smoked illegally in their fireplace-less rooms, and housemaster Rocky Drake was kindly about it. But Dave often batted tennis balls against his room's wall, and Rocky was unkindly about that. As for R, late at night he brought his illegal radio out of his under-the-bed strongbox, and Rocky did not (apparently) know of its jazzy existence.

The illegality of radios in Andover rooms remains a wonder to R but there it was. So his fine small Philco went underground — or rather underbed — for three years and brought him secret happiness such as Benny Goodman on Saturday nights. At home he had rigged up an astonishing device for turning on this radio — which was then displayed openly across the room from his bed — while lying in the bed. It was such a fine arrangement that he later wrote a story about it for the *Yale Literary Magazine* (published as "Modern Science at 1930 Prices" in R's *Fascination of the Abomination*) in which the hero, Alec, at great labor hangs a string around three walls of the room — with pulleys from his Erector set taking care of the corners — so that he can lie abed yet listen, starting at precisely 12:30 p.m., to the luncheon music of Sammy Richey and his Connecticut Smoothies from Hartford.

> Twelve twenty-nine. So there he was stretched out taking it easy, not a care in the world, and yet he knew it was 12:29 and that without moving hardly a muscle he could reach over in fifty seconds and pull that string and there the band'd be. And of course if he wasn't absolutely sure it was 12:29 he could just get up for a second and check the other two clocks — that was another thing, with three he always had a way of checking — and then get right back and get ready for it, so that when he pulled the string, and when the ten seconds for warming up had gone by, the first thing he'd hear out of that radio would be bango that old bong in Hartford ringing twelve-thirty and the announcer saying This Is WTIC, with the Richey theme song then coming in perfectly.

But then Alec's whole day is ruined by "Mother coming in and pushing the bureau back" or she is calling from downstairs that lunch is ready. In the 50s, *The New Yorker* published "The Radio Under the Bed," a poem that drew on those memories of the Andover prohibition.

> Why was a radio sinful? Lord knows. But it was.
> So I had one,
> Which I kept locked in a strongbox under my bed
> And brought forth, turned on, tuned and fondled at night
> When the sneaky housemaster slept and vice was all right.
>
> The music played in my ear from the Steel Pier,
> Nob Hill, the Astor and other housemasterless
> Hebrides where (I heard) the loved lived it up.
> I listened myself to sleep, the sweet saxes
> Filtering in my future, filling my cup.
>
> All prohibitions have vanished. Radios bore me
> As do the two-step debauches I used to crave.
> But the songs still remain, the old vulgar songs, and will play me,
> Tum-te-tum, tum-te-tum, tum-te-tum, into my grave.

I submit that R listening secretly at Andover to Benny Goodman at midnight out of a strong box was at least an improvement over luncheon-listening at home. He also played, on a windup phonograph, records of Louis Armstrong, Bing Crosby, Ray Noble, Glen Gray, Fred Waring, Red Nichols, and Jimmy Lunceford.

R later published another story from his youth — at 13, perhaps, maybe 11 — in "How I Bicycled Seventeen Miles No-Handed on Cape Cod." While his memory of that feat is still vivid — daughter Cate put this one too into a painting — the story's narrator makes the remembering of it much less reliable. "Nobody ever believes me when I tell them another boy and I once bicycled eighteen miles no-handed.... We did it on Cape Cod," the older narrator says at the outset. The course was Chatham to Hyannis, or was it Orleans to Wellfleet, or Barnstable to Truro, and how did they end up in the middle of Provincetown and then get back to Northfield, Minnesota? The reader is never sure, just as he is never sure if the course was 17 miles or 18 or 21, or if the friend was Sam or Tom or Ronnie. The story itself was R's venture into unreliable narrating.

Cate Whittemore's version of R bicycling no-handed on Cape Cod.

And so back to R's second (Junior) year in a normal dormitory, Taylor Hall. There he and Dave combined their smoking with one or two civilized Saturday-night drinking bouts (from two half-pints R purchased on a dangerous weekend quest to South Boston). I think it is fair to say that R, with Old Overshoe and Old Golds and Dave supporting him, could now think himself a man. Yes, he now knew the way life was really lived.

There did remain the difficulty that the Taylor Hall housemaster was strict — smoking was among the things he disapproved of. Luckily Taylor Hall's double rooms had fireplaces up which one could spew fumes — though the luxury did not make smoking legal. That year Dave roomed alone and R had a mathematical genius for a roommate — he too disapproved of smoking and tried to be out when the smoking began. But not Dave who slept in a single unfireplaced room and so came to R's for a last safe smoke. R has a photo of their rears, their heads in the fireplace — he doesn't know who could have taken it but it provides definite evidence

that the evil was exciting, therefore worth remembering. And without evidence, old as R now is, he remembers that one Saturday night the stern housemaster did knock on the door, at which instant the cigarettes were shoved up the chimney, their little bottle was hidden under something, and Dave stashed himself in a closet. Dave had drunk about half a bottle in the sudden way that the young begin by doing. R opened the door sleepily. The housemaster looked surprised, apologized for waking him, and simply left! R was amazed at his own acting skill, opened the closet to let out Dave, and found him asleep in the dirty shirts.

Of course such a mystical triumph over authority was rare at a place like Andover in the 1930s — for sin at that time had many fewer teenage opportunities than at this writing. R was lonely mostly, depressed by, but struggling with, classes such as French and solid geometry. And then came the fraternity mess, since Andover at this time was not only all male but also frat-plagued. R became pledged to one, accepted, found he didn't like his "brothers," nor his brothers him. (One called him Whittishit.) Predictably Dave was in none. Once or twice R even found himself with his frat brothers in a windowless room voting for new members by secretly placing a little round white ball or a little less-round black ball into the side of a box. He soon stopped going to the "house" entirely and Junior year became very long. It even had in it several books as dull as *The Vicar of Wakefield*.

So Junior year ground slowly on until late spring when on a bright, clear Saturday evening — with Dave off somewhere — R was climbing the stairs alone to his room and the building's janitor oddly stopped R, proposing that he look out the window at the moon. R stopped, looked, and yes, there was the moon. Then the janitor asked him, also oddly, if he could see the girl in the moon. R could not. He could see that the moon was a bright clear moon and that the man in the moon was there — but a girl? No. "Oh yes she is there," said the janitor. "She's a Gibson girl." He then explained that the Gibson girl was in profile and her hairdo was the right eyebrow of the man in the moon. And sure enough, there was R's first sight of a Gibson girl.

Not explained by memory here is why the pedagogical janitor was there at all — and at work — on a lonely Saturday night. But there he was. And there was the moon girl, one of the few females that R was to run across during his Andover years, despite Abbot Academy, a girls school only a few blocks away. Of course R did think about girls a lot then, but mostly they were in memories of New Haven, especially at "dancing school" at the New Haven Lawn Club in vacation time. A fierce sergeant of a tiny woman, Miss Darling, who was always dressed in a long white gown and equipped with both a whistle and a noisy clicker, conducted that educational institution. He immortalized Miss Darling and her "Step-slide-change; One-two-three-four" in "A Child's Christmas in New Haven," another story he included in *Fascination of the Abomination*, the title parodying Dylan Thomas's more justifiably famous and nostalgic one. R's story was anything but nostalgic as it alternated between ballroom dancing with Miss Darling and Christmas dinner with Nangma and family — this was life at 193 East Rock Road seemingly as fiction.

My grandmother presided at that dinner. We we were not a clan family; there were just my grandmother, my parents, my brothers and I — no aunts and cousins, no kinfolk traveling from remote places to join us and tie on, as my brothers put it, the feedbag, and no special clan dishes, ceremonies, customs. Indeed it was a cold-blooded affair in an unfamily-like family, just another Sunday dinner.... My grandmother would sit silent, erect, stern across the table, flanked by my brothers; my mother would sit to my left trying to start some conversation about the neighbors while telling me to keep my hands off the table and sit up straight and stop chewing my napkin....plates would slowly be filled and passed and placed in their proper places before the proper parties where they would slowly cool and harden; and my mother would say, "no R," a few dozen times; and my father would at last sit down and we would begin.

Miss Darling was backed up at the piano by a large sloppily dressed college student who banged away at the keys without sitting up straight. He played slow fox trots and furious waltzes in the same position while Miss D clicked and whistled at her two or three dozen teen-age inmates. She regularly backed up her whistle and clicker by shouting — when the musical ruckus seemed insufficient — "Step! Slide! Change!" The "Step" had to be accomplished (by the leaderly male) (with the obedient female retreating) by moving the left foot forward, so that the "slide" could be achieved by the right foot, thus making necessary the "change" that brought the feet back together and ready for the next step. The girls, R noted, were always better, though retreating, than the boys at this art, which he never really mastered. Usually he felt confident with small responsive girls, but with large ones his right hand would squirm help-lessly on their hefty backs as he tried to steer them — like a bureau on wheels — temporarily around the dance floor. His favorite partner was the girl whose family's backyard abutted on R's grandmother's house. She was nice — though of course a snob — and he *did* think that *she* thought he was a good dancer. So he had her often in his mind at Andover until late in his junior year when he was shocked to learn (by mail from his offended mother) that she had run off with — been happily abducted by? — an elderly lawyer for pete's sake.

Yes, he was miserable at Andover but at least his stay there was broken — in the summer before his senior year — by a summer Cook's Tour to Europe inspired by general fatigue that R's mother had with East Rock Road. The *S.S. Pennland* left New York near the end of June 1936 and arrived first in Antwerp. I have before me a tattered notebook, R's diary of the trip, and can report on the scribbled and fragmentary in it, always reminding me that what memory remembers is not always true, for instance, that R hated the trip from the very beginning. The first entry reads this way:

After spending a pleasant hour standing in front of the Hotel Commodore, our bus came and took us to the pier in Hoboken by roar-ing through the Holland Tunnel. When we reached the pier we wrestled with the luggage for a time. Then we found the gangplank.

So there was R's writing talent — phase one — suddenly busting out all over. I note especially the verbal vigor of the roaring and wrestling and finding the gangplank. And can add that the vigor continued throughout the account. For four whole days he liked the ship's bingo and horseracing games since he "netted a clear profit of about eleven bucks." And he nervously admired describing the ocean's elements, such as a storm with "swishing foam" that "rolled the ship gently from one 45 degree angle to another" while a moon "snapped out of its lethargy."

Then he turned with qualified pleasure to a few young passengers such as one seventeen-year-old who had gone on the wagon, and another whose "favorite grudge" was "the average Princeton man" but who was "funny in spite of everything." He was even content when they came to a country "as flat as Holland, for in fact it was Holland." And he rather liked Brussels with its "wonderful stores and modern buildings," though there was a breakfast "tragedy"

Big R, Mother and R — departure for Europe, summer 1936.

when "Mother ordered two boiled eggs and they brought them in a little container out of which one stuck half way." In Paris, however, life grew grim. It was raining and the first restaurant they ate at was "tres cher and lousy." Then in Switzerland the people expected visitors to "gurgle 'beautiful, beautiful, beautiful' about Lake Geneva," and the Grimsel and Furka Passes scared him to reflect that they were, "respectively and respectfully, 6700 and 7500 feet above a normal situation." After that the misery grew. The diary neglected all of Germany and England, and ended abruptly as they reboarded the *S.S. Pennland* in Southampton on August 6th. R wrote, "I have gone back over these pages and am convinced that they are the worst pages I have ever read. To go further would be criminal."

He was not wrong but what strikes home now is that he was taking his pages seriously. The writer in him was revealing itself, and he hadn't known about that personage before. In sitting down to his diary he must have felt that going through the world with a cynical wit was simply a writer's daily job, since what after all could a writer *write* about going through the Holland Tunnel or looking at an Alp.

R's father also kept a journal, though his was a different affair. R happened to find it in among his own papers at the University of Maryland Hornbake Library while looking for something else; he wasn't surprised to rediscover his father's meticulousness in keeping track of almost everything, from hotel rooms to meals to sights to souvenirs — including the cost of everything — to breasts, to R himself:

> Monday, July 13.
> R Jr. developed a "cold" which circulated amongst our party & felt so punk that he stayed quiet. He's recovered enough to join the whole crowd and we went to the Casino de Paris. Revue. Very undressed. The breasts of the choruses etc. are entirely uncovered. Practically the only clothing a "fig leaf." But the dancers were not as good nor the choruses as well drilled as many of the shows at home.

> Wednesday, July 15
> Going home from café, Prof. S got us lost; but R Jr. who has a fine sense of locality steered us back again to the hotel.

> Thursday, Jul 16
> R Jr. was much impressed by Geneva & decided he would like to spend a summer there — an ideal resort.

In the coming war he was to write R overseas daily about *everything*. While letters were his life, R was not like that; his were spotty and brief. Andover had not stirred him to writing personally, but his literary horizon was at least broadening. He seems to have entered "Literature."

—

It might have happened in his last year at Andover that R was possessed of this new vision of himself. While struggling with solid geometry and evil world history the year before, he had actually branched out into a bit of contemporary fiction. Did he first then read Sherwood Anderson — the novel *Poor White* and a story collection, *Winesburg, Ohio* — and

Thomas (not Tom) Wolfe's *Look Homeward, Angel* and *From Death to Morning*? At least R's bookshelves have Modern Library copies of these books that seem to go back to Andover days. Going through them for clues to what impressed R about those books at the time doesn't help much since Anderson seems now to have been a very mixed-up "period" author. Yet Anderson in his narratives did mix — and ambitiously — small-town talk and proletarian commentary with much evocative detail about individuals; and such details may have been what struck home with the novice R as he looked seriously for the first time at the writing trade. He could only have been impressed, for instance, with the hero of *Poor White* — who was at first an ignoramus and then suddenly an inventor-genius (surely one of the truly improbable transformations in modern lit) who helped start the industrial revolution in an Ohio farm-ing town. And of course he would also have liked that hero for being a shy recluse walking endlessly at night thinking deep, and then (most suddenly) marrying — the deed was almost like sleep-walking — an enterprising upper-class woman who quickly put the facts of life into his head.

At least it now seems clear that R was definitely attracted to an Anderson short story, "Hands," featuring another loner, Wing Biddlebaum, whose hands kept getting out of hand and caressing (male) people. Was this sex at work or just the depths of an innovative subcon-scious? R knows not, and the mysteries of most of Anderson's characters' actions now seem frivolous; yet R must have liked that handyman loner, for he even wrote a short poem — now luckily missing — about hands. The hands were seemingly unattached to any person and R has no further memory of it other than the first line: "Simple hands they were." Presumably his own weren't.

As for the Wolfe influence, that seems clearer though it may not have amounted to much until college. Wolfe was surely one of the most com-pulsive writers in modern history, and his productive capacity continues to amaze everyone who has dipped into him. R still wonders how the author ever had time to walk lonely through the long nights like his hero Eugene Gant, and at the same time to write and write and write and then ship off a million or so words to his faithful editors — first Maxwell Perkins and then Edward Aswell — for cutting, chopping up and piecing together. Yes, there was much in Wolfe to impress R, especially his absolutely tireless write-write-write commitment. Wolfe had been to

drama school and he loved to catch the flavor of talk and to describe the
thought and feelings behind the talk (and all the furniture in the room
where the talk was taking place). So while some of the dialect he experimented with now seems crude (in, for example, "Only the Dead Know
Brooklyn") Wolfe can be praised for wanting any hero of his to be whole
and complete in his being. Here is an ambitious short sample, the first
paragraph of an early chapter in *Look Homeward, Angel.*

> Eugene was loose now in the limitless meadows of sensation; his sensory
> equipment was so complete that at the moment of perception of a single
> thing, the whole background of color, warmth, odor, sound, taste estab-
> lished itself, so that later, the breath of hot dandelion brought back the
> grass-warm banks of Spring, a day, a place, the rustling of young leaves or
> the page of a book, the thin exotic smell of tangerine, the wintry bite of
> great apples; or, as with *Gulliver's Travels*, a bright windy day in March, the
> spurting moments of warmth, the drip and reek of the earth-thaw, the feel
> of the fire.
>
> He had won the first release from the fences of home. He was not quite
> six when....[!]

Whew! After typing that R just had to go back to *Gulliver's Travels*,
being pretty sure that Swift had never made any such fuss about the drip
and reek of March. Not that it mattered — and R couldn't find his copy
of Swift. The point here simply proceeds from R's envy at Wolfe's furious
capacity to put everything in his head into words — and instantly it
seems. R's own machinery would never (as he slowly learned) purr at that
speed; still, at least Wolfe's talent could dazzle him.

But onward. Making it at Andover with average grades to senior year R
was then again in a single room, with his closest friend Dave now off in
a different dorm. He knew no one on his floor well and didn't particularly want to. He walked alone at night near campus, a 120-pound
Eugene Gant thinking deep thoughts but being also, rather simply,
unhappy. And taking and hating German. So on a warm fall Saturday
afternoon when there seemed to be no hope he packed his book-bag with
a shirt, a sweater and a pair of socks, walked downtown to the railroad
station and left the place.

He took a Boston & Maine train to Boston, then transferred to a
Greyhound bus that headed south on Route 1. He had no destination in
mind — except possibly Rio de Janeiro by tramp steamer — but he rode

through the night to New York, passing right through New Haven at 4 a.m. By dawn he found himself in the big city's bus station where, after twenty minutes in a coffee shop, he decided against Rio. He took a cab to Grand Central, rode a train back to New Haven and reported in at No. 193 East Rock Road around noon. He was low.

———

Let this account now pause for a moment for a memory of Thomas Carlyle that seems relevant to R's Andover "problems." Carlyle was the 19th century British thinker who wrote of British culture and ideas, the French Revolution, and the lives of heroes as though he were delivering the truth (Truth) from Mount Sinai. About 1850, Carlyle turned to John Sterling, a young poet he liked but didn't think highly of. Sterling was rich and sickly and ran away from his equivalent of Andover. He wrote home to his mother saying that he was in the next town but would soon be sailing for France. Then he decided he couldn't sail for France — and came back home. Of course Carlyle — who was never without direction — then made his point about Sterling, that Sterling was flabby at the core. Unlike R, however, Sterling at least had the justification of sickness, and was soon wafted off to expensive warm places where he wrote small poems and died. Yet like R he did have an ego problem, that of coming to think of himself *as* a poet. Carlyle's biography of Sterling interested R because, unlike his other biographies, which were of heroes who possessed some measure of "divine essence," the Sterling boy kept disappointing Carlyle by emerging, in one way or another, as not a divinity but a dilettante. No poet himself, Carlyle decided that poetry was what encouraged low self-thoughts in the poor chap. His physical weakness had been aggravated by the spiritual contamination of a flaccid genre, and had led to a few dull evenings at the Carlyles when Sterling read his poems, with Carlyle noting that he did not read well. Furthermore, poetry just did not lead where a Man of Letters ought to be led. Yes, on first meeting Sterling, Carlyle sensed a great missionary in the man, and he watched him leave the Anglican Church for the world of letters with serious notions of saving everybody. Then, somehow, he did not take hold. The underlying theme of Carlyle's biography became just that: the tragedy of a literary person not taking hold.

This tale, R has sometimes felt, may be a parable for his own life.

———

At No. 193 Mother and Father were not angry about R's escapade. Nangma was failing — she would die in a few weeks — and the prospect of selling her house now took much of their attention (for this was 1936 and Father had managed to lose most of his life's investments — and a few of Nangma's — in a now unknown stock debacle). When R visited Nangma in her chambers she did not recognize him, and her nurse — for now there was one — said as if confidentially, "You know that your grandmother is very sick." By then R was himself sick, and repentant for being there at all. He said little. For the rest of that day he lay on his old bed without even his radio to listen to. He moped. The next morning both his

R looking smartly in his last Andover year.

mother and father drove him back to Andover where there were embarrassing conferrings with authorities including a pleasant English teacher, Alan Downer (who was about to help R begin to think that he really could "take hold"), and the Day Hall housemaster (whom R disliked though he was to play a role too). During the conferrings nobody raised an eyebrow though R — being timid, cowardly, and irresolute — had told no one of his Rio plan.

After his parents' departure for home an alien plan, a therapeutic institutional plot to save him, began to unfold. The first agent of the plot was the Day Hall housemaster who knocked on R's door to ask if everything was all right. Everything was all right, the housemaster left, and ten minutes later the second agent appeared, a certain Larry S who was taking Downer's poetry course with R and who now entered R's room — as he never had before — to ask if R would like to play a little two-handed rummy game called ratfuck. R had never played the game but it was an easy one and Larry was easy to get on with. Soon they were playing the game every night and Larry seemed to like being a plot-agent if he was one. And if he was he was probably in cahoots with a third fairly obvious agent, teacher Downer himself, who suddenly had R writing an enormous historical essay on the whole of modern poetry. R no longer has the opus, but A.E. Housman must have been included because Larry happened to like Housman and could recite him while playing ratfuck. Soon R also could recite a Housman poem ("Stars, I have seen them fall,/But when they drop and die/ No star is lost at all/ From all the star-sown sky"). Christmas came upon him easily with his mind full of such matters. It seemed that the plot to keep him at Andover had succeeded.

—

The unexpected reward for R's misery was that he wrote two chapters of a novel about being miserable, then destroyed them and switched to writing poems of misery. The poems somehow arranged for him to be put in a seminar conducted by Alan Blackmur in an elegant leathery room in Bulfinch Hall, and it was there that he had sudden dim insights into his future. Blackmur was the first teacher in his experience to try a bit of positive reinforcement. R was to be more than a decade out of Andover, though his "travel trick" had started there, when he wrote "Preface to a Projected Guidebook," an eccentric sonnet that he later included in *An American Takes a Walk and Other Poems*.

> Travel is a trick I learned
> From my betters
> For trifling with the troubles that attend
> All that matters.
>
> The pains, the wear and tear
> Of living in the closeness and loving
> By the year I forswear
> By simply leaving.
>
> The regions in the distance are my homelands.
> The cities with the shimmering walls and steeples
> House my gibbering friends,
> My peoples.
>
> The whole world I inhabit except the bit
> Where I at the moment sit.

The words are and are not speaking for him. He does not mean "betters" except ironically (and the irony is wasted), nor does he believe what he says that staying home is all that matters. He flogs himself for fourteen lines for his love of homelessness, his failure to settle down, but in the process he shows himself rather pleased about his failure. He is thematically mixed up, for all his irony, but he is aesthetically very very neat. He must have written every line ten times, and has been bowled over by such technical triumphs as his "tr" tetralogy in stanza one ("travel, trick, trifling, troubles"), and his long line-short line balancing throughout. For weeks, he remembers, he lacerated himself deciding whether or not to put "chosen" before "peoples" in stanza three. The poem has finish if not, R is sorry to say, wisdom; still, it is one of the few poems of his own that he was able to recite without a trot for more than thirty years.

~~~

Then during the holiday Nangma died and his half-brother twins, now out in the world, came home briefly, one of them with a wife, the other alone (having an ex-wife), to honor the deceased. They had not been at No.193 at all since their college years, during which, R remembered, they usually imported two roommates each for a Thanksgiving feast so that eight rather than the usual four sat at the dining room table while R's Father carved the turkey and chewed his tongue. So now, for the mournful Christmas without Nangma, there were seven. And R's mother? She was particularly upset. She was silent at dinner, and after dinner she made herself busy trimming the already-trimmed Christmas tree. Then when she could not find a single place for another trinket she could only drink and talk of the next cruise she was planning for the time when they had sold No.193 and paid a few debts. Money for cruises was to come from Nangma's inheritance plus the sale of her house, but soon after that she and R's Father would give up the big house and move to a two-bedroom apartment five blocks away on Livingston Street. In a few years, Ezra Pound would sit in an armchair for an evening and hold court in that apartment. R by that adolescent time was busy disapproving — privately of course — of his mother's drinking, not only because he was at a good age for disapproving, but also because he had long resented her feelings about Nangma. He wrote "Mrs. Benedict" much later about his state of mind then, though its autobiographical source is not in the direct manner of what came to be called the Confessional poetry of the 60s and 70s, coming at memory through an aging man, more slant than direct.

Oh where are you now, Mrs. Benedict?
The last time I heard your voice over the phone
I was a child and you were drunk but orderly
And I called mother
                    That you and she could talk
Until I was grown

Talk talk
About nothing that I can remember
Or that you would remember
Talk slowly brokenly angrily and without respite

As the years filled with bottles

Where are you now? Where have you taken your permanent bun?
Mother is dead father is dead I sit here old and silent
Yet somewhere somehow you are still saying and saying
                    Something not to remember

Yes, as a fairly timid soul, R seems often to have enjoyed writing about what he knew better than to say.

Yale & Furioso

Much later in life R found himself reading an old anthology of essays about life as lived at Yale and Harvard by various notables in classes from 1922 to 1972, and was struck by the authors' fairly uniform opinion that the two schools' main role was to protect a student from Real Life. They were upper-class cocoons providing learned advisors and books for some, sports for others, and friends (who would last a lifetime) for all. They did not favor the presence of rude persons who had emerged from rude places like New Haven High School, and even in the Depression Thirties they managed to shut out hard times. William Proxmire (Yale '33) summed up this view ironically while describing the arrival in New Haven at the Schubert Theater of a Cole Porter musical (Cole Porter was Yale '13) called *Red, Hot and Blue*, with its cast including — at a dinner with the football team — Bob Hope and Jimmy Durante:

> Meanwhile, outside our happy cocoon, breadlines were forming, veterans were marching, Hitler was putsching in the name of the master race in Germany, Stalin was starving or shooting or working to death the last vestiges of Russian free spirits, but at Yale it was Cole Porter.

Then a little later at Harvard Robert Coles ('50) agreed about the cocoon condition — or rather had the poet William Carlos Williams agree for him — when Coles, an admirer who had written a "desperate, stuffy, self-important" school paper on Williams's work, sent the paper to the poet and then visited him at his Rutherford, New Jersey, home. (As had R in 1940 after he and roommate Jim Angleton had begun their little magazine, *Furioso*.) Coles found Williams extremely friendly, encouraging and tactful, but also found him asking pointed questions about Harvard life, such as "When do you catch your supply of fresh air?" (In the mid-70s, Coles wrote a monograph about Williams, around the same time as R's biography — more on the WCW biography in due time.)

The first Yale contributor to the volume, Dr. Benjamin Spock ('25), surprised R because he hadn't known the good doctor was a Yalie, much less a townie and a graduate of Andover. Yet there he was in the anthology, a seemingly representative cocoon-type who happened to have written *Dr. Spock's Baby and Childcare*, a book that has been translated into 40 languages and sold more than 50 million copies. So that was the real world? — if so Spock was for R a poor model, having had no literary interests at Yale as he rowed and high-jumped. Furthermore he lived at home while at college. Imagine. But at least he seemed modest as he finished off his memoir, saying only that upon leaving Yale he was able to turn his mind to the "outside" world. R could also look forward to that, couldn't he? No, there was trouble for a freshman trying to fathom even Yale's inside world. And since freshman R was still busy being a loner he might well have damned the anthology's whole cocoon thesis if he had been a contributor. He might even have suggested that the contributors had never left the Yale cocoon at all and had never found the outside world at all, but remained smug Ivy League insiders all their lives. Yes, freshman R had not yet adjusted to the college cocoon, being largely in a cocoon of his own.

But being an outsider to the place as a freshman was hardly unusual since the "college" system put freshmen off to themselves as if they were not yet even inside the cocoon but waiting to be let in. Also, though R could be unpleasant and surly in his scribbled European journal of the previous summer, he did make actual friends on the third floor of Welch Hall. And he did play bridge and go to dances at the Lawn Club and drink (even outsiders at Yale drank) and play a then fashionable Extra Sensory Perception game in his Welch room with other addicts late at night. Despite their handicaps Freshmen could survive, though sometimes they felt like hicks from the hills wandering lost in the big city. For Yale was big. And Andover, though also big, had none of Yale's aura of bigness. Furthermore Andover's senior-year plot, if it had been one, to save R had worked to the extent that he had not gone to Rio but had gone back to school to play ratfuck, write his great essay on poetry, walk off with his $25 prize, and become an obvious contender for a future Nobel prize. But as a freshman?

He took a basic lecture course in Geology in a large lecture hall and a basic lecture course in Biology in another large lecture hall. It's dubious that this latter inspired such poems later on as "The Tarantula" (in the voice of a tarantula) and three shorter ones gathered under "Biological Thoughts": "The Sand Dollar, "The Starfish," and "Bacteria." Not surprisingly, the poems are more urban than naturely, e.g., these few lines from "The Sand Dollar": "It serves its tiny economy (plankton for dollars)/ For its term, and then passes on// To its own fancied heaven ashore where the higher powers/ Make, it has heard, millions of dollars with flowers." He sat, I now think, in a large elementary German class and despised it. (Why despise? He cannot say, except that he and languages other than English were not compatible. And yet, he went on to publish translations in the little magazines he edited, the post-war *Furioso, The Carleton Miscellany* and then in the 1980s *Delos*, a magazine whose primary focus was translations of poetry and prose.)

Yale did not allow him to take any English course except Freshman Comp, though one day he audited a mighty lecture course in the Romantics taught by the mighty Chauncey Brewster Tinker. Right there he decided the rhetorical Chauncey was not for him. By the time R arrived in his classroom, Tinker was in his early 60s and had amassed scores of publications below his name, among them, a translation of *Beowulf* in 1910, learned treatments of Samuel Johnson, James Boswell, and Fanny Burney, and an edition of Matthew Arnold's letters. In R's freshman year, Tinker was giving the Charles Eliot Norton lectures, *Painter and Poet: Studies in the Literary Relations of English Painting*. R would learn later that Chauncey was also not for many of the young English teachers R would come to like, especially Arthur Mizener who was to take on a major role in his life. And, inevitably, in taking Freshman Comp he discovered his own talent was still obscure and unrecognized in the Yale cocoon, since he was expected to write infantile 300-word themes three times a week.

His teacher was Maynard Mack, then a young instructor who had begun teaching full-time in 1936, a year before R's arrival. Mack clearly needed to be shown the caliber of this prizewinner. So R took it on himself to terrorize his instructor by producing a many-paged, single-spaced, definitive account of the whole history of the short story plus a few novels. (After all, at Andover he had covered all modern poetry for $25.) Crafty Mack only wrote "nice" on the monster and gave him a depressing

C plus. Twelve years later, having by then run through Yale and WWII and a bit of graduate school in History, R found himself teaching Freshman Comp (and the Sophomore Lit Survey) at Carleton College in far-off Minnesota where he became a defender of short-theme assignments and found himself recommending that senior professors (like Tinker) teach Freshman Comp in order to improve their own pedagogy. Mack, the author and editor of many books on Shakespeare and 18th century writers especially, went on to become an English Department star, by then presumably spared teaching the elementary course. It is fair to say now that he did well for R in that course. The memory of the C plus has lingered for seventy years

At the time the C plus also had the merit of encouraging R to search out other readers for his work, that is, the wise upperclassmen running the *Yale Literary Magazine*. Of course he soon characterized its editors — or some of them — as insipid. For instance, on top of the first story of his they accepted some snob wrote, "This is better than the author knows." Most of the *Lit's* editors were out of step with the times and had not yet even heard of Modernism; but R put up with them anyway. By the beginning of his sophomore year he had printed the necessary number of stories and poems in the *Lit* to become a snobbish sub-editor himself. In November 1938 the magazine officially "announced" that R was now a member of the Associate Editorial Board, a level below the four Executive Editors, one of whom was Richard Ellmann. Ellmann wrote poetry but went on to literary acclaim as a Yeats scholar and biographer of James Joyce. Perhaps R's most memorable contribution was an extremely bad sonnet, his first (I think), about an "airman" who had been dumb enough to crash (unhurt) in somebody's cornfield, thereby annoying the farmer. R wouldn't dare print a line of the poem here even if he could find it, though it might have served as evidence that the accepting *Lit* editors were also mixed up. Looking ahead for a moment, R took up flying after the war while teaching at Carleton College and coming in for a landing had nearly done the same dumb thing himself.

A more promising magazine venture that year was a brand new publication he found himself working for in the spring. Simply called *'41* (the year of graduation for the class of 1937), he may even have helped start it — preoccupations with little magazines, let alone starting them, were to become a habit if not an obsessive part of his literary life. The purpose of *'41* is now thoroughly obscure but suddenly there it was. R wrote a little of it and then it went out of bounds for him by becoming '42. Luckily it remained, as '42, sufficiently in R's sophomore life to introduce him to the new class of freshman '42 editors, three of whom were to become life-long friends John Pauker, Bill Johnson, and Ambrose (Ambie) Gordon. They carried on for their year, and then presumably passed the sheet on to '43 novices, though R never worried about '43. It was the '42 writer-editors who became fellow-editors with R after the war, then working on round two of the most rewarding of his magazine ventures, *Furioso*, soon to be described. But most important for R at the time was the arrival of a Ford roadster, which meant more to him in his Freshman year than all English Lit.

The figure of $760 sits in R's mind now as the car's total cost, and while he may not have thanked the good Uncle Sandy (who gave it to him) with proper enthusiasm, R was enthused. It had plastic curtains, a good motor, and ridiculous transverse springs incapable of keeping the car on the ground on a washboard pavement. R had it through college and wrote reams of important material while seated in it, often on top of East Rock Road. Under its influence he would walk out Whitney Avenue after a hard midwinter day of learning (possibly in the back row of Professor Tinker's course in the Romantics) to where the car was garaged, near his parents' apartment, and then often drive twenty miles east on Route 1 to Madison on the Long Island Sound shore. There, still sitting in the car, he would look out on the Sound's cold waters and scribble icily (the plastic curtains leaked a little) for perhaps an hour before driving inland for half a mile to Madison's small movie house (shows at 7 and 9). Of course the city of New Haven had five movie houses near the Yale campus steadily showing all the latest films, but they were large movie houses with balconies where cocooned students hooted and whistled. Sensible loners with roadsters did not hoot. Furthermore R was a townie, and as a townie with wheels he was also the possessor of the town's surrounding territory, not trapped with the boorish visitors.

Yes, R often had negative sensations about Yale — as about Andover. Naturally the establishment air of both places had to be lived with — he knew that fact of life and respected it — but by mid-college he had become busy as a political dissident of sorts. Oddly his Republican father had originally encouraged R's dissidence by bringing up with him one childish afternoon, while driving him somewhere in his boring Chrysler, a fine (complicatedly political) Victorian word that his father liked simply because it was long — twelve syllables — and could be recited slowly and distinctly. The word was "antidisestablishmentarianism" and child R was much impressed. He soon could recite it himself, loudly, and would shout the climactic "iz-zum" — without needing to know what was and was not to be established. (If readers are now wondering I suggest they check the religious situation in England around 1870.) So perhaps it was with that fine word that the whole depressing history of human establishments (including, later, committees) began to creep in on R. Certainly by the time he found himself sitting about in the offices of the *Yale Lit* (publicized as the oldest literary magazine in America) he was familiar in a rough way with quite a few of the "anti's and dis's" of establishment life. He had found for instance that the *Lit* itself — not to mention much else at Yale — often badly needed disestablishing; further, that a sound writerly mission in all of life could be made out of coping with establishmentarianism.

Not without labor I have now managed to put the verb "to cope" into play. Down the years R became increasingly annoyed with an economic meaning for the verb "to cope" that he ran into in the Yale textbook for Econ 10, another freshman lecture course. The textbook authors were three Yale professors — Fairchild, Furness and Buck — known then as F, F & B. In their book F, F & B declared that the pursuit of profit was basic to all humans. And as if that were not enough they added a footnote clincher to the effect that certain anthropologists had located a primitive tribe in darkest Africa whose members did not choose to *cope* with life by working each day a moment longer than was needed to purchase a day's liquor supply. Now while taking Econ 10, R happened also to be reading Herman Melville's *Bartleby the Scrivener,* and found that putting F, F & B's footnote and Bartleby's problem — of "preferring not to" — together in his head at the same time was most suggestive. It then seemed to him that he was trapped in life to serve F, F & B's wishes, much as Bartleby had been trapped to scribble what a wicked Wall Streeter invented by Melville wished him to scribble. It followed, did it not, that (perhaps after a few drinks) he should say, "I prefer not to."

In general Yale's climate was indeed that of secular capitalist establishmentarianism — that is, of wholly accepting the creed of F, F & B. R was not a socialist yet — and would never really veer further left than Norman

Thomas's leftish anti-establishmentarianism — but his chief problem was not of left vs right, nor was it even political. His was a character problem. He was not exactly cowardly, yet he was not a powerful *dis*establishmentarian. For instance, he could only admire from a distance his daring new friend John Pauker, '42, who was a fine disrupter — though not exactly political. Pauker dramatically proved where he stood in relation to Yale's freshman establishment by plotting one Saturday night to lock up the whole class of '42 right on the freshman campus, which was one square block enclosed by walls and gates. Yes, he bought chains in order to incarcerate them all there on a quiet Sunday morning.

What spirit *that* hero had. And how remarkable the disestablishmentarian consequences would have been if, for perhaps the whole of that Sunday morning, the campus police, the New Haven police, the New Haven Fire Department and the University Association of Deans, Department Heads and Coaches, as well as Yale's President (it may have been Charles Seymour that year) could have been seen *outside* the quad wrestling with the hero's massive locks and chains at the quad's four separate gates, while *inside* the quad the frosh flocked frenziedly to and fro without breakfast.

Unluckily the campus cops caught the hero as he sealed the last gate. Too bad. For even then R knew he himself was not up to such daring. As a quiet literary disestablishmentarian he could only perform underground or alone in his Ford roadster, where he would scribble Bartleby thoughts for his own private benefit. His college career might never have been ruffled by active thoughts if he had not become friends in the spring with another activist — but far from leftist — Jim Angleton, who was later to become a top CIA spy (more about his spy side later). For freshman year Jim (on record as James Jesus) — possessed of an excellently alien English accent — had a single room next to R's on third floor Welch. Throughout the Fall they hardly spoke even on the stairs, but after Christmas something happened — whether the something be fictional or no, imagine the name Ezra Pound rang out on third floor Welch in the middle of a Saturday night — and suddenly they hit it off, deciding to room together the next year.

Their decision came so late that they were assigned an isolated off-campus room on the third floor of a rickety house outside the cocoon at 312 Temple Street. Fall 1938. They did not eat with classmates that year but only with (boring) law students at an odd club on Wall Street. R's mother, fascinated by Jim, produced an immense drape to divide their room between sleeping and living, though even with the drape it was hard for one Sophomore to sleep when the other was playing Artie Shaw records. At least there they were coping.

Jim was two years older than R, and though born in Idaho he was definitely a foreigner when he thought about it. After all he had been living in Italy and England for some years, wore expensive Italian suits, and had met Ezra Pound. (Just when R is no longer certain. In August 1938, Pound was already writing familiarly to Jim in Milan at his parents' address —16 via Dante, yet — on how long he'd be in Rapallo if Jim wanted to visit. A few days later he wrote again to say he'd be there probably until the 21st.) Jim's mother was Mexican but the Mexican in him showed in his complexion rather than manner. His father was a genuine Idahoan like Pound but unlike the poet he was a businessman, and had become a vice president of the National Cash Register Company, had taken over the company's operations in Italy, and had moved his family of four children — Jim being the oldest — there to live. When Jim was ready for prep-school polish the father sent him off to an English equivalent of Andover. Accordingly Jim arrived in New Haven with an English accent and a lofty manner that complemented his Italian suits. His accent, mixed with Italian pleasantries, made R feel like the townie he was, but Jim liked R as a townie, especially since townies had ready access to cars in a time when Yale had rules (mostly ineffective) against students having them. By late sophomore year Jim had become an avid trout fisherman — in the Ford roadster.

He would wander off (to the best of R's knowledge then) to strange streams in far-off northwestern Connecticut where he would stand in cold waters for hours casting for trout (though R never saw a single catch). Then after the casting he would happen to visit, while driving home, a certain female he had known early in life in an unspecified locale. He was a fine mystery man — mystery became him and was to do so even more, rising rising in the CIA, until controversy brought him down (historians have since tried figuring him out in numbers of books). Jim turned out to be a fine friend too, for forty years — best of all his life abroad had made him a literary modern. After all, he *had* met Pound, one of the great early disestablishmentarians of 20th century literature.

Jim had become a sub-editor of *Yale Lit* several months after R and published a couple of not very exciting poems there. Here's one of them, for the record at least, "The Immaculate Conversion":

Jim Angleton took these photographs and more of Ezra Pound in Italy in 1938, mailing them from New Haven. Pound replied, "I am really very grateful to you. Magnificent photos, and by far the best treatment the subject has ever had from a camera." (No Poundian CAPS, no underlining.) For a time, Yale Lit's masthead listed Angleton as photography editor, though the magazine published no photographs.

When the pollen drips from stamen
Urging womb-fruit for next year —
I murmur to see the sun and rain
Quicken to dust the flowers again
Quicken to flowers the dust again
Quicken to dust
Didn't they smell for life this year
Didn't they smell for death
Didn't they smell I ask

At night illiterate I saw these things
Lying cadaverous in the parlour hall
Then quickening to the priest who sings
They sprawled as writing on my wall

So going quick to religious places
I inspect the graven gargoyles there
And finding myself among the faces
Affect a bow and tonsured hair.

Somewhere in Pound's published letters there is a characteristically sweeping Poundian remark describing Jim as one of the few literary live wires extant in backward America at the time. Apparently Jim was this to Pound because Jim had mentioned his dream of starting a little magazine — this while playing tennis with EP in Rapallo. In January 1939 (for Pound, on his stationery at least, it was Anno XVII), he wrote Jim a long letter in his Poundian punctuation, letter spacing, hyper capitalization and spelling: "Now what about WORK ? any chance of starting a li'l seeryus mental life at Yale ??" Jim had obviously advanced the idea of Pound contributing to this new magazine, "Yes, I'll back up any and all the proposals in yrs/ But we had better think out WHAT will do the job best. A 'text book' ought to be ready soon/ you can quote from advance copy of that." As well as instructing Jim on history and the deficiencies of Yale — "Yale Lit/ might cite my article on 'Mencius' in last summer's *Criterion*/ as evidence of insanity (or the reverse .../ I don't know why the student body shd/ wait twenty years to learn things quite well known in Europe)." Pound probably saw in Jim and the new magazine to come — no name yet — a chance to get his words into print again. As he wrote, always emphatically, "I have at the moment NO American connections: No American magazine which I can rely on. I mean not even to print the simplest correction or statement, not only re/ econ/ but about literature."

For the sake of literary history, I suppose it's too bad that Jim's side of the correspondence has disappeared — he must have set out what he and R were looking to do as evidenced by Pound's reply, who set out *his* conditions and instructions if he was to help.

If I am to be the padre eterne or whatever of one or more of the mags/ mentioned/

a group of you/ at least 3 , and I shd/ think not more than five ought formally to ACCEPT at least a few principles from

ABC of Reading

And/or KULCH. ,   and prob. the preface to Active Anthology.

at any rate get the GROUP to <u>TELL me what they agree on</u>.

I can't start writing criticisms just in the vague/ it has got to procede from a known context.
                    (is this clear ?)
....

To ORGANIZE or <u>make</u> a mag/ the editorial board must do what I did in
          Little Review/
                    i.e., assert which authors they respect
/ can't be an unlimited number /

Stick to what you actually believe and agree on.

then mark out a field for discussion/ points that is, that are <u>WORTH wrangling</u> about.

I have said so much in Kulch etc.; that it is hard for me to go on UNTIL the receiving station registers reception.

AFTER you GET, Active Anthology/ ABC of Reading/ KULCH (or Culture) my program is/ REFORM of TEXT BOOKS along the lines I have projected/

     WHICH BEGIN with definition of terms/ (Money, Credit/ Property/ Capital etc. in econ)

     2. Knowledge of vital FACTS of history AND of literature.

Second segment/ Reprint of gists and piths/ of FOUNDERS of the U.S.A.
(this is a special line and PART of plan for reform of curricula....)
                                    leaflet will follow in a few weeks.

So General EP with his CAPS and underlinings was setting out directions
and an agenda for two undergraduates — possibly three but not more
than five.

Probably the name *Furioso* itself was Pound's idea — it sounds like
Pound — and Jim and R were happy with it. With the Pound imprimatur
they set out a prospectus, since lost, though it made some references to
having "axes to grind" and quoted a few poets on the new venture, including William Carlos Williams, whom they had written for an endorsement
and who wrote back with all modesty, "I am never certain that my name
will do anyone any good. I feel that there are so many in official positions
who detest me." Meanwhile, Jim and R began writing letters asking for
poems *and* subscriptions to more than a dozen bigtime Modernists,
among them E.E. Cummings, Archibald MacLeish, Marianne Moore,
Wallace Stevens, T.S. Eliot, Richard Eberhart, John Crowe Ransom,
Dudley Fitts, and John Peale Bishop. On Feb. 20, 1939, Williams was
back with a subscription: "I'm all for you and will give you the best I have
in poetry — now being revised in whatever spare moments I can find."
He also cheered R and Jim on.

> You don't need help. Just go to it. We need your youth more than you
> need us — in one way. Go to it, and more power to you. It's a tough racket.

> The name FURIOSO is a knockout. Nothing could be more to the
> point. If youth ain't furioso at the shitty spectacle the world presents today
> with all its backhouses propped up on the official stilts — then it ain't
> worth a damn. Start furioso. You'll be geniuses if you can bring it out. But
> if you can by any farthest chance really put over the idea of furioso, in half
> its salutary implications — you'll deserve the greatest praise of the era.

Meanwhile, Jim and R sent Williams poems as well. Two weeks later he
wrote back.

> I hope you won't mind my having taken a shot at your two poems. Both
> of them appeal to me as material. What you do, to my thinking, and you
> both do it, is to restate things by trying to be too explicit. All you have to

do is touch the meaning. You don't have to hammer it down with a maul. You state the thing before you have led up to it. Instead you should state its qualities and then come in with the thing itself at the end, as a confirmation. Tell me to go to hell if you want to. I don't care.

But Williams wasn't finished — so I'll quote from the third paragraph in which with his Jersey directness he laid down in an authoritative but different voice than his difficult pal Pound what a poem should do.

> In a short poem cut everything down to the last significant word, shave it, prune it, leave certain parts floating — if you have sufficiently implied them earlier. Don't forget you're writing for the IMAGINATION, to stir it, to confirm it, to convince it — to PLEASE it. You don't have to say more than just precisely that which will give the meaning. I've slashed your two poems to show you what I mean. Hope you'll forgive me — you know. Boloney.

R himself was soon emboldened and sent Williams criticism of a poem — though the years have clouded his memory of what he wrote, he has Williams' reply that his "criticism is justified…[it's] incurably romantic in a bad way — not Cummings's way which is all for accurate detail but the way which induces to vagueness and the borrowing of supposititious [?] values due to a swooning mind. To hell with it. Send it back for treatment or burial."

That was pure Williams, as was his open invitation to come visit, which R and Jim had asked about doing. "Come on along. We're here most of the time," he wrote. "It will be a great pleasure to meet you."

⁓

A brief digression here on the one trip that R made to meet Williams in Rutherford, N.J. He wrote about that visit some years later in the post-war *Furioso* in a review of *Paterson (Books I-III)*. I'll quote from the opening because it gives a further sense of what Williams (and Pound) meant to him and to Angleton at that time.

> I have met Dr. Williams only once, but I associate him personally with many matters which were terribly important to me at a terribly important time, the time of the founding of this magazine. He was wonderfully generous then, as I believe he has always been on such occasions, in his sup-

port of our enterprise; but more than that he was in his generosity a figure Jim Angleton and I could think of as an ally with special and genuine credentials whenever our own credentials were exposed as the forgeries they were. He was someone solid, someone whose literary history was Literary History and who, in addition to knowing so-and-so and so-and-so, was himself an active ingredient of that revolution we had arrived too late for but admired fervently. To sum up he was, with Pound, for us a reassuring symbol of successful revolt against authority; and though we did not at the time, I think now, know what the revolt consisted of or who the authorities were, we were confident Williams and Pound knew, and that was all that mattered.

So during spring 1939, their sophomore year, Jim and R labored to bring *Furioso* into the world. No. 1, a 28-page issue dated summer 1939 had 19 poets *ironically* sandwiched between an introductory letter from Archibald MacLeish to "My dear Mr. Angleton" — recommending that *Furioso* not be precious but speak to people "who understand the feel of things and the thinking of things, naturally and simply" — and a one page "Introductory Text Book" by Pound consisting of quotations from John Adams, Jefferson, Lincoln and Washington, all decrying usury (aka Capitalismus); the latter was followed by a Poundian "Note" correcting the readers' ignorance about such matters. Why *ironic*? Because MacLeish in his high-toned manner was pumping for plain American speech in poetry — getting poems to the American masses, for example, on radio — while Pound, with his fascist broadcasts to come, had been at the forefront of a Modernism that also pumped for plain speech in the ancient art. But the plain speech each advocated pulled in opposite directions: MacLeish was interested in an American poetry that reflected the country's great promise; Pound wanted an American poetry that could take its place alongside the work of ancient China, the Greeks, the French Troubadors. For Pound, all great poetry was contemporaneous — at least ideally.

Among the several Pound-friend poets in the issue were Williams, Dudley Fitts, Cummings and James Laughlin, founder of New Directions and publisher of Pound and Williams. Others included Horace Gregory, John Peale Bishop, and Richard Eberhart, whom R was to carry on an intense critical correspondence with. Of undergraduates there were only three — one from Yale, two from Harvard. In other words the issue was not an undergraduate event. More important, it contained no words at all from the editors themselves. R was publishing in *Yale Lit* and that winter, Jim was on the masthead of *Vif*, an intercollegiate French review, as (of all things) Redacteur en Chef. The issue had "Deux Poemes" by J.J. Angleton and a story by R, "Le Matinel." (R has no memory of who did the translations.). Their silence in *Furioso* would continue until their last undergraduate issue (I, 4) for which Jim produced an unrebellious one-page introduction.

In the meantime, Jim was engaged in literary entrepreneurship, promoting the magazine and also promoting Pound and his coming to the U.S. especially to speak at Yale and Harvard. How much had Jim instigated the trip and how much Pound and his other confreres? A couple of months after his visit, Pound wrote from Italy admonishing him: "It is inexact/ in fact it aint so at all, to suggest that I went to the U.S. in order to lecture at Yale. I said I wd/ be pleased to do so/ but it was NOT a reason for going to the U.S.A. I appreciate yr/ intentions, and local issue etc/ but the statement could have been exact, without damaging yr/ point." EP the teacher concluded:

> In another 30 years you will see reason for greater exactness of expression. at least lets hope so. Idea of precision used to bore me when I was yr/ age. so take this as part of attempt to eddikate you. not as mere crab.

Pound arrived in New Haven near the end of the school year on his well-known jaunt to keep "Patria Mia" out of the coming war. He may have first visited E.E. Cummings in New York, to whom (said Cummings himself) he lectured steadily about usury. It occurs to R now that Jim must have gone to see him there and spoken about *Furioso* because of another admonitory letter Pound wrote him, this on May 12th. "If you think you know more about what a magazine ought to print than I do, I just haven't time to argue the matter. Magazines either feed contributors or they serve to set certain scales of importance — proportional value of concepts." There! But Pound was not one to hold a grudge, not against Jim. Not yet.

He traveled to Washington where, with help from Senator Borah of Idaho, he visited or tried to visit other senators as well as FDR himself but was steadily rebuffed. His next engagements were scheduled in advance — at Harvard, and then at Hamilton College where he received an honorary degree. On the way to Cambridge he spent a night at Williams' house in Rutherford. After that visit Williams wrote a disparaging article about Pound — R doesn' remember where — which Jim wrote Williams about. Jim's letter is gone but what R has is WCWs' reply:

> You are quite right, what I have said about the semi-divine Ezra had better be modified. I was so infuriated with him when I talked to him here this spring that I never wanted to have more to do with him. I still feel somewhat that way but — there's no confusing him with the William [sic: Robert] Penn Warrens of the world or the young instructors at Yale. He is as I meant to imply in my article, a poet. I greatly admire your defense of him. It does you credit.

The next night the semi-divine Ezra arrived in New Haven at R's parents' apartment. Though the first issue of *Furioso* was near-ready, it was not yet back from the printer. Pound's visit was brief and R described it in the years following so many times that as he wrote in an essay in the late 50s, he wasn't sure if he remembered "what it was really like." Nevertheless, that visit was important to him and I'll quote from "A Brief History of a Little Magazine, and Other Matters" since it was written only 20 years after EP's visit rather than the nearly 70 it is now:

> Although he "visited" with us only briefly he did one thing that made it worthwhile: he tried to snow us. Having seated himself in a large armchair, he spread himself out in vast disarray while we gathered around and waited for the word, whatever the word was to be. It took no time coming: "Mrs. Whittemore, would you be so kind as to fetch me the book I left on my bed?" My mother fetched the book — it was a book of Chinese ideographs — and gave it to him. He opened it (from the back) as if we were not in the room at all and he was settling down for a quiet evening alone with Mei Sheng and Rihaku. But in less than thirty seconds he looked up, reacknowledged our presence, sighed noisily, and said, "How restful!"

R's parents and R later agreed that Pound had been a stuffed shirt, though in his defense R could say that the angry rebel in him must have been embarrassed to find no "serious" lit'ry folk other than two undergraduates cheering him on in all of New Haven. But more than a stuffed shirt, R came to feel that Pound's behavior was a "deception" and that he hadn't carried that deception off. R's position, as he wrote in his late-50s essay, "was one of unenlightened skepticism," his attitude, "no, thank you." That was a new position for R at the time. "Had Pound been a quack selling patent medicines, or a circus barker, it wouldn't have been remarkable; I had been told not to take any wooden nickels. But Pound wasn't offering any wooden nickels." Rather, "he was offering peace — Mussolini's kind — and he was a man for whom I had, and have, a great deal of respect."

> That I should be suspicious of him and of his position was, therefore, quite a blow. I found myself, like Troilus when he discovers Cressida's infidelity, doubting my senses. I became suspicious of Pound and at the same time suspicious of my suspicions. And out of these suspicions emerged, as I like to think, one of the important convictions of my college career, the conviction that there were lots of wooden nickels even in the temples of Apollo, Dionysus and Mei Sheng.

But back to where we were. The next day Jim and R drove Pound to Cambridge for various festivities — arranged by James Laughlin among others — where, according to Archibald MacLeish's biographer Scott Donaldson, he was indeed serious. MacLeish told Donaldson the following.

> Pound spent the time at Harvard letting everyone know what an awful place it was. The students were being cheated of their $400 tuition fee, he told them. They were not getting the "straight tip" on economics and American history. The straight tip, as Pound saw it, was that fascism posed no danger. "It is as idiotic to be anti-fascist in America as it would be to start a movement to prevent Javanese temple dancing in Massachusetts." At a party later at Theodore Spencer's house Pound continued in the same vein. MacLeish thought he was not only in error but boringly so, and left as soon as he could.

Meanwhile, summer came on and issue No. 1 finally appeared, the cover dominated by the "zany" figure with feather duster designed by Graham Peck. Jim and R heard from Williams on June 7th — "Dear *Furiosos*" — on their "good start in a difficult game.... You've definitely put yourselves on the spot," he wrote, then continued on what was required of the *Furiosos* to come.

> You will find plenty of friends ready to root for you if you keep up the clean front but if you slip, they'll crap all over you with glee. Print the kids, print 'em bald, fragmentarily, scattered, in part, a line, a bit and paragraph

FOR THE GOOD IN IT. I'd like to see a fragmentary issue of the kids, kid stuff, at its best — eliminating everything but the good pieces which may later appear as a considered work. But do print more of the unknowns. It's all right to salt in a few like myself but it's not the major function of FURIOSO unless I mistake your aim. The issue seems to me a little tight, too ordered — coming from two kids. I want to see what might be presumed to be more of you, as you, in it.

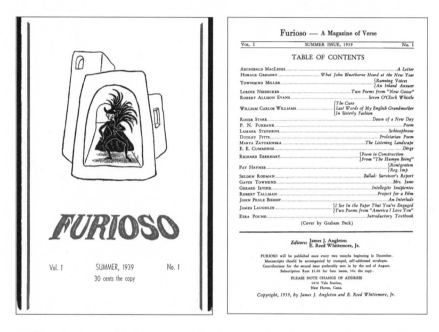

Williams returned a few days later with a hand-written note: "To explain myself perhaps better: what I wanted to say was that the poems were too neat, too finished — not furioso at all — not bolstered [?] by whatever passions they expressed. Their form was too calculated. I'd like to see them scattered in pieces — ending nowhere...."

Cummings wrote at the end of May with, what seems now, a remarkable modesty: "in certainly printing a certain poem, you and your confrère have paid me one deep compliment, and I heartily thank you both." Richard Eberhart wrote with detailed remarks, from the design — "a certain stiffness.... The furious Image is clever and diabolical — man casting his evil shadow into the lake" — to comments on nearly every poem. On Cummings's poem, he apologized for his prejudice: "How can you justify this poem? Its main point would seem to be its 'sophistication,' which,

ANNO

XVII

VIA MARSALA 12-5

E. POUND RAPALLO

Dear Jim

Cummings' poem will keep No I. on the map.

No. 2 should contain notice of (F.madox) Ford's death announcing No 3
as memorial issue to him.

The English Review was during the year and a half
he had it (started it) the greatest little review of our
time I908/I0

and much more is due Ford for all that is
alive in our verse than is generally known, all the drive
toward live language as distinct for Hopkin's ' retrospect.

As I told you, a review shd/ augment and the different issues
be NOTICEABLY different and rememberable one from another.

A memorial issue as No 3/ shd get you over one of the
technical problems in differentiation/ one and two bound to
differ, and the six months between two and 4
wd again provide a natural difference.

No one in our time has done more for young writers than poor
old Fordie. + Not over a long
period.

yrz.

Pound's letter of congratulations to Jim Angleton on Furioso No. 1.

March 23, 1939

Dear Whittemore:

Your criticism is justified, the Lillian piece is
incurably romantic in a bad way - not Cumming's way which is
all for accurate detail but a way which induces to vagueness and
the borrowing of supposititious values due to a swooning mind.
To hell with it. Send it back for treatment or burial.

Due to a curious sequence of circumstances you are
to have back the very poem I want you most to have, the Last
Words of My Grandmother. I had a feeling and still have it that
that poem was published somewhere, in some forgotten magazine
fifteen or more years ago. I don't know what magazine it was but
I feel certain that the poem did appear to some microscopic
audience then. This I told to the editors of Poetry who straight-
way sent the poem back to me. In the belief that this circum-
stance won't bother you I ask you to take it and use it now - if
you care to.

Come on along, we're here most of the time though
we shall be busy April 2nd. Better to call up, it will be a great
pleasure to meet you.

A good prospectus though I always feel a little
self conscious when I see myself quoted as you have quoted me. I
am never certain that my name will do anyone any good. I feel
that there are so many in official positions who detest me that
I regret, really, not to have been anonymous as one of your backers.
Howbeit, the quotations by three such names gave me a big laugh.
If you can survive that you're close to genius.

The little figure made me think of Cotton Mather, a
good American, not to say New England touch. Splendid.

Keep my poems as long as you like, hold them that long
I should have said, they're yours to do as you please with - and
I distinctly mean what I say : any of them that seems inappropriate
to you please send it back so that I may substitute another. I'll
try to get the prose bit ready but for that I shall have to wait
until Southern Review comes out of its southern lethargy and sends
the scripts of mine they are holding (including postage) back to
me.

                                    Sincerely

9 Ridge Road
Rutherford, N.J.   W. C. Williams

Letter to R from William Carlos Williams.

however, anyone should be beyond at the age of 18, whereafter its bug-ger-rectie impeti become merely boring. This poem again is comic, pulls the silly verbal wool over myopic eyes."

Pound chipped in a few weeks later from Rapallo, his one specific response: "Cummings' poem will keep No. I on the map." (No wonder Eberhart had written R earlier, "I am sure Pound would disapprove of me entirely.")

With No. 1 out Pound sent new instructions. "No. 2 should contain notice of F. Madox Ford's death announcing No. 3 as memorial issue to him."

As I told you, a review shd/ augment and the different issues be NOTICE-ABLY different and rememberable one from another.

A memorial issue as No. 3/ shd get you over one of the technical problems in differentiation/ one and two bound to differ, and the six months between two and 4 wd again provide a natural difference.

"No one in our time," he ended, "has done more for young writers than poor old Fordie and not over a long period."

The industry that went into *Furioso* impressed Jim and R's teachers, R wrote years later for a special *Tri-Quarterly* issue on little magazines; he couldn't help adding that "they must have understood the industry was not matched by wisdom." R's mother and father were also impressed, though they "took the position that *Furioso* was a strange and marvelous invention that was quite beyond them." That did not stop R's mother from selling subscriptions to her friends.

⸺

Summer 1939 came on and while Jim spent those months in Cambridge R went on an immense uncollegiate cruise with his parents (money from the sale of No. 193 East Rock Road) on a Canadian Pacific ship *The Duchess of Richmond* that slipped through the Panama Canal, then visited Southern California (Hollywood), Hawaii, Alaska and, yes, Acapulco, at which point most passengers were motored from the port up to Mexico City and then put on a train taking them down on the other side of Mexico to Vera Cruz where, on September 1st, the cruise ship — having slipped through the Canal again — met them. (That is quite a sentence but it was quite a cruise.) All would then have been well in Vera Cruz if World War II had not happened to begin on September 1, 1939, a date memorialized, at least in poetry anthologies, by W.H. Auden's poem of that title.

But it did begin then and the passengers of the *Duchess* found themselves in a thoroughly novel blackout as they steamed for New York via Havana. Of course all of them came home safe — the ship was not sunk until a few months later — and in their safety the war for them became a largely foreign event for two years.

Back at Yale in the fall, R and Jim found themselves living at last quite elegantly *inside* Yale's cocoon — that is, in Pearson College as Juniors and the next year in Silliman College as Seniors. And they went right ahead with *Furioso*. In No. 1 they ambitiously announced that "FURIOSO will be published once every two months" — only three more issues were to come over their junior and senior years, though the last was a whopper. Among the Modernists there were more poems by Williams and Cummings, Auden, Eberhart, Louis MacNeice, Marianne Moore, Pound and Wallace Stevens, William Empson, as well as reviews by John Crowe Ransom, Fitts, and Eberhart. Jim and R meanwhile proceeded with their ordinary college studies, though Jim's labors were erratic and produced many incompletes. Years later in a letter to Allen Tate, R wrote that "Jim could hardly be gotten to go to class in four years at Yale."

Whether his literary entrepreneurship had something to do with this, R doesn't know. During 1939 and 1940, for example, Jim was writing T.S. Eliot about arranging for Italian translations of Eliot's poems. He had originally written him in Spring 1939 about poems and a subscription for *Furioso* — Eliot, in his cool Brahmin manner, wrote that he "had to decline all invitations to contribute poetry to periodicals on the one final ground that I have not written any poems." In the meantime, he asked Jim to send the first number and wrote, "if I think it is good enough, I will subscribe." But Jim was not finished. After the first issue was out, he wrote again, this time proposing that Eliot's poems be brought out in Italian translation. Eliot advised Jim to line up an Italian publisher first who would then "communicate with Faber & Faber.... It would be a pity," he wrote, "for your friends to undertake the labour of translation unless a publisher could be secured." Who were these friends? R no longer knows, nor may Jim have. Still, he persisted. In June 1940, Eliot wrote to say there were several translators who were at work on his plays, some with permissions, others not. "If you could do something toward centralising these various activities and getting the various things published by one firm, you would certainly be doing me a service, and I should be glad to see my firm make an arrangement with you." That was the last of the Eliot letters and the enterprise itself — the world war had begun.

Meanwhile, R had been carrying on a correspondence with Eberhart that had begun before the first issue when R wrote back with detailed criticism of a poem Eberhart had sent. "Your letter seemed to be ultra-conservative," Eberhart admonished: "the kind of critic-snippets you give represents university criticism." Nevertheless, Eberhart revised poems and asked in one letter, "Is this an improvement" and wrote in another, "You are right about p. 3," while adding a P.S., "You may be quite right on p. 22 last 2 stanzas — reading them aloud your way is effective." It was a heady literary time.

———

In the middle of Junior year Jim defected rather oddly from responsibilities with *Furioso* long enough to write — secretly of course — a mimeographed pamphlet that he called *The Waif*. Perhaps relevantly that year he also picked up a temporary but disturbing family responsibility when his father, stranded (comfortably) in Rome, was unable to move money readily to the U.S. for his three children at school there. Therefore: instead of money a large shipment of elegant Italian purses and footwear suddenly arrived in Pearson College for Jim to sell. Jim quickly harnessed R's mother to the selling, but Lord knows how much was ever actually marketed; some of the shipment was still under Jim's bed in senior year. At that time Jim's sister Carmen at Bryn Mawr, his brother Hugh at Yale and Jim himself were somehow solvent when 1941 and Jim's graduation arrived. A bank or two in Switzerland seems to have been involved — but all that is another family's story.

Pound's *Furioso* labors continued. He contributed several light verses — a side of Pound not often seen— for No. 2, including an arch masculine poem called "Spaggia 1937": "A lesson no school book teaches:/ Women's bums are often/ Too big for their breeches." No. 2 also had "A Letter" from Williams addressed to "Dear Whittemore" — he was throwing fast balls at R, raising issues that "certainly should be covered right now in *Furioso*. Propaganda in Poetry. Poetry that tries to influence people. In other words, just what is the function of poetry?" This question was already nagging at R, continued to during his war years in Europe, in essays and reviews and late-night muddles over the next 50 years, and still does.

"What has a poetry magazine to do with a war, with a country's policy, with a new bunch of quintuplets, etc.?" Williams asked, then laid down his conclusion — and this after only one issue: "In publishing *Furioso* I think that's one of the things we've been trying to find out, and so far I haven't found anything." (It was to be a topic that Andrews [Andy] Wanning took up in "Ruminations over the Dilemma of Poets in Wartime" in the one wartime issue of *Furioso*, in 1943, which Carmen Angleton handled with help from Emma Swan.) "My idea," Williams wrote, "is that poetry deals with the generalities of human conduct, with questions that are important for more than ten minutes, with movements greater than the French occupation of the Saar Basin." The end of poetry, he wrote, "is a poem" and instanced Pound as "one example of someone whose economic ideas didn't amount to much, that they could be said much more concisely and clearly: Peter Cooper said a number of years ago, Exorbitant rent (commonly called interest) silently — I think this, in one sentence, says more succinctly than Pound ever dreamed, everything he ever conceived of economics. But Peter Cooper was not a poet. Pound is a poet, so we forgive him."

Williams ended his personal-public letter with an exhortation to R and by extension to all poets.

> Be the Shakespeare of your day, write well, skillfully, covertly, deceitfully, with every faculty under a hood or blanket concealed from public view, write of that which is nearest to the skin (to hell with the heart!) but write well."

Issue No. 3 (Summer, 1940) opened with Pound and Williams' fine memorials to Ford Maddox Ford. Pound in his two-page homage elaborated comically and self-deprecatingly on the warm words he wrote to Jim about Ford, picturing Ford rolling on the floor "when my third volume displayed me trapped, flypapered, gummed and strapped down in a jejune provincial effort to learn, *mehercule*, the stilted language that then passed for 'good English' in the arthritic milieu that held control of the respected critical circles.... " Pound was not finished.

And that roll saved me at least two years, perhaps more. It sent me back to my own proper effort, namely, toward using the living tongue (with younger men after me), though none of us has found a more natural language than Ford did.

Williams had written Jim in the fall that he'd do anything for the so-called Ford number. "I'll think up a poem," he wrote, "there must be one there waiting. It's a real opportunity to get something said. He was an old man, a fat old man who wheezed when he spoke, an old man who was something of an outcast at home — we'll see." He did think up a poem, "Ford Madox Ford in Heaven" — and in Williams fashion got the fat old man into it. Here's an excerpt:

I laugh to think of you wheezing in Heaven. Where is
          Heaven? But why
do I ask that, since you showed the way. I don't care a
          damn for it
other than for that better part beside me here
          so long as I
live and remember you. Thank God you were not delicate,
          you let the world in
and lied! Damn it you lied grossly sometimes. But it
          was all, I see now,
careless, the part of man that is homeless here
          on earth.
Provence! The fat-assed Ford will never again strain
          the chairs of your cafés,
pull and pare for his dish your sacred garlic, grunt and
          sweat and lick
his lips. Gross as the world he has left to us he has
          become
a part of that which you were the known part, Provence,
          he loved so well.

The issue was delayed — it didn't come out until the spring — though Williams expressed satisfaction that it was finally coming: "Its reception, if it is noticed, should be of interest. I'd like to know what Pound thinks of it — if anything; in all probability he'll say nothing being inhibited from noticing anything but his own peculiar interests."

An odd announcement in No. 3 probably had Poundian origins: it advised that the next issue would "be printed somewhere in Europe, possibly in Italy." Of course the next issue was not printed in Italy but by the same drunken printer in New Haven whose erratic typesetting had some *Furioso* contributors asking for proof after proof. Cummings, for example, wrote, "I suppose it'll take at least 6 or 7 proofs to get this right — so let's start in!"

R did not read until much later a letter by Pound, not to Jim but to another young editor thinking of starting a magazine, to the effect that another magazine was now needed by the world since *Furioso* was not getting "the job" done. Thinking of that put-down later on, R could never really stop wondering and worrying about what in the world "the job" *should* be for a little magazine — or a little poetry magazine anyway. He assumed Pound had in mind what it should be in terms of his own thirty-year role as a message-filled bard and little-magazine reformer, and while R had no plans for following in Poundian political footsteps he would continue to respect the basic "jobbing" notion for poetry and little mags. Half a century later R even made small gestures (in letters only) opposing the establishment of a "National Poetry Month," a high-powered promotional scheme that he was pretty sure Pound also would have opposed as well. (It's continued for a bit, despite R's cantankerous opposition.) In R's view the trouble with poetry was and may still be that it is jobless except in the production of beauty, sweetness and light. For better or worse Pound would surely have filled the air with angry remarks against such effete nonsense being dreamed up by commercial publishing interests for the preservation of a poetic status quo.

One can readily argue that such political *jobbing* was what got Pound in trouble on Rome Radio during the war. And yet, interestingly, MacLeish in 1939-41 was also an urgent jobber about going to war and also concerned with making poetry (and literature generally, and academia generally) a jobbing business. In *The Irresponsibles*, he split the pre-war American academic community in half, and set most of *Furioso*'s contributors raging against him. MacLeish (and Van Wyck Brooks more simplistically) attacked American academics and writers for not taking a strong stand on the side of democracy. Edmund Wilson accused MacLeish of being himself a propagandist. Two of Yale's young untenured teachers, Arthur Mizener and Andy Wanning were among the MacLeish despisers; they had also become involved with *Furioso*. At a time when such academic-political-aesthetic maneuvering was constantly in the papers and being expressed at public meetings, *Furioso* printed two intelligent New Critical reviews by Wanning that, without rancor, put poetic warriors down.

In "Interim Report on the National Poetical Effort," he took aim at the hackneyed work that MacLeish's call for a more patriotic poetry most often leads to. Edna St. Vincent Millay's *Make Bright the Arrows* was one of the exemplary targets — Wanning quoted the following as an example that "cannot be much more kindly described than as cartoonist's imagery."

> Yet matters from without intrude
>   At times upon my solitude:
> A forest fire, a dog run mad,
>   A neighbor stripped of all he had
> By swindlers, or the shrieking plea
>   For help, of stabbed Democracy...
>
> Oh, God, let not the lovely brow
> Of Freedom in the trampled mud
> Grow cold!

Jim and R also enlisted the anti-warrior enthusiasm of Horace Gregory, a prominent New York literary politico of the 30s, who in the same issue attacked this warmonger volume with a one-page caricature review — a drawing of a pure poetic maiden throwing herself and her lute off a cliff. These doings provoked — before WW II — constant serious controversy about a poet's *proper* job, and R at that earlier time was confronted night and day by the controversy.

Twenty-one years old, R listened and found temporary leftist reinforcement against America's

CRITICISM

Make Bright the Arrows, by Edna St. Vincent Millay. Harper & Brothers. 65 pp. $1.75.

"It was my evil star above,
    Not my sweet lute, that wrought me wrong;
It was not song that taught me love,
    But it was love that taught me song.

If song be passed, and hope undone,
    And pulse, and head, and heart, are flame;
It is thy work, thou faithless one!
    But, no!—I will not name thy name . . ."

(Arrangement by *Horace Gregory*)

R, Richard Eberhart and W.H. Auden at Yale, c. 1940.

E.E. Cummings and his painting of wife Marion behind him. Photograph by Jim Angleton, c. 1941.

going to war from an English communist graduate student at Yale, Arnold Kettle, whom R was to have an intense correspondence with during the War.

Kettle was a pleasant, open, vocal Soviet backer who had nothing but contempt for American warmongers as he likened MacLeish to as long as the Soviet-German non-aggression pact seemed real. Then in late 1940, reading of the German betrayals, he suddenly became ferocious — and went home to join the British Army. For R at the time Kettle's passionately political approach to literature made the temperate New Critical views of many of the Yale literary faculty of the time seem, if not wrong, at least feeble. And certainly Kettle helped bring R around to believing that poets could be political without, like MacLeish, falling off the platform. R's problem with Kettle was that he kept calling Pound a fascist and Pound kept showing that he was.

Characteristically R was struggling with the big word "commitment," worrying about how he as a writer might move beyond self-study and congratulatory fabrications of beauty, and might learn instead to back something beyond his typewriter. Accordingly he much admired an adolescent poem of commitment that had come out of Harvard for *Furioso* No. 2, an angry piece by an unknown named James Higgins with a thoroughly local view of a needed "job." In it Higgins was neither for nor against war. He was just fed up to the teeth with his own classmates for their inveterate joblessness. Addressing the lovely crew of fops at poem's end he wrote, "Gentlemen there is not one/among you can smile/ a coherent smile/ By Jesus,/ Take note of *that!*"

And R didn't feel up to smiling a coherent smile either — perhaps he suspected he never had been up to such a smile, not since he sat stonily on a tricycle in a cement driveway. Worse, the war's urgencies seemed to boost his indecision. If only he could have been moved back six or eight years and forced to live in the Depression's climate he might at least have busied himself writing hot verbiage for little radical Thirties magazines like *Anvil* or papers like *The Daily Worker*. But in the frenetic war-but-no-war climate there was no avoiding the fact that clear left-right positioning was dumb. And even if it was not so for humanity in general it was dumb for him since as a leftist he was no proletarian but a genteel middle class New England son of a quiet capitalist doctor. He could complain and complain about this condition. He could also complain about "pure poetry," a phrase that kept coming up in high academic circles and making him, like Higgins, angry since purity in a seedy war-torn world did not seem — to use Pound's favorite word — a serious option. So there he was, feeling that he ought to have meaningful disestablishment commitments but not having them. The result in his own college poetry was generally miserable, and nothing of his that appeared in *Yale Lit* seemed to him, later, worth much except for "A Winter Shore," a heavy long poem in five parts that was published in the last issue, May 1941, before graduation. R later sent it to *The Kenyon Review* for what John Crowe Ransom called the "Younger Poets Competition." Though R would come to call such poems Sappy Nature Sop, he did reprint it in 1990 in *The Past, The Future, The Present: Poems New and Selected*. Here is the first stanza — the best part:

> What the sea does winters,
> What to summer's wreck,
> It does well.
> > What old hull is
> Not borne under, swept bare,
> Shattered, buried in the sand,
> A broken shell?
> > Winter has
> No other undertow like this,
> The sea. No other burial
> Makes skeletons so fast,
>
> What the sea does winters,
> To summer's corpse,
> It does for all.

To read R's letters to Arthur Mizener at this time (Mizener had spent much of R's senior year away from Yale, and would soon be settled at Wells College in upstate New York) is to realize that by R's junior year he and Mizener were fast friends and though their tie was that of student and teacher — with R bothering Mizener in his Pearson College office every Sunday morning — they steadily talked about each other's work. Best of all, their relationship would continue through the war with their correspondence (now in the University of Maryland Hornbake Library) filling pages and pages — and seldom touching on the war itself but only on the rightness and wrongness of particular verse lines. Mizener was the helpful agent, even before R's graduation, in connecting R to Ransom and *The Kenyon Review*.

And what of Jim at college's end? His commitments were perhaps more scattered than R's since his parents were still in Rome as WWII began. Yet his manner remained generally assured, while continuing his literary salesmanship. There were the Eliot Italian translations, a proposal to Pound that a complete bibliography of his work be put together — Pound wanted little part of it, primarily because it would be too much work — while to Cummings he proposed printing his plays, which Cummings was greatly appreciative of. At the same time, he was a persistently confident debater, and his arguments had a way of turning into sales talks. In this respect he took after his father, a strong-minded businessman who knew how to manage, make decisions, sell.

A brief aside about Jim's father, James Hugh Angleton, whom R met in New York just *after* the war when R was fresh out of uniform and wondering what to do next. The father knew. He had good reports from Jim about R, so offered him a job on the spot — and sold it hard right there in a Fifth Avenue hotel over drinks: R could be an executive of a brand-new big-time newspaper (in English) in just-being-reconstructed Italy. How could R refuse?

R did refuse — refusals were perhaps part of his usual coping procedure — and the father was disappointed. So was Jim, and more than a half century later it seems likely that Jim himself was then on the edge of taking the newspaper on. Right there he might have given up the intelligence business rather than making the move he was about to make, from the OSS (which he had joined early and worked for in London during the war) into the new peacetime CIA, where he ascended nearly to the top before his catastrophic fall. It should be noted that Pêre Angleton was also in the OSS.

It even seems possible that a grandiose post-war scheme Jim had for *Furioso* could have been part of his thinking before the war hit him. As his widow Cicely says, *Furioso* was everything to him in those years before he was drafted in 1943. Here is a quotation from a 1940 letter he wrote to one of the magazine's steadiest contributors, Richard Eberhart.

We are going on with *Furioso* after we leave Yale and we are going to have a better and more appreciated magazine than all the others. I know this as a fact. I know that we will mold a large audience and that they will support us. I know also that we are going to improve to the point that we [shall] have all the best poets wanting their material in *Furioso*, not because of payment but because we will have the more informed and appreciative audience.

Whew! There is the voice of a salesman-editor indeed, with more of the salesman-side showing than that of the little mag editor. Yet lest there be a misunderstanding it should be said that Jim was often a very sensible promoter. *Furioso's* final undergraduate issue — appearing on the very last day before graduation in 1941 — was in all respects a product of his best promotional talent, particularly a section of it labeled "Aesthetics" that emerged from Jim's successful parleying with several high academics at Harvard and Yale. The parleying began with the unexpected arrival — early Junior year — of William Empson in Jim and R's rooms in Pearson College.

Why was he there? Where did he come from? The chain of circumstances would seem wiggly enough to have pleased Agatha Christie, but probably the explanation lay largely with Jim's English schooling, English accent and effective salesmanship. Empson had just come to the U.S. from China, but before that he had been a prize student in England of I.A. Richards who had much admired his *Seven Types of Ambiguity* and had recently migrated from England to Harvard. Richards quickly moved into the circle of Harvard academics who were familiar with Pound's (and Jim and R's) *Furioso*. Empson apparently visited Richards at Harvard for advice and comfort in a new and strange country. He was given the names of influential persons in New York and was in the process of traveling to New York when Richards or some other Harvard man suggested that on the way there he drop in on Angleton in New Haven. He did. R and Jim were in their Pearson quarters at the time and, pleased with their catch, quickly drove him to supper in R's roadster at a shore restaurant near Madison. They were on their first course and had hardly begun to discuss literature, little magazines and life when Empson began to tremble and shake. The shaking problem was new to Jim and R — something out of China no doubt — so they hurried him back to Pearson, put him in R's bed and sat out in their living room debating their next move. Suddenly they heard R's typewriter clacking and soon Empson, not trembling and shaking at all, emerged with a poem — which of course would soon appear in *Furioso*. The episode ended happily with Empson's continuing on his New York journey, returning a few weeks later to deliver a lecture at Yale, one that Jim had arranged and that *Furioso* promoted on campus with a four-page brochure — "*Furioso*: A Special Note - January 12, 1940" — that included an introduction by none other than Richards. Jim had written him about doing one — Richards sent a hand-written piece and apologized for its being "roughly scribbled and probably too long." As he didn't have his books then, he asked Jim's help to "verify the line I quote from the Shakespeare sonnet and spell villanelle right, will you?" There was more.

The flyer-and-lecture episode led — through many twists and turns — to Richards himself being invited to Yale to deliver its important annual Bergen lecture. Behind the twists was the remarkably persuasive undergraduate Jim, and the lecture itself became the heart of *Furioso*'s last collegiate brainchild, an "aesthetics" section.

In its scope and intention the lecture was a grand interdisciplinary affair. That surprised R, since Richards (in R's newly scholarly mind) was an early New Critic, a forerunner of Cleanth Brooks and Robert Penn Warren's *Understanding Poetry*. He had produced a convincingly documented, poet-shaking volume — *Practical Criticism* — with "practical" right in its title, showing that readers of poems had an evil way of reading whatever they pleased into poems. So R, expecting more bad shop-news in the lecture, instead heard Richards begin with a kind of sales talk for his own pet project, "Basic English," and then shift cleverly into high philosophy in order to mention — pleasantly of course — a Yale philosopher, William M. Urban, who had "made a hash" of the Richards book on Basic English. Urban happened to be right in the audience, and afterwards he harkened to a request by the *Furioso* editors that he comment on Richards' comments — by writing a brief "Note 'Anent' Dr. Richards." (The "anent" was Jim's idea.) In the 700-word note he praised Richards' interest in philosophy until near the end, when he observed — pleasantly of course — that "he had always admired Richards' writings even though it was often his errors that had been the source of the stimulation."

Well, this naturally delighted the serious if not mischievous minds behind *Furioso*. And with the "note" instantly taken to the printer, those minds wanted more, more — so went out and captured two other campus philosophers. One was an instructor in philosophy, Martin

Furioso *A Special Note*

January 12, 1940

WILLIAM EMPSON
BY L. A. RICHARDS

William Empson made his name first with *Seven Types of Ambiguity*, a book which came into being more or less in the following fashion. He had been a mathematician at Cambridge and switched over for his last year to English. As he was at Magdalene, this made me his Director of Studies. He seemed to have read more English Literature than I had, and to have read it more recently and better, so our roles were soon in some danger of becoming reversed. At about his third visit he brought up the games of interpretation which Laura Riding and Robert Graves had been playing with the unpunctuated form of 'The expense of spirit in a waste of shame.' Taking the sonnet as a conjurer takes his hat, he produced an endless swarm of lively rabbits from it and ended by "You could do that with any poetry, couldn't you?" This was a Godsend to a Director of Studies, so I said, "You'd better go off and do it, hadn't you?" A week later he said he was still slapping away at it on his typewriter. Would I mind if he just went on with that? Not a bit. The following week there he was with a thick wad of very illegible typescript under his arm—the central 30,000 words or so of the book. I can't think of any literary criticism written since which seems likely to have as persistent and as distinctive an influence. If you read much of it at once, you will think you are sickening for 'flu; but read a little *with care* and your reading habits may be altered—for the better, I believe.

While we were discussing it somewhat later he suddenly jumped up in a sort of rapture and shouted "Why we are *talking* Metaphysical poetry!" Certainly he was talking his own poetry; and that, at its best, has always been pregnant conversation fitted miraculously into the most insistent formal patterns. A villanelle is just the thing he is most at ease in. To quote the close of one,

> Slowly the poison the whole blood stream fills.
> The waste remains, the waste remains, and kills.

The unconscious echo of Tennyson's

> The woods decay, the woods decay, and fall

is characteristic. There is always a huge hinterland around everything he says in verse. The peculiarly grim wit and the savage gusto come perhaps from our awareness of the beasts which are roaming there. I remember him saying that there are things in *Alice* which would give Freud the creeps. There is plenty in his poetry to give us all the other parts of the poetic sensation as well. But, far more important because it orders them, is its intellectual grasp of the deepest traditional themes. His poetry is metaphysical in the root sense.

For a time the poetry lost itself in over-compressed conceits and turned into a guessing game. But now it seems to be back again at railhead working on the track.

Editors: JAMES J. ANGLETON
E. REED WHITTEMORE, JR.

1456 Yale Station,
New Haven, Conn.

Among the contributors, Archibald MacLeish, Ezra Pound, Arthur Mizener, E. E. Cummings, Horace Gregory, Andrews Wanning, Richard Eberhart, John Peale Bishop, Emma Swan, William Carlos Williams, Dudley Fitts, Marya Zaturenska, and others.

As graduation approached, the editorial board of Yale Lit *posed for an august final photograph: R (second row, left), Jim Angleton and Bill Johnson, future co-editor of the postwar* Furioso *(second row, last two), and John Pauker (first row, center).*

Lit, vif, furioso

Two views of Jim Angleton: at Yale in 1941, his senior year (from The Yale Banner*) and in military uniform, c. 1942.*

Eshleman, who sat right down and wrote a learned piece praising Urban's most recent book. The other was a full professor, Filmer Northrop (better known, more forbiddingly, as F.S.C. Northrop), a specialist in the truths of science but also, as if incidentally, the Master of Silliman College where Jim and R were by then housed. In his own masterly fashion Jim persuaded Northrop to write a piece for the fast-growing "aesthetics" section on "The Functions and Future of Poetry" — and tie it up somehow with Richards' piece.

And as if all this were not enough, Jim drew up a tentative plan (also described in a letter to Eberhart) for distributing 6000 copies of the grand new issue (the print order for the issue before it had been perhaps a thousand) to "all classes in modern thought, criticism, poetry, etc., in American universities." (R was particularly struck by the "etc.") He even persuaded contributor Northrop to have Silliman College buy 200 real copies of the apocryphal 6000 for placement on Silliman students' last-lunch plates for the spring term.

The 100-page issue opened with a brief introduction addressing the question, "What is poetry?" Jim penned it and it's worth quoting here, especially because he refers to the *Furioso* logo that Graham Peck had first designed and which was to serve as the guiding spirit for the postwar *Furioso* as well.

"What is poetry?" The unusual bulk of prose appearing in this issue might constitute our reply.... P-o-e-t-r-y, like its fellow actualities, Beauty, Wisdom, and Truth, exists behind the veil darkly of the Incomprehensible. While nose, ear, eye (and other organs) make homo sapiens of our questioner and editors of us, their worst or best efforts do not begin to penetrate one true mystery. Poetry may be experience, yes: it cannot be editorially defined....

Were we the absolute judges our contributors and readers demand, our occupation would perhaps be that of saints; certainly not that of editors. As editors, and no one else, we beg to reintroduce the little zany whose figure appears upon our magazine's cover: he is not any, but the *oonly trew juge of poesye*. Peering through his unshatterable goggles and brandishing a featherduster, he scampers over all epochs; rejecting there, quickening here. The number of words he has swept into the bottomless dustbin since Homer and Hesiod spoke, since Lucretius and Dante lived, defies computation. We, his lesser henchmen, humbly hope that he may spare a section of *Furioso*, or a poem, or a line, or a single metaphor — finding which, some seeking person of the future's future will in amazement exclaim "This Is Myself!"

When Jim and R finally put the aesthetics section together, it included a 5000-word Richards lecture, 700-word Urban note, 5000-word review of the Urban book and the interminable 7000-word piece by Northrop. In addition to this vast section there was work by MacLeish, Auden, Stevens, Cummings and Lawrence Durrell fluttering through the poetry pages, and book reviews in back assessing Pound (John Drummond), Auden (Dudley Fitts), Cummings (Theodore Spencer), John Peale Bishop (Richard Eberhart), and Richard Eberhart (John Crowe Ransom). R, typically, had some doubts about such grandeur — doubts that would show up again in his workings on the magazine after the war — yet he could only be pleased. Even the immense (and in R's opinion wrong-headed) poetry essay by the good and kind master of Silliman had the merit, perhaps unmeant, of humor. For instance, Northrop, in explaining how a poet could be a useful "handmaiden" to scientists, suggested that the marvelous poetic phrase "babbling brook" served to clarify, for lay readers, difficult truths that a full-blooded physicist might omit about the brook. The physicist might instead "speak of molecules falling from the top of one stone to a stone below and moving in a path which is a parabola, compounded out of an inertial force with a constant velocity in a straight line, and an accelerated motion perpendicular thereto defined by the constant of gravitation." Yes, "babbling brook" was an improvement.

⁓

Of course, this chapter should now move away from *Furioso* in order to get at R's Yale education as a whole before going on to the next stage of his education, WWII. The point is that *Furioso* was a large part of his education, even though the education pretended to go on separately — with its readings, classes, term-papers and finals. By graduation *Furioso* had somehow involved itself in the whole academic process, not just because of Northrop, Wanning and Mizener's work in the magazine but also because the magazine had brought all sorts of human ties to teacher miseries, teacher jealousies, teacher politics and so on. R would be spared personally the basics of pedagogy until he became a teacher himself — and Jim would always be spared those though he would be trapped with similar miseries in the "Agency." Yet the magazine's heavy presence for both of them, amid normal student affairs, made them feel a little *like* faculty, though degree-less.

They were particularly struck at the end of senior year by the plight and feelings of four teachers they liked, including Wanning and Mizener, who failed to receive tenure. They discovered — as if taking a no-credit course — that though Yale seemed a big impersonal place the daily working life in it could be like life in a small town, with teacher A in an office next to teacher B and hating teacher B, and with the scholarship of C being discovered to be fraudulent by D. On a big campus a student might easily miss these human normalcies and stay innocent. Jim and R could not, but at least they had the satisfaction of becoming educated (a little). They could also be pleased to think that with issue No. 4 at the printer's they had done a good Poundian "job." They therefore dedicated the issue to the four teachers — Mizener, Wanning, Raymond Short, Alan McGee — who had not been rehired.

And with that gesture did come, at last, graduation. The graduation class assembled in Woolsey Hall to be praised and cautioned, and then to be entertained by the long-retired English professor William Lyon Phelps reading an honorary degree citation for Walt Disney. Yes Disney himself was there and was praised by Phelps for having "labored like a mountain to produce a mouse" — perhaps a fitting conclusion for much of the class. But it was not fitting for Jim simply because he wasn't even there. He had not concluded at all but had rushed off on other projects such as delivering boxes of manuscripts as well as *Furioso's* subscription list to his sister Carmen in New York, and beginning his own sales campaign for admission to Harvard Law School. As mentioned earlier, Carmen published the one issue of *Furioso* during WWII.

At that point Jim was suddenly gone from R's life for the next three years, since R had just been drafted and was to be inducted in October. (Readers not familiar with the timetable of WWII are inclined to think the war began with Pearl Harbor in December. No, no. Hitler and the war in Europe had already brought about conscription for ripe young men.) Much later R learned that Jim had indeed been admitted to Harvard Law, completed one year, married Cicely d'Autremont, who was at Vassar, was then drafted and sent abroad in November 1943, finding his way into the OSS. Meanwhile, however, R's future was fixed and he was the one who had become the waif.

What to do? For a few days he lay on his bed at home in his parents' Livingston Street apartment wondering what had happened to his life. Then, still wondering, he climbed into the Ford with his usual pad of paper, drove out to Madison on his usual back road and found his usual shore place, the one where he had often looked out on lonely Long Island Sound with appropriate thoughts. But it was not the off-season. The beach was crowded with heartless unconcerned undrafted sunbathers who quickly drove him inland. There he came to a dirty rundown motel he had noticed for years without ever imagining that he would enter. He entered. He spent a sleepless night in it on a lumpy mattress, drove home, and the next day drove downtown in New Haven to enlist early.

His three months of basic training began not in October but August. Completing them he came home on furlough and then drove up to Cambridge to see loyal *Furioso* contributor Andy Wanning who had a temporary teaching job there. He was sitting in the Wanning living room on December 7, 1941, listening to the radio when the news of Pearl Harbor came through.

Wartime

chapter four

R's mother and father saw him off at the New Haven railroad station. His destination was Fort Devens, Massachusetts. He was twenty-one. His height was 5'8", weight 125. He had black hair, prominent ears, thin wrists and small feet. Yes, and he also had good hard teeth that would nonetheless cause him trouble later and drive him to write a tedious dental story (never to be mentioned again) with irrelevant data about porcelain crowns that he had picked up from his father's 1910 *Encyclopedia Britannica, 11th Edition*. The *Enc Brit 11* he has carried with him in all his journeying.

More data. He was near-sighted but wore no glasses. He had a medium-grade mind and managed to mix intellectual modesty with sudden arrogance. He was not cut out to be a mathematician, a philosopher or a teetotaler, and some of his best friends were as commonplace as he. He preferred to think of himself as a genuine rebel yet couldn't help being polite. Also he was remarkably unobservant, had a poor memory and slept too much. At Yale his grades had been B's or even C's except when he was interested. He had belonged to no fraternity and had been uncomfortable sipping tea among solemn minds at the Elizabethan Club. In poetry he would soon gravitate, though in uniform and surrounded by war, to innocent sonnets about literary characters. More of this later.

Despite his now aging mind R can still remember details of basic WWII training as they crept up on him. What surprises him now is how intensely preoccupied he remained with Poetry and Literature (in caps). All this came back much later while sitting for a day at the University of Maryland Hornbake Library looking at scores of letters that he and Arthur Mizener wrote to each other more than sixty years ago, with Mizener serving as a sounding board for the poems he was writing. As for R's living with the war itself, the first thing to be noted now is that he was comically ignorant about army life — and how to cope with it. The coping theory of economics professors F, F & B — that if one couldn't cope one quit — had become thoroughly irrelevant, and even the derivation of "cope" in R's father's *Century Dictionary*, that it came from "coup — a powerful stroke" or perhaps "kola — to strike resoundingly" also seemed odd when practicing hospital corners on a barracks cot as one readied for inspection. It was a new world. And by the second week of training he was cowed by just being where he was — already *in* training at Camp Croft, South Carolina. Yet he tried to show a bit of jobbish resounding-ness by writing a snippy letter describing sinister military evils — espe-cially in the mess hall — and posting it to an editor on the *Yale Lit* board. He designed it for dissemination among ignorant student civilians back in civilization, but right after posting it he learned that no, it had been captured by the enemy — mail was being censored — and a Colonel wished to talk with him.

He was led to that Colonel, and though that Colonel was the highest-ranking tyrant he had met he was a pleasant man behind an ordinary desk. He sat there chattily amused by R's revolutionary words and pretty soon "persuaded" R not to send them. So there R was, helpless. He wrote Mizener on the last day of August 1941, "the change of life is so enormous for me that I wonder if I'm going to be able to accommodate the change, or if the change is going to overwhelm me...of being shouted at from 5:30 a.m. until 5:30 p.m."

> Every day wears poor draftee out. Next week worst week of all, probably. Bayonets. So far we have received rather elementary training. Marching — handling of arms. We have, however, been lectured to on how to defend ourselves against tanks, airplanes, & gas. Moreover, we have *practiced* what to do when attacked by a dive bomber, and we have been pushed through a gas chamber with and without gas masks, learning how useful such an instrument can be. There was tear gas in the chamber. First we stood in the chamber with our masks on all the time. Then we stood in there until told to take off masks. Coughing and crying we left. Finally we *entered* the chamber *without* our masks and had to put them on while coughing and crying.... I have had a cold since I entered the army, and I am being driven slowly crazy by it.

R apologized for his complaints but not before complaining once more about "not having read anything but Kenneth Patchen's new book

(Awful!) since my induction. And not having written anything, not having had the opportunity to put myself in a critical dilemma of any kind, I am left high and dry for impersonal material." To John Pauker he wrote at the same time, "my writing is sloppier and sloppier. Usually it is done under extreme conditions of tiredness, noise, or bad light. All three at present." He wrote Pauker about reading Patchen's "last opus" as well, that he "reviewed it (panned it) for the *Tribune.* "I don't know if Mrs. Van Doren will accept the review. If she does there'll be a sore Patchen."

For the rest of Basic Training he coped as obediently as he could, by saluting all possible superiors — the going joke was that if it moved salute it, but if it didn't paint it — and constantly policing the area, especially around his bed. But poetry was still not far away, at least in those hours when there was time. *The Kenyon Review* had come out with younger poets, including R, Howard Nemerov and Pauker, as well as poems by Howard Moss and Jean Garrigue whose work led him to think about just what he was looking to do as a poet.

> I am — awful — coming to believe, you see, that it is perhaps NOT proper for a poet to take the common opinions of his time as a base — as Garrigue has, for example. Somehow he must deviate. In other words I deny Prof. Northrop (don't mutter under your breath). He is all wet even in his basic premise, that a poet must express the philosophy of his age. I mean that in some sense a poet must be a revolutionary. This does not mean that he has to be a communist. He may, as well, be a Republican or Shaker. But he must deviate from the so-called "common beliefs."
>
> To continue — the "young poet" is faced with a variety of what I have called "common beliefs." There are the agrarian and the radical political beliefs. There is Freud. There are the various usual negative statements to be made about love, religion, society. It would be absurd to say that he can avoid TRUTHS — if there are such things. At the same time it seems to me that a poet's individuality is not derived simply from his methods. He must have, in some sense, a philosophy or belief of his own, not of Allen Tate or W.H. Auden. So I am trying to make the poet's (yes the artist's) choice of *subject matter* a more thoughtful choice. I am tired of the ass-end-first approach commonly applied — a new situation for an old theme. It may be that I have not put my finger on the real trouble, but I think that I have. It is this. The "young poet" approaches the whole problem of creation blindly. He knows that he wants to build, but he doesn't know what. Like my roommate Jim [Angleton] he is full of ideas about methods of production and materials to be used, and yet he doesn't give a damn

whether or not the finished product is a speedboat or a house or a jigsaw puzzle. Therefore he picks some finished product (any one) of his predecessors and sets about to build it by his new production methods.

While thinking poetry was all well and good when there was time for it, one morning before breakfast he found himself up against a less conspicuous force than the Colonel who had persuaded him not to send subversive letters. A sergeant leading R's rookie platoon in close-order drill suddenly halted the platoon, faced it forward, stood it at ease, and asked it if anyone could type. R raised his hand about six inches and was instantly sent to headquarters to be a clerk. First hidden military coping lesson: do *not* raise hand.

At this time not even the sergeant knew of any serious consequences from hand-raising, though it did pass through R's mind that he might be kept at Camp Croft clerking forever. At headquarters in front of a typewriter for at least a week he did not imagine that he was doing anything wrong except typing uncommunicative communications badly and fussing to himself about the ridiculous conventions of military correspondence. For instance he did not imagine that even while he was sitting there doing his non-Poundian *job* he would suddenly be removed for what amounted to incompetence by being kicked upstairs. But that was (approximately) what happened. Suddenly his company commander arranged for him to be sent off — following a furlough — to Officers Candidate School at Fort Benning. Within a month Pearl Harbor had occurred. R — still on furlough in Boston — got together with Jim Angleton, his sister Carmen, and Yale classmate Bill Wick. At that time, he wrote Mizener, "*Furioso* is all around me. It is really very pleasant to be surrounded by letters and literature and bills and checks. A great change has come over the magazine since last I functioned actively. Carmen has been working very hard." R's letter was post-marked Dec. 7, 1941.

After 15 days, R was back in still more Basic Training but with a different serial number — a new man. And it was about this time that the military folk, lecturing to him about the properties of leadership, began to prove to him what he had long suspected about himself, that as a leader he just could not be resounding. But did this mean that he would not be able to cope at all as an officer? That he would — as F, F & B had said — "give up the battle and do nothing?" Hardly. For by this time R's trainers had lessoned him in the practical military coping truth that idle social-science theorists F, F & B had naturally never learned. Hidden military coping lesson No.2: in the Army one can neither give up the battle *nor* do nothing.

For some weeks then he struggled to do what he couldn't do, especially on the parade ground. There he couldn't shout as a leader was supposed to, so he was put in an awkward squad for Saturday morning exercises. In how-to. Each incipient non-leader in the squad had to lead the squad for ten minutes at a time in close-order drill, that is, in drill persuading the squad to start, to stop, and to start again. He wrote Mizener about his daytime life that began at 6:00 a.m.

> In theory our working day does not begin until 8 and ends at 5. This is so much rot. Reveille at 6:45. Terrific pressure on tricky bed-making, silly arrangements of clothing and equipment make the hours between six and eight as busy as any. We have, for instance, sheet and pillow [problems]. We have capacious shelves but we are allowed to put very little on them.... We have 40 minutes for lunch. We finish work 3-1/2 minutes before supper. About fifteen minutes after supper we go to a stupid study hall (all study halls are, in my opinion, stupid, but this one is tops) until 7:30. And so far I have had enough homework to keep me going (a total wreck, of course) until 9. Then I have time to take a shower, care for my person, and maybe write a letter if I am not suddenly required to move all my belongings to another barracks and start life anew. I have moved so often in the past few weeks (with all my property) that I think my post-war activity will be, not artistry, but trucking.

And yet R still made time to write because he had someone who was listening to him intently. "You had some very good things to say about my poem [what poem is not indicated]," he wrote to Mizener, "not so much about the particular poem as about the general striving for a mixture of the dull and fancy words."

> I'll add that the poet's most difficult job is covering up the technique which he must use to write a poem. In other words he is at cross purposes, having to rhyme BUT UNOBTRUSIVELY, having to alliterate but unobtrusively, having to use metaphor but not in such a way as to divert the reader into a study of method rather than result. I think you see what I mean though I'm saying it badly. Technique is, after all, a means. When the reader trips over the means he may not get the ends at all.

In the meantime, back at the war, R was one of those who kept flunking his own challenge. His earnest Saturday morning training officer tried and tried to help him cope with the squad in ways that the squad could hear, but R was not ready to be helped. Finally the officer — so R liked to think years later — actually cried. Was R not a Yale man? He was, but that was incidental on the parade ground. On the parade ground one was expected to cope even if one couldn't. How, then, did R do this? He quickly picked up scarlet fever.

He was put out of action for several weeks. He didn't have a typewriter and was forced to use "pencil and scratchpaper" in replying to Mizener who had sent a poem of his own, asking R to "take some pot-shots" at it. "The general criticism I'd make," R wrote back, "is that you have been a little awkward in some places adapting yourself to the form (I know how difficult it is to 'adapt oneself' so I intend no disparagement). Specifically you had difficulty making the run-on lines run on in significant places. I don't see, for example, why (except for the formal reason) the sentence 'Is it enough that we should talk/ Of freedom in the usual way' should be divided where it is. The same applies to the next sentence."

Several weeks later he was writing again to Mizener, in part about his sick leave furlough.

> I caught up on the [latest] literary scandals by visiting Jim in Cambridge for one night (and Andy Wanning) and John Pauker in New York for one night (and Oscar, no less, Williams). I deny emphatically, of course that my purpose on these visits was primarily scandalous.... I learned, for example, 14 separate versions of whether or not the KR [*Kenyon Review*] would proceed. I met a fellow named Edouard Roditi, a poet, who told me that one must either conform with society en toute (and protest violently on paper naturally), or commit suicide. I heard Oscar Williams proclaim that a true poet never considered his audience when he scrobe.

After scarlet fever, R — at Fort Benning — found himself in training unit No. 38. (He had started in No. 11.) And when he had somehow completed the training he also found that he had been removed from the infantry world he thought he had been trained to live in, and had become a second lieutenant in the ground services of a still unshaped *Air Force*. That unit was about to be shipped off to England for reshipment to nobody knew where. "I am still here and have been here for three weeks now, as an officer," he wrote Mizener on June 16, "waiting for orders.

Waiting for orders is one of the most unpleasant jobs the army has given me. I am sorry to say," he added "that in my three weeks as a 2nd lieutenant I have not at all times maintained a suave, untroubled look. Nor have my commissioned friends in the same unhappy boat."

> No, we have been bad officers so far, getting drunk a lot, sleeping in the day rooms during the day because there is nothing for us to do, setting a bad example generally for "the men" by playing poker in the day rooms or reading magazines and mystery stories in the orderly rooms. We have been bad officers and shall continue to be bad officers, with an ever-mounting vengeance, if the adjutant general does not soon determine whether or not he needs us some place.

Then the determination came: R was moved with dazzling speed, first to an Air Force base in Florida and then to Fort Dix, N.J. On August 30 — by now it was 1942 and R was closing in on age 23 — he was somehow able to play as censor himself, and to write Mizener in such a way that though he didn't actually say he was going overseas it was quite clear that he was. "At present," he began,

> I am not in a position to say where I am, but I am allowed to give you an address (which you should not noise about), an address that will probably last me for some time. It is:
> 2nd Lt. Edward R. Whittemore, Jr., 0-1287107
> A.P.O. 3052, 12th Fighter Command,
> Care of Postmaster, New York, N.Y.
> Guard that, pleeuz. Censorship restrictions are very peculiar here, thoroughly inconsistent. It is very difficult to know just what to do about them.

The letter continued in part:

> At any rate, the Air Corps has been exciting. Somehow the army is bewitched by the old theory that a man should be a jack of all trades. Overnight I have been associated with supply in a high office. Supply is very very complicated in the army and appears even more so to someone who knows nothing about planes and who has recently graduated from the Infantry School. While I was a clerk at Camp Croft I learned a little about everything except supply. And now that I have become associated with supply in a high office and am catching on, I am threatened with

transfer to supply in a low office. The difference is not in the importance of the job (not, in other words, a demotion) but in the kind of supply work involved. The supply officer in a low office really handles supplies, checks what he has on hand (counts shovels and guns, one by one, packs and crates, distributes supplies). The supply officer in the high office works on paper, checking on the supply officers in the low office, turning out little papers on methods of procuring supplies, issuing orders, anticipating supply requirements, etc. In other words the high supply officer has a much less aggravating job, although he too has his troubles.

Meanwhile *infantry* class No.11 had already been shipped off to the south Pacific and R's life may well have been — who knows — copinglessly saved. Hidden military coping lesson No. 3: Never imagine that you will or will not be rewarded whether you do or do not do what you can or cannot do.

Pause. The clear sense of being wholly in others' hands and doing only as others wish is naturally very hard on idealists who worry about human rights. Camp Croft was hard on their kind and Fort Benning was harder. Fort Benning thought that positive decision-making could be useful and necessary even if impossible or stupid, especially for leaders like second lieutenants. Therefore second lieutenants were ordered to give orders no matter how bad the orders might be.

In fact this particular, superficial killer commandment proved to be more important than all the rest, and R learned slowly to respect it while sneering. At Benning one memorable exercise of the commandment was handled by a memorably hard-boiled sergeant who put in front of R's class a blackboard with a crude diagram of an open field to be traversed against an enemy armed on the left with machine guns, and on the right with poison gas. The school question: should a dutiful second lieutenant lead his platoon in a charge to the right or the left?

The hypothetical statistics behind the school problem were not important — perhaps 80 percent would die when ordered to the left, 90 percent to the right — but the point was not in the statistics. The point was that an officer, a leader in war, a second lieutenant *had* to decide. It was Fort Benning's big either/or point. It was Kierkegaard's point too, but with no little gold bar on each shoulder.

R at the time was merely depressed by the diagram, thinking very quietly that he would have led *his* troops *quickly* to the rear while he looked on a map for another place for charging. Yet fifty years later he was reminded of the weightiness of the exercise while reading a book about World War I by Paul Fussell who provided a good and a bad instance of leadership coping. First there was Marshall Douglas Haig whom Fussell gave an "F" for sending 160,000 men to their death in a head-on assault at Vimy Ridge. And second there was General Sir Herbert Plumer who received an "A" for having — though "stout, chinless, white-haired and pot-bellied" — imagination. (Plumer blew up the waiting Germans before attacking.) At Fort Benning in early 1942 R's education in leadership was largely based on World War I experience, and from a great distance I now suggest for him very humbly that World War II's Normandy landing was in the Haig mode. At any rate both R and Plumer might have suggested a ploy of some kind, any kind for avoiding the Benning option between guns and gas.

Luckily in the real war R did not have to face any decision like the one insisted on at Benning. Instead he had to confront mindless headquarters machines where decision-imperatives were apt to be misprints and where a second lieutenant planning to order a charge on the enemy might find that his troops had been lost in convoy on the way to the charge. For R became a behind-the-lines supply-and-transportation coper, living overseas for three years in a coping dimension wholly unlike Benning's training world. Most days it was a sedentary sitting-at-a-desk mode, a keeping-of-charts mode, a bad-phone-connections mode, and toward the end it was a luxurious apartment poker-and-alcohol mode. As this kind of coper he often had trouble persuading himself that the 100 octane gasoline he was busy phoning about and keeping charts about was real gasoline being pumped into real planes, and that the bellytanks (explanation to come) his office trafficked in were real, and that....

At any rate R as a new Lieutenant now did not question his presence in the war at all. He was indeed in it, and in mid-1942 soon after the quoted Mizener letter, he found himself in England, having steamed out of Hoboken with 16,000 others on the *Queen Mary* for an eight-day cruise to Liverpool.

Had the *Queen Mary* been waiting in Hoboken because some great leader like Marshall Haig single-mindedly on his own decided to face

America's vast transportation dangers, doing so by personally renting from Mr. Cunard that single weaponless hulk?

With R's war knowledge long behind him he would have to say no. He would say WWII was not managed by Haigs and Plumers but by an anarchic headquarters structure with experienced army executives at the top talking things over while playing bridge and dozens of adjutants down below passing on (via dozens of hapless clerks) their conclusions *as if* they had been reached by Haig-types though there were no Haig-types, only cold hard heads who knew the basic blackboard rules of war: that one had to decide even if one knew better than to.

And in the case of the borrowed great *Queen M*, that fatalistic mystique worked. The *Queen* went about her business *without* losing thousands. Nonetheless the soldier-passengers huddled on her decks and in her staterooms on her many voyages were handy potential victims anyway. War always needs them, as even the hard-boiled Benning pedagogue with his primitive WWI options between machine guns and poison gas knew. So more than half a century later the great ship now sits at a California dock in the role of museum — to commemorate what? Haig-ism? No, perhaps the ship's success was even a sign of human progress in the 1940s, though the thousands of potential victims it served did worry a bit.

The poet Karl Shapiro was aboard the *Queen* on its one Pacific trip, just before R's, and he seems to have felt less helpless. The ship went right around South America — being too big for the Panama Canal — and managed to treat her inhabitants (many fewer than on R's trip) humanely. Shapiro was able to lie on a cot pretty steadily for forty days and write poems — see his memoir, *The Younger Son*. (I'll add parenthetically that in 1963, R invited Shapiro to give the first Ward Lucas Lecture at Carleton College; they went on to become friends as well.) R had not even a pencil for crossing the Atlantic, and no cot either. Each victim lay or stood on deck for half of each day, and spent another half standing in line for food, and spent a third half below rubbing elbows on floors with other victims. Roughly speaking 8000 victims were on decks and 8000 below decks at all times, the alternation having been devised so that 8000 at a time could taste real air.

The ship cruised at 35 knots and changed direction, tipping sickly, every eight minutes. Happily its route was tricky, and German submarines seem to have been as baffled by its movements as they were supposed to have been. Across the Atlantic's open spaces it cruised its 80,000 tons as if invisibly, then sneaked around the west and north of Ireland in order to slip like a (large) Indian canoe down through the North Channel to Liverpool's safety. Just living in it was an education in nightmare, and as for leadership-coping, well, R could not even obey the noblest of OCS rules — that a leader eat only after his troops have been fed. R did nothing leaderly for the eight days except count "his" troops' noses and be, with them, nervous. It was a long long eight days.

Thinking back on the trip's challenge later, I have run hastily through the names of WWII poets that R was familiar with, wondering who wrote most tellingly — let us say copingly — about war. And have settled on Auden. Auden had a talent for being casual, confused and worried, yet witty, eloquent, moving. Furthermore he seems to have been able to do some of his best writing while traveling. Further yet he was lucky or unlucky enough to have touched on three wars — in Spain, China and the big one. There was just one problem in choosing him. He was never actually — actively — *in* any. Did that disqualify him as a war poet?

Yes and no. Yes, of course he should be left out because he was free as a bird, never committed to coping. And no, he certainly should be let in because he was a warrior in spirit anyway, in that he knew he could not cope and kept saying so. R and Angleton had published poems by Auden in *Furioso* and though R had posed for the photo with him and Richard Eberhart at Yale, he only spoke with him at length once, sometime in 1960 in Minneapolis, at an Allen Tate and Isabella Gardner gathering (cocktail party in those days). There a number of guests sat around Auden as if at a campfire and heard him declare that his war poem "September 1, 1939" as well as his elegy to Yeats (also 1939) were "fake." He was complaining about his affirmations in them, and about "the devil of inauthenticity" in others — "false emotions, inflated rhetoric, empty sonorities." And these complaints turn out to have been a staple with him early and late. For example, take two stanzas (out of six) in a poem that he wrote for *The Ascent of F6* way back in 1936, and then didn't use. They make him a warrior.

> When I was only so high I was amiable and gay
> But mother left the larder door ajar one summer day
> And that night before he smacked me I heard dear father say
> "He's nice but he's weak."

If there's one thing more than all the rest I simply can't abide
It's drunkenness, I think it's such an insult to man's pride
But when I pass a public house I find myself inside.
    I'm nice but I'm weak.

To deal with our ruthless managers as in old Russia one might for instance ask — as did Chichikov in Gogol's *Dead Souls* — "how many present souls do you have in your outfit?"

And if Gogol were alive now, and teaching Creative Writing, he might advise the class that his art was largely the art of padding. For *Dead Souls* is a satire on the very art that Gogol seems to have practiced. His easy attitude toward death is perhaps the strangest feature of the work. Imagine buying (or playing chess for) dead souls.

With such matters in mind my readers will note that this war chapter has so far taken R safely to England and no further. Yet England was temporary, a staging area, and for a month he did much that was military but little that was warlike. He spent two or three afternoons describing — to ignorant new soldiers without Fort Benning training — the parts and purposes of such strange weapons as M1 and 03 rifles. For the most part he could have been a clerk again at Camp Croft except that he wore gold bars now and had a clerk of his own, a small modest PFC from West Virginia (with relatives as it happened in Rome) who was also not ready to be warlike. The two of them worked daily from 9 to 5 in a dark Nissen hut, one of several behind an immense castle on a hill not far from London. There were other lieutenants with clerks also working in the huts, and to the best of R's knowledge all of them were preparing for the same war — but no one was supposed to know where the war was to be. R and his PFC's daily labors involved inventorying their squadron's primary warrior equipment — helmets, canteens, typewriters, trucks (but where were the trucks?), flashlights, erasers and training manuals (on such matters as correct military correspondence and correct foxholes). Yes there was a military manual on how to dig a foxhole.

At 5 p.m. each evening some of the workers in the huts would race to a Nissen-hut mess hall, some would trudge to sleepable huts and some — such leaders as R — would bicycle in the rain down a steep hill to the town of Waterford where they were billeted. R was billeted on the third floor of a dentist's house on the town's main street, and on most evenings after work he would go almost directly to the house — stopping perhaps with another lieutenant for a single pint at a pub half way down the hill. At the house he would then be greeted by the dentist's motherly mate who would wonder if he would 'ave a spot o' tea. Normally he would, and as they sipped the motherly mate would ask him questions about his family and country in front of a tiny fireplace containing two sullen coals. After tea he might go out again for another pint with another lieutenant, usually the fat one who could put down twice as many pints as R but who did not smoke and who, when offered a cigarette, always said he had no bad habits. Then R would return to the dentist's, climb the stairs and sleep. So this was war?

Yes the blackout spoke war, and riding a bicycle in the blackout with tiny lights that lit nothing spoke war. And the mood of American soldiers working behind the castle — which was off limits (was it occupied by Germans?) — spoke war, especially in the week before R's world sailed again. By that time everyone in R's HQ (for Headquarters) squadron had counted all the equipment that was theirs and the squadron's several times and had nothing further to cope with except destiny. And drink. On one night when R decided not to come "home" for a spot o' tea he arrived in his room late and drunk and sick. The motherly person, always alert, climbed the stairs, cleaned up the mess and put him to bed with "That's all right dearie, I'll bring you a spot o' tea."

So it is with this second mention of tea that I can turn to history, which is often thought of — and not wrongly — as a mere matter of "whenting." What is that? The misspelling for some inexplicable reason grabbed hold of R's fancy as certain words or phrases will do, like his father's "for pete's sake" or "hundred percent"; they take on a life that cannot be explained and used over and over, they can become a mark of eccentricity. The origin of "whenting" is in a letter that William Carlos Williams' older son Bill wrote in a letter home from camp; R found it in Wiliams' files in the 70s when he was writing the poet's biography.

Monday morning we whent on the four-day hike...we whent through Wilmington and from there we whent to Arlington High School and had dinner and whent to Bennington monument. We whent to Lake Bomoseen and stayed on Crystal Beach. In the morning we whent to ....

That is quite enough to illustrate at least one principle of history —
that is its childishness and hominess despite or in conjunction with war.
The next cup o' tea here will be after much *whenting*, starting with R's second sea voyage. On this trip, the ship was a slow one-stacker, part of an
immense convoy heading — secretly of course — for the Mediterranean.
One could stand on deck, look out on calm water, and see secret but very
conspicuous ships, ships, ships as far as the horizon. And one could find
a little space to walk on deck and pretend to be a tourist. But where in the
Mediterranean — if one happened to be going there — was one going to
land? And when would one arrive? Few details slipped down to the lieu-
tenant-set and if there was clarity in higher places it must have been tentative. The whole convoy had left port before an unannounced D-Day
No.1. And when the Day actually took place the information about it
aboard was scanty, suggesting that resistance at three landing points —
Casablanca, Oran and Algiers — had been slight. In the meantime the
great convoy was seemingly nowhere and seemingly unmoving for day
after day (see Coleridge's "Ancient Mariner") under a cloudless fall sky
until, on a dark night, it squeezed perhaps two-thirds of itself through the
straits of Gibraltar — and planes were heard overhead. Germans?

Apparently not. At least they did nothing, and when dawn came two-
thirds of the ships were in the Mediterranean and the troops had news at
last. The Germans had put up no resistance on D-1 at any of the three
ports, and R's ship would land at the Oran docks (Mers-el-Kebir) on D-3
as (it was then revealed) scheduled.

Before passing through the Straits Lieutenant R had nothing leaderly
to do except before breakfast when he was expected to raise his voice to
lead his troops in calisthenics on the promenade deck. But when they
landed in Oran some of his other duties appeared, for he was now definitely in A-4 (supply and transportation). Where then *were* the trucks?

They were mysteriously elsewhere but soon two or three dozen
appeared, with a few jeeps, in a line on the dock. Someone on high had
also mysteriously decreed that he was to be in a front jeep, hence the
leader of eight trucks. And someone had also slipped him, via his PFC
who was now his driver, and would soon be a sergeant, a map with Oran's
La Senia airport marked on it. What efficiency, what clarity. So a portion
of R's HQ squadron hopped into the trucks, and with barracks bags piled
high a small convoy of young low-grade air force bureaucrats motored off
the dock and headed east through Oran to the airport as if on a Fort

Benning training exercise. Soon they were even where they were supposed to be, and parked in front of a fine French military barracks. Who could have arranged this perfection?

R never found out the Who but he was soon sure that a certain major who had suddenly become R's boss had not. The new boss was a bald-headed arrogant know-nothing stuttering-muttering reserve Major left over from WWI. He had no mental tie to the scene he sat in, and when the A-4 department achieved an airport office at La Senia he sat opposite R at a large desk and told him everything he knew about the earlier war. He would pick up the phone — which normally only crackled — and shout angrily into it until he slammed it down. After two or three weeks of this he suddenly vanished — having been kicked upstairs? — and the phone worked better.

So did R, and his morale at La Senia was soon unreasonably high, partly because he knew so little. He had nothing to do with the actual servicing of planes, and didn't even know what one of his responsibilities (bellytanks — explanation coming) looked like. Of course the faulty phone was a serious problem, but to do his job he at least could limit his fragmented talk to his A-4 counterparts in Casablanca and Algiers, plus six or eight lower-echelon supply officers (S-4). Also everyone in North Africa was having phone trouble so he was beyond guilt.

For a time the Oran HQ was labeled IISAC (meaning the Second Service Area Command) and was expected to serve (if HQs can honestly be said to do that) all American combat planes in or near Oran. ISAC was off to the west in Casablanca, IIISAC was east in Algiers, and for several months only Germans and Italians (and North Africans) were to be found significantly east of Algiers — that is, in Tunisia. At the La Senia airport in Oran IISAC took over a modern French barracks that was much solider and less bed-bugged than the old wooden ones at Camp Croft and Fort Benning. It was also exotic because of its toilets, which were seatless with their waters swishing around their occupants' feet when the feet were placed on top of slippery, foot-shaped, tiled mounds. Therefore R and the HQ staff were in clover. There was not even an enemy and the roads for R's trucks — when R "did" trucks — were good, paved and empty roads, since there was no gas for North Africans. Also those roads were peacefully lined by Arab vendors selling fat and very sweet oranges to new customers. How unwarlike. Yes, and it was here that even R began to like the military.

Of course he told no one about this failing since everyone with hearing would have sneered and shouted, "So you found a home!" He had
not found one, and after the war he would not consider (for more than a
week or two) joining the Regular Army, though he did remain in the
Reserves. Still and all, North Africa and Army life were slowly revealing
their wonders. Also he had plenty of transportation to take him away
from the Base in order to see North Africa, and to help him mix A-4 matters with his own literary matters — such as those that used to take him
to the movies and shore in Madison, Connecticut, a world away.

In early February, 1943, he wrote Rosemary Mizener almost light-
heartedly that this was "indeed a good country, fertile, livable, and worthy of conquest. I did not think so in December in the mud, but I think
so now and I rather wish I had more time to travel through it at peace
with the world, not worrying about the unloading of freight cars, the dis-
position of troops or gasoline, or forty trucks stringing along behind me."
And more:

> I am at present occupying a sort of logistical hot seat where I am tor-
> mented from early morning until late at night by people who want to go
> places or have things go places — by train, truck, air, and boat. I am devel-
> oping a powerful right arm from cranking up a field telephone, a mean
> disposition from dealing with so many cantankerous customers, a fatalis-
> tic attitude from having so many cancellations and changes, and a com-
> plete library of excuses. Most complicated of all activities is the railroad
> which is run by the French although used almost exclusively by us. There
> are so many offices determining what is to be shipped that all advance
> planning by them is worthless.

But of course it should be understood that he was never inattentive to
his own A-4 matters. This is proved by a remarkable blurb, written late in
the war by a close friend in the HQ recommending that he receive a
Bronze Star. The blurb shamelessly omitted R's fine service in North Africa
(and even later in Sicily), and was wholly wrong about what he did to
solve major supply problems during the Anzio landings in Italy and the
invasion of Southern France. Yet it did suggest that the Allies would not
have won the war without him; the close HQ friend who wrote it was
clearly on R's side. The document may be referred to again later but for
now just one misleading remark in it needs correction — it has to do with
bellytanks.

Bellytanks in WWII had two basic uses. First they were used to extend the range of fighter planes such as the P47 and P51, usually on missions providing cover for bombers with distant targets such as the Rumanian oil fields. Second they were used, late in the war, as fire bombs to render untenable the "environment" held by the Germans north of Florence. Now this firebomb tactic — which later played a big part in Vietnam — was not, R insisted, his idea. Indeed he only learned by chance, during cocktail time much later when he was stationed in Siena's Grand Hotel, that such firebombs were being dropped. Yet the Bronze Star citation mentioned above reported that R "ably supervised the distribution of 14,000 [of the firebombs and the others] and that at no time were operations ever hindered for lack of them." Now R has said on a number of occasions he had nothing at all to do with any of the firebomb tanks and that in fact, like any sensible HQ person, he never saw one of them. In further fact, during the North African campaign, he did not even see any of the plain bellytanks though it was then, he has admitted, that he learned what a bellytank box containing a bellytank looked like. This learning moment occurred at night in the rain in Mostaganem (a town between Oran and Algiers) when....

No, an even earlier A-4 learning moment must first be mentioned, a truck convoy moment that took place only three or four days after arriving at Oran's La Senia. One night R was summoned from his French barracks bed to convoy a brand new shipload of Air Force troops away from the Mers-el-Kebir docks to a staging area. He did know of staging areas, having been in one called Fort Dix before sailing on the *Queen Mary*, and also in the dentist's house in Waterford when he was served tea. But until he was given his convoy orders in Oran he knew nothing of the staging area that the high copers there had settled on, a hill just south of town. He was simply given a map with an X marking the hill so that at midnight in the rain he could lead thirty 2½ ton trucks with their drivers from the La Senia motor pool to the Oran docks, there to pick up several hundred wet new arrivals bearing barracks bags for delivery to the hill. He did what was ordered, and about 2 a.m. the trucks stopped along the road beside the hill.

The hill was already well occupied by others and it was a muddy hill with no buildings or other shelter. It seemed a poor place for tired troops to spend what was left of the night but orders were orders so the trucks were emptied. Then R counted his trucks and found that there were only 29. He put his loyal PFC in charge of the 29, ordering the empty convoy back to the La Senia motor pool. He returned alone in his jeep to the dock and found the missing truck still on the dock, empty except for its driver who was pleasantly asleep.

Soon after that came his trip to Mostaganem, which is (or was) a point at which two different railroad systems merge. In 1942 the tracks of the system to the West, all the way to Casablanca, were of a certain width or gauge, while the tracks to the East were of a slightly wider gauge. Of course R had known about tracks and gauges since childhood when he possessed a standard gauge Lionel train-set of which he was proud, since he could look down upon the smaller gauge as childish. In grown-up Mostaganem, however, the lesser gauge was also grown-up, being the gauge of the whole Western rail system bearing supplies from Casablanca, and there meeting the standard gauge of the Eastern system. So in Mostaganem the Casablanca freight had to be transferred to other cars. Now while R with all his Lionel experience had a fine intellectual awareness of the Mostaganem problem, the high transportation copers of North Africa had not brought the problem to him in Lionel terms. Nor had they told him that most of the bellytanks being shipped to North Africa in the early stage of the Moroccan/Algerian campaign had been consigned to Casablanca. R's shouting Major was the one who early learned of the matter — on the impossible phone — on a wet afternoon in Oran. As soon as he did he slammed the phone down in order to shout at R that a trainload of bellytanks was sitting in Mostaganem and someone was needed to *shift them*. With that he walked out for the day, leaving R and his PFC to arrange for bellytank shifting, whatever that meant. The two of them drove to Mostaganem in the rain, arriving at dark still wondering what a bellytank looked like.

What they saw were bellytank boxes. For shipping purposes each light (expendable) bellytank came in a wooden box perhaps eight feet long. Of course no headquarters is equipped to imagine 100 of them in boxes on flat freight cars, but R's childhood helped him here. They were stacked on four or five childish flat cars parked next to four or five grown-up flats. R and his loyal PFC actually saw the boxes, touched them, lifted them and transferred them to the other flats and soon the mission was complete. R had still not seen a bare bellytank, but he had been close to 100 and hadn't been shot at. All of mysterious romantic Africa was becoming explicable. R was now truly there. So years later, out of the service and reading Winston Churchill's memoirs, R was mightily offended by Winnie's saying — of his meeting FDR in Marrakech after the successful invasion — "It gave me great pleasure to see my great colleague here on conquered or liberated territory which he and I had secured." Who was Winnie to have talked about what he personally had secured? R complained indignantly about him in an essay for *The Yale Review*, "Churchill and the Limitations of Myth." (I recently reread the essay and am even more indignant now.) At any rate, the military point here is that R had an advantage over Churchill in describing North Africa since he had actually secured a few bellytank boxes there. Also he had actually toured the country a bit and discovered how inappropriate it would be for him to say that he, R, had secured it. He took two memorably irresponsible trips to learn this.

The first was merely vacation, a long Saturday off in Oran when he and two other lieutenants, unable to squeeze a jeep out of the motor pool, somehow secured a fading Renault and drove to an officers club of the French Foreign Legion in Sidi Bel Abbes. That city is south of Oran in not-quite-desert country, and the club was a colonial establishment whose precarious serenity was a carryover from the "great" days of the French in Africa. For literary R it was even suggestive of Joseph Conrad's experience with Belgian colonialism on the Congo River (*The Heart of Darkness*) though the "horror" was missing. And for three Americans sipping gin and tonic it was also suggestive of *Beau Geste*, a 1930s movie with Gary Cooper chasing a Hollywood enemy heroically across sand dunes. Some years later, R pulled a poem out of the experience in which he was not at all pro-Gary. But on his first Saturday off in Africa he did not have a cultural agenda to worry about, so that his trip to the desert was almost one in which his own real war was at least catching up with his childhood. The poem, "A Day with the Foreign Legion," is somewhat long and while it has qualities of the burlesque, it is a dark burlesque as in Shakespeare's comedies, which viewed from another perspective, could easily turn tragic.

> On one of those days with the Legion
> When everyone sticks to sofas and itches and bitches —
> A day for gin and bitters and the plague —
> Down by Mount Tessala under the plane trees,

Seated at iron tables cursing the country,
Cursing the times and the natives, cursing the drinks,
Cursing the food and the bugs, cursing the Legion,
Were Kim and Bim and all the many heroes
Of all the books and plays and poems and movies
The desert serves.
And as they sat at the iron tables cursing the country
Some sergeant or other rushed in from the fort
Gallantly bearing the news
From which all those many heroes take their cues:
"Sirs!"
          "What is it, sergeant?"
                              "Sirs, the hordes
March e'en now across the desert swards."

Just like the movies.

Now in the movies
The sergeant's arrival touches off bugles and bells,
Emptying bunks and showers, frightening horses,
Pushing up flags and standards, hardening lines
Of unsoldierly softness, and putting farewells
Hastily in the post so two weeks hence
A perfectly lovely lovely in far-off Canada
Will go pale and bite buttons and stare at the air in Canada.
And in the movies,
Almost before the audience spills its popcorn,
The company's formed and away, with Bim or Kim
Solemnly leading them forth into a sandstorm,
Getting them into what is quite clearly a trap,
Posting a double guard,
Sending messengers frantic to Marrakech,
Inadvertently pouring the water away,
Losing the ammunition, horses and food,
And generally carrying on in the great tradition
By making speeches,
Which bring back to mind the glorious name of the Legion,
And serve as the turning point,
After which the Arabs seem doped and perfectly helpless,
Plenty of food is discovered in some old cave,
And reinforcements arrive led by the girl
From Canada.

But in this instance nothing from *Beau Geste*
Or the Paramount lot was attempted,
It being too hot for dramatics,
Even for Kim and Bim,
Aging under the plane trees,
Cursing the food and the bugs, cursing the sergeant
Who gallantly bore the news because he was young,
Full of oats and ignorance, so damned young
In his pretty khaki; nothing at all
So late in the day, with everyone crocked
And sweaty and bitten to death and all,
Was attempted despite the sergeant
Who whirled on his heel and marched, hip hip, a true trooper,
Out of the bar as if to the wars.

So the lights went on and the audience,
Pleasantly stupid, whistled and clapped at the rarity
Of a film breaking down in this late year of Our Lord.

But of course it was not the film; it was not the projector;
Nor was it the man in the booth, who hastened away
As soon as the feature was over, leaving the heroes
Cursing the food and the bugs, cursing the Legion
As heathendom marched and the sergeant whirled,
Hip hip,
But some other darker cause having to do
With the script perhaps, or the art,

Or the time,
The time and the place
The place, the time
For how could one blame them
Seated at iron tables cursing the country?
What could they do,
Seated under the plane trees watching the sergeant
Whirl on his heel, hip hip, in his pretty khaki?
What could they say,
Drinking their gin and bitters by Mount Tessala,
For what after all could be said after all was said
But that the feature had merely run out and the lights had gone on
Because it was time for the lights to go on, and time
For them not to dash out and be lost in the desert

But to rage,
As befitted their age,
At the drinks and the country, letting their audience
Clap, stamp, whistle and hoot as darkness
Settled on Mount Tessala, the lights went on,
The enemy roamed the desert and everyone itched.

This is not an obvious WWII poem — not like those that Randall Jarrell and Karl Shapiro wrote (nor like "Black Cross" coming up). Perhaps its emphasis on mere itching was a bit cynical. R could not have written it without *his* war experience, yet that experience has been so transmuted that its autobiographical origin has been subsumed. The self as subject in poetry is one that has preoccupied him like most other American poets. It's a subject I will return to.

R's second fine trip was at least ostensibly business, soon after the big battle at the Kasserine Pass — where the evil enemy was turned back, leaving the Americans in charge and making their forward movement to Sicily and Italy possible — and after his HQ had moved eastward from its fine quarters at La Senia to Constantine, which was even grander. Many American planes were said to have landed then on Tunisian fields and R drove east alone in a jeep from Constantine to the coast to see if they were really there and what in the world he could do about their supplies if they were. In two days he covered much of northern Tunisia just after the fighting ended. He then drove on to 100-octane business at one of "his" airfields near Bizerte and spent the night. The next day, rising early he inspected the port at Bizerte where he had a glass of milk (not tea) on an American warship. Then he visited the nearby famous *ruine* at Carthage, finding it so boring that he hurried right on to a lonely but littered beach at Cape Bon where many Germans had, within days, left by sea. He stripped, swam, redressed, and continued with his one-soldier adventure by skirting Tunis itself and heading southwest on a straight flat road alongside an immense ancient Roman aqueduct. Forty miles? Fifty? At aqueduct's end he found the reason for its being, the minimal remains of an ancient settlement, Sedrata, baking in the sun in desert isolation. It was a much more persuasive *ruine* than Carthage, and for perhaps an hour R sat on centuries-sanded stones in the deadest of worlds, feeling sad, empty, foolish, even academic and back in classical Civilization 101 — yet wildly alive too, like stout Cortez (Or Balboa) (or just Keats in his "On Reading Chapman's Homer") staring at the Pacific. It was still only noon when he headed west again, right through the Kasserine Pass. The Pass itself was now another *ruine* but only two or three weeks old, with signs of battle everywhere, especially a few temporary grave markers scattered along his route — fuel for more poems? In a letter to Arthur and Rosemary M that June, he wrote about his seeing "along all roads the small minor graves of German and Allied soldiers, the charred minefields, and old bivouac areas (over here every orchard has been, at one time or another, a bivouac area for at least one nation and more probably six)."

> The wreck of Bizerte is spectacular, and it is a question to me if an attempt should be made to rebuild the city or rather leave it grow to the stature of a majestic old ruin like Carthage or Sedrata. If such a procedure were followed a great upsurge of that peculiar industry of the archaeologists would be necessary after this war. Myself, however, I despise ruins.

At this point R seems to have converted his two-day excursion into a great literary adventure. But soon he was again driving, tired, toward "home" in Constantine — it was summer and the days were long — and he decided to stop just once more for a break. He pulled off the main though largely empty road, and walked down a desolate path for perhaps a quarter of a mile to a little pull-off that would have been equipped, in the U.S., with 50-cent binocular gadgets for tourists to look through. The view was fine, a fitting lonely climax to a day's silence, so he chose simply to lie down beside the Jeep for a bit and savor the wonder of it — a country left to itself by both sides. He slept for five, perhaps ten minutes, and was startled awake by three curious Arab boys, each with a burro, who had come out of all the emptiness and were just looking at him. They were friendly, shy. He was friendly, nervous, jumped up, and left fast. It seemed that the magnificently empty, silent Africa wasn't empty at all as soon as the warriors were asleep. He didn't know how to write the poem then of that emptiness, but only much later did he write "Black Cross," when he recollected passing peacefully through the Kasserine that day and seeing the lonely crosses on the side of the road.

I would like to dispense with certain sorrows,
Having no room for unessentials
Like a German death, and travel light,
A better soldier than I am.
Black cross on new lumber, a medal,

The guttural letters of vital statistics,
A helmet — besides, I never knew this man,
How tall, how small,
Digging with sweat on his shoulders, marching,
Loving a dark-haired girl he was.
And where he was born and moved with grace
Through a pretty little pattern to this desert place
Is no concern of mine.

The front-lines war, which R was to remain on the periphery of, was of course always present with him since he was — in his supply officer role — a full-time participant. As a result he had "war poetry" in mind steadily and took the subject up later in a series of lectures at Beloit College on aspects of modern poetry that was included in *From Zero to the Absolute*. There his focus was poetic rebellion or alienation since, as he put it, it attacked "a prime social premise that has been a pillar in the long-term coherence systems of Western nations, the old Horatian platitude, 'It is sweet and honorable to die for one's country.'" He began with Wilfred Owen's bitterly ironic poem, "Dulce et Decorum Est" noting how Owen wrote from the inside ("In all my dreams, before my helpless sight,/ He plunges at me, guttering, choking, drowning."): "Owen's soldier plunged at him," he wrote, "got inside him, became part of his dream life. Reading the poem, I got the sense that Owen lived that other's death…. To Owen the death was a horror because it was so close, so relevant — to *him*." Then reflecting on the few war poems that he wrote, R asked himself, "Why didn't I cope thus with *my* war?"

> The center of the war for me was administration and dullness. Dying soldiers were not plunging at me. I was stuck with tons of inanimate supplies, with paperwork, with lost trucks and gasolineless planes, not with death mostly. The few occasions I did seize were outside my humdrum war life, and they were about death — but death at the war's edges, for that's all I saw.

He wrote about"Black Cross" and "White Cross," a "companion" poem from a few years later (they were to appear next to each other in *Heroes & Heroines*).

> Blatz was drafted, act of God and neighbors,
> For God and neighbors and The Better Life

As Bangor, Boston, Bethlehem, and Boise
Live it. Blatz was drafted in the spring.
By summer he had gone abroad to see
What he could do. By winter he was buried.

Poor Blatz. His absence stirs the sale of bonds
On Linden Road, brings tears and pride and emptiness
To Linden Road, alone to Linden Road.
But in another country, by the road
That stretches east to Kairouan and west
To Kasserine, Tebessa, and Thelepte

(Kairouan is a place to buy a rug,
A noon dune scene, a trinket dug in the desert,
Not honour. A Souk, a watering point,
A white and holy city, it buries its dead
On the outskirts, under a few weathered stones.
Those are the stones that line the western hills,

The wise dead, the ready dead, the prayed for,
Beards and wrinkles come to their elephant graves),
But in another country strangers pause,
Observing a special silence before his cross,
Reading his name, poor Blatz, and possibly
Dreaming of heroes.

Of the first stanza, R lectured, "All the patriotic jazz at home — the recruiting, the send-off, the basic training — leads very swiftly and senselessly to death in the desert." But then what? No answer except that of dreaming. Moving to "Black Cross," he added, "in both poems I am terribly concerned with how I ought to feel (I ought to feel 'no'), and at the same time I'm annoyed that anybody should tell me to feel that way."

> Both poems are also heavily ironic. In the German poem I say that I should have no concern — that is, the system tells me I should have no concern — for a German death; but then I discover that I do have concern. I indulge myself in a little daydream about the German's heroic and humane properties, and then I pretend to stiffen up and be soldierly again, ending with the ironic lines: 'And where he was born and moved with grace/ Through a pretty little pattern to this desert place/ Is no concern of mine.'"

In some odd way, it *was* R's concern — and yet to say so directly would undermine the bitterness of irony. Irony is another issue I'll take up as we go along — it's generally a pejorative among American poets that is said to reflect defensiveness and hiding. Sometimes. But it's served poets and their small audiences very well. For starters, consider Swift, Byron and Owen himself.

War's End & Home

The first priority of a high headquarters is to find itself quarters worthy of itself. R's Service Command started off poorly in England, with nothing but two Nissen huts to call its own. Oran on the other hand was fine, with a modern barracks building plus a comfortable airport office to live and function in. Then after Oran came Constantine, a housing delight with an incredible view (though characteristically nowhere near the airfields of any of the planes it was designed to service). But after Constantine the wonders of French-North African quarters came to an end, being replaced by the miseries of Sicily.

In July '43 R was flown there in a C-47 full of HQ functionaries and barracks bags. They landed on an airstrip near Gela on the south coast, and there they lived next to sudden foxholes in an adjacent orchard for nearly a month, mostly wondering where the war and their tactical units were. At that troubled time only the veteran English troops from the long Libyan campaign knew, pinned down as they were by the Germans in this island's southeast corner, next to the famous classical city of Syracuse. All the American ground forces were soon led by General Ride 'em Cowboy Patton and his tanks. Patton galloped everywhere and secured, chiefly, the big port of Palermo on the north coast (which R also never saw) where many crucial air force supplies were soon landed. Then suddenly the Germans backed off from Sicily and retreated north, rapidly, all the way to Italy. As a result R's HQ moved from its field near Gela and found itself at last inside something, namely several unfurnished summer seaside cabins — in the shade of Mt. Etna — that looked out over the Ionian Sea (near where Odysseus had had trouble with the Sirens). The practical difficulty there was that the HQ's high officers still didn't even know where many of their own tactical units were, and they certainly didn't know how to be wise and definite about what to do with incoming supplies.

Where was the war anyway? R knew then that he was lucky. Men were dying in the most terrible and brutal ways — but he was still far away from all that.

As the Allied invasion of Italy at Salerno crystallized it seemed as if the Germans would back off and the Salerno landings would be a breeze, enabling American planes to settle in on fields near Salerno. Yet the Germans did not back off. They resisted from the hills to the north of the beaches, with the result that a clever headquarters plan — to have a shipload of 100 octane drums then standing offshore at Palermo steered directly to Salerno — had to be scrapped. What to do? HQ strategists decided that all the planes covering Salerno from Sicily would have to be relocated instantly in East Italy. That meant (a) having the gasoline freighter waiting off Palermo re-routed to Taranto and (b) having crucial Sicilian fields in the Messina-Catania area supplied for the moment by air from Palermo with emergency 50-gallon drums already on the ground there. At one point R learned that only a one-day supply remained for certain crucial units flying Salerno cover. A crisis was at hand and R, depressed, even dreamed of going to his immediate superior and resigning from the armed services. Luckily the superior officer helped him think of a better solution, which was for him to be jeeped over to the nearby (as it happened) Desert Air Force HQ of the British at Catania. There he happily picked up a 3000-gallon loan (by truck) of the needed petrol, and the kindly donor-sergeant then asked him if he'd 'ave a cup 'o tea.

At this time poetry was still alive in him, if not regularly. R wrote Mizener that he had "started a poem which of course I shall never do another lick of work on which is something like this":

> Those of us here think of those not here
> As comrades, strangers, lovers, foes,
> Across a water gap. And those of us here
> Have crossed and may recross but never close
> Again this. [He certainly didn't know how to end that sentence.]

And then I have a tentative line which goes:

> This is the grave blue gulf
> Between two villainies.

But "gulf" floors me. Nothing that rhymes with "gulf" gives any lead at all. And a poet cannot operate without rhymes to give him leads. He doesn't know what to do without leads.

Meanwhile in cabins under summer skies east of Sicily's Mt. Etna on the Ionian Sea, the Americans (theoretically planning the Salerno invasion while being quite out of touch) lived it up evenings with a small crew of Britishers who didn't seem to know what was happening either — so in blackout darkness they sang happily from romantic balconies as German planes flew overhead to bomb Catania. In memory these scenes have the look of '40s war movies where the hard fighting, battle-scarred men lived life to its fullest — for this was Sicily's Hollywood moment, and a fine one — though it ended fast when R's HQ personnel found themselves boarding, trucks and all, an LST (Landing Ship Tank) from Messina for embattled Salerno. Soon they were actually on the beach there but with orders to proceed instantly east, by road in convoy, *away* from the fierce battle scene and across the mountains (a two-day trip) to Taranto. So with R in the lead jeep they did, and when they stopped for the night en route he even managed to steer the whole convoy into a muddy field where, in the morning, they found themselves mired. After unmiring they proceeded without further trouble to Taranto and it was there, billeted in warehouses near the harbor, that they — and particularly R who was now inescapably in the POL trade (Petrol, Oil & Lubricants) — had to face up to the fact that they had little reason to be there at all (not an unusual military discovery) since all their planes were elsewhere. Thus, as far as battle goes, continued R's good fortune.

At this point a mighty strategic decision floated down from Algiers and Washington by which all American air power in the Mediterranean was split in two, becoming the XIIth and XVth Air Forces. The XIIth then became the "Tactical" Air Force (two-engine bombers and P-47 fighters that would be needed on the West Coast when the Germans retreated to above Naples) and the XVth becoming the "Strategic" Air Force (four-engine bombers and P-51 fighters to fly distant missions from East Italy around Foggia). And also at this time came the annoying news that the wandering freighter with needed gasoline diverted to Taranto had docked in Brindisi instead, that its cargo had been loaded on a train, and that the train was lost. Comedic? In retrospect, yes. Then, no.

R was now of course ready to resign again since he didn't even know where Brindisi was (about 50 miles east of Taranto) and could not comprehend how a whole train could have been lost. But a strange Colonel from a worrying tactical unit suddenly appeared, a personage who had a military Cessna and took R up in it to look for the train. He was very old, or so it seemed then, possibly sixty, and his hands shook, and he didn't smile. But he had a map in his lap and soon had the two of them in the air canvassing the tracks between Taranto and Brindisi. No train. Then he undertook to canvas the tracks between Brindisi and Bari. No train there either. South of Bari he spotted an airfield and was descending to land, perhaps to ask if anyone had seen a lost train, when R noticed an impediment on the runway, perhaps a truck. Had the old codger seen it? R pointed at it but the old codger said nothing at all and R was not sure that he had even nodded his head. What to do?

It should be understood that so far R had actually flown only once, that flight being from Africa to Gela in a C-47 "on the deck" (a precaution against German planes) while he sat scared in the back with ten others and many many barracks bags. Certainly he had not — in war or peace — sat up front in a small plane with dual controls. (A decade later he would be piloting his own single-engine Cessna far away in a college town in Minnesota.) Also he knew nothing at all of the Colonel. For instance he did not know that the Colonel — who would later be his own immediate commander — had some sort of palsy so that his hands, even while resting on a desk, might be expected to shake. But R had been watching the Colonel's handling of the wheel and it looked easy. He thought that if he just pulled back on it a bit it would be a signal to the Colonel that there was this impediment on the runway. Accordingly he reached for the wheel and may even have touched the wheel when, very rapidly, the Colonel reached over and slapped R's hands, very hard, before shakingly but safely flying over — and landing beyond — the impediment. A little later they were back in the warehouse where they learned that the missing train had appeared at the place it was supposed to.

The War then resumed and improved. The Germans abandoned Naples and moved thirty miles north. R's HQ squadron westwardly recrossed the mountains — without deviating into a muddy field — and found itself at last located in three unbombed modern apartment buildings in Naples' best residential district. There R shared a three-bedroom apartment with two other officers, and there the most critical part of the Mediterranean war seemed over — not to ground troops thirty miles north in range of the Germans, but to R and his compatriots at HQ who two or three nights a week settled around the marble table in R's apartment to play poker. And it seemed over and even worth celebrating on New Year's Eve (1943) — R had a few months earlier turned 24 — when a large group of Aussies somehow appeared (Naples was full of surprises) and sang drunken songs around the apartment's German grand piano until nobody knows when.

"The recent quiet on my particular front," he wrote to Mizener, "has allowed me to renew an interest in ARTISTIC CREATION. I am dreaming of a book of war stories right now. They must be stories, I think, and not diary entries." Why? "The actions I would like to describe, are somehow not suitable for poetry (how I should hate to explicate that statement)." And though he had only written half of a story at the time, they preoccupied him mightily. "I have the titles for three which are uncensorable and unwritten," he wrote. "'Waterford.' 'La Senia.' 'Constantine.' The titles for three more are censorable right now, strictly speaking."

In the one I am working on I am a Tech Sgt., and am rather involved at the moment in assuming the attitude of a Tech. Sgt. When I began it I thought, somehow, that the enlisted rank has a privilege of outrageous expression which an officer rank has not. And so I am a Tech. Sgt. and fearing that I sound a little like one of these big healthy dopes sitting in the middle of no man's land eating "C" rations with a big smile for the Campbell Soup Corporation. It is quite unfair to the average enlisted man, but then I am a novice with attitudes. [R continues] I am awake until late at night dreaming of how to make a rather ordinary event in Oran, a long time ago, now somehow not ordinary and somehow meaningful. That is why the artist must resort to Tech Sgts. I could not show these stories to anyone around here because they would say "they are not true" (that is, if I had them written). And yet I *think* that it may be helpful to me to have some genuine actions as a basis for work, if only because I find the genuine actions more spectacular than any actions I would dream up on my own.... The motivation of real action (like knifing somebody in the back) is very difficult for me personally, perhaps because I can't imagine an adequate motive ever, in my own mind. My characters can talk and think and play around but never get up the gumption to DO it.

During all the motion of the last half of 1943 and early 1944 the mail to and from civilization had been spotty, though by the time R's Service Command was settled in Naples all was well. And among the correspondents appearing in the mail at odd intervals — in addition to Mizener and his father — were Yale friends Bill Johnson and John Pauker. Johnson wrote from Denver earlier in 1942 where he had met Weldon Kees "who runs the bibliographical dept. of the Denver Public Library, collects little mags, writes damn good verse, talks the good language.... Maybe you should know him. Maybe he has contributed, or been rejected from *Furioso*." R's English Communist friend at Yale, Arnold Kettle, had returned to England and was quite a bit behind R in becoming military, though, as usual, thoroughly up-to-date politically. While denying that he was preaching he lectured R pretty steadily for expecting too much of the world's reformers, and he even quoted Lenin: "'The old Utopian Socialists imagined that Socialism could be built with a different sort of people, that they would first train nice, clean, splendidly educated people and [then] build Socialism with them.... We have always laughed at this and said this is playing dolls, that this is pastime for romantic young ladies but not serious politics.'" Then, ending the quotation he seemed rather happy to report that his dubious English ally Eric Bentley (who had been with him at Yale's graduate school), had been "chucked out" of UCLA for having joined the Communist Party and was living in New York while writing for the *Partisan Review*, but had "decided to stop because *PR* is run by Trotskyites(!) He is full of antifascist passion."

Kettle's later letters (also remarkably to be found in the U of Maryland's file of R's papers) were similarly focused on the big social picture of the time — always confronting true Commies with Trotskyites and so on. They were indeed wartime letters, and when Kettle found himself in basic training at home in England they continued to cover the waterfront. Thus, while he at one point (Fall, 1943) reported that "the last eight months have been the most unpleasant of my life," he also wrote:

> Many people here are worried by the apparent preferences of the British and American governments for conservative authoritarian stooges rather than left-wing democratic governments. I am not surprised by the preference but it is not encouraging. The hope lies in the internal strength of the left wing movements.

Then he raged quite a bit about the conservatives and other villains at home, and by the beginning of 1944 he had himself made it through basic training and decided that he was happier in the English army than he would be in R's, though "you have more money, more democracy, more comfortable uniforms."

> I will even grant that most Americans are nicer than most Englishmen and that the behavior of the American upper class is preferable to that of the British, but the more I see of U.S. troops here the more shocked I am by their reactionary views (all ranks). I talk to all the Americans I can, in trains, pubs, cafes, etc., and I can say without exaggeration that not one in ten appears to have the remotest idea of what this war is about or even to care.

Kettle wound up his lecture with a few words of hope that with help from the Red Army it might become possible (for the first time since 1914) "for this continent to advance to a higher stage of civilization. I am not quite certain why this is so very important but it is."

In a subsequent letter he then indicated a bit of dissatisfaction with R's having (shamefully) written that it was important "to stomach and accept, not to [try to] change" the world. Then he moved away from the "cosmic" and became the pleasant Kettle that he always tried to be — but it *was* hard for him. Suddenly he was overseas himself, in Italy but unable to make connections with R, and the war was ending. By the time R had made it home Kettle was still stuck in Taranto, happy about the future but worrying lest R not realize that the British Tory party had received its greatest defeat since 1642, making "the way at last open for advance."

In contrast to Kettle, R's father was a conservative. But he was a steady war correspondent and backed up his fine newsy letters with packages of books (at R's request), respectable ones such as Jane Austen's *Emma* and DeFoe's *Moll Flanders*. His father even wrote to Mizener (teaching then at Wells College) and soon the two of them were corresponding about their hero abroad. Years later, when Mizener returned all R's letters, he also sent the couple R's father had written him, which included the following:

> Your letter about R made me very happy. I can't remember when my ego has been so well fed. For all parents enjoy praise of their offspring. It's a sort of sublimated egotism without the selfishness.

I do wish R were less secretive about his plans, activities & ambitions. But children always are with parents. Until this recent letter, he has never once spoken of writing anything since he went overseas.

You refer to frequent parental horror at having their progeny take up poetry (or for that matter, painting, sculpture, the stage or any form of artistry). It is due to lack of artistic understanding — an atavistic fear of the unknown. A very fundamental instinct stemming from the inborn fear that animals have of the strange. Then too parents view with alarm a vocation, which, at best, may not be very lucrative.

I fear my own literary taste, if I ever had any, has become pretty well debased — magazines and detective mysteries. I go for the "story" not the "form," while poetry is all form, the story nothing. Moreover these modern poets, who rise above rhyme, rhythm and meter become so rarified as to be quite over my head. To me William Carlos Williams is chiefly conspicuous by his typographical trick of using no capital letters. My reaction to R's poetry is mostly a sort of mystified wonder.

....

Thanks again for your letter. If, as you say, R has poetic promise, I should be very glad to have him develop it. If he enjoys that as he seems to, let him by all means stick to it. I am convinced that of all parental folly, the greatest is to try to force a child into a, to him, unattractive vocation.

I keep calling R "child." But remember he was just out of college when he went into the military and it's almost three years since I saw him. Doubtless I shall find him quite a bit changed, if he gets home (on "leave" or on "rotation") this summer, as we now hope.

About the same time, R wrote to Mizener about R Sr.

> I have discovered what a good man my father is. Perhaps I am only now over the period of thinking that parents are dull and stupid, but I have found in the past few months that I look forward to his letters with eagerness. He writes fine letters and often I am rather ashamed to think that I had to leave home for two years to discover this.

In early January 1944 both Arthur and Father had learned of R's promotion to Captain and were able to congratulate him and worry (perhaps even seriously) lest he was now being "bowed down under the cares of the whole Mediterranean front." Arthur also guessed wittily at R's whereabouts (since censors had snipped a line out of R's last letter) while his father at least favored Corsica.

Father, meanwhile, keeping R up to date, mentioned new rationing and price-fixing rules at home, adding that one of their Livingston Street neighbors had just sighted a sea-going jeep — clumsy things nicknamed "ducks" — on Willow Street and he hoped that R had not been making any beach landings in one of those. Then he turned the last page over to Mother who "had a cold." Mother reported that one of R's college classmates had been lost in the Pacific, that she felt "lousy" but was o.k. and she loved him.

On the same day as the letter a cable from Father arrived at R's headquarters announcing her death.

The follow-up arrived a week later and began, "My dear son it is with heavy heart that I sit down and write you one of the sorriest messages which can be penned." A long account followed, praising her, telling R how much he had loved her, how much she had been forced to put up with in Nangma's house, and how damaging to her health alcohol had become before pneumonia set in. He wound up with a quiet suggestion to R himself about alcohol.

So that was that. R was numb, then distraught, then numb again. Much later he would write "Mrs. Benedict," the unpleasantly honest poem that tried to catch his early adolescent feelings about her alcoholism. Yet in Naples, with cable and letter at hand, he was more childish. He told himself he would try to balance hatred and love most subtly, would present an emotional complex of great depth, and would do this with great understatement. So he struggled with his complex feelings and the poem was (predictably) terrible. A bit later he wrote "On the Death of Someone Close."

Neither the least nor the most
Sorrow is becoming
In this instance.
A certain gravity,
A solemn pose denoting
Grief well-borne
Is probably correct.

At parties be reserved.
Restrain the raucous chuckle
And the dirty joke.
Drink less,

Incline to thoughtfulness,
And dance, dance
Those melancholy tunes.

At night of course, alone,
A little more abandon
Is permissible.
A tear perhaps,
Or holding back a tear,
Or simple sobbing —
May be correct.

Whatever the time and the place
Remember the fact of shock.

On October 14, 1944, he sent the hand-written poem to Mizener who
singled it out as one of R's best.

> It makes something out of the fact, which is important and valid in itself,
> which goes beyond the fact. It is the particular instance of the general
> problem of deep feeling: how to handle the relation between the always
> partly artificial outward act — public or private — and the inward feeling.
> Is there any inward feeling worthy of the name, however, until the out-
> ward fact exists? But the poem never falters in maintaining just the right
> tone here, the irony at the expense of the mere "theater" of outward act is
> fully marked without smothering the fact of shock.

R's feelings of failure may have helped push him away, if briefly, from his
own life. He retreated into the normal cubbyhole of a properly rational
up-tight New Englander, where he could take on classroom subjects like
famous novels. There he could pretend to be an English department fix-
ture (in about three years he would actually have students) asking students to write 300-word papers about, say, the midnight ride of Paul
Revere, or Moll Flanders. Soon he became his own student, but in sonnets
— not related to the war but to books he was reading. The first three were
on Thomas Hardy's Tess, Hemingway's Lady Ashley, and Daniel DeFoe's
Moll, these being among the many works his father had sent him overseas. He would then sit — during the lunch hour — on a pleasant balcony in the sun and play the part of a poetry sage, first in Naples and then
in lovely Siena.

His idea was "to write a series of sonnets about heroines — which I think is a useful idea from the poet's point of view," he wrote to Mizener, "because it gives him some fundamental data to work with." "Paul Revere's Ride" was one such poem.

Is it one if by land, two if by sea?
Or two if by land? Or what?
What farms, what villages are those to be
Roused from their midnight rut?

Worry, worry, worry. There! A light?
Of course not. But for an empty head
I'd quit this profitless, cold post to plot
The Revolution home in bed.

Yet if the British do the Tower hunts me down.
Then I mount swiftly; then I fiercely ride,
Bearing fresh news of the infamous Crown
To agitate the countryside.

But if the British do,
I wonder, is it one if by land or two?

Even while writing these sonnets, he was also worrying "whether this sort of stuff isn't precious.... There's something obscurely stinking about writing about writing." Mizener replied that there was "of course a danger in writing about other writing."

This only threatens if you depend on the other writing for your effects [and] don't create the effect yourself but depend on the reader's recollection of what is in the original for the resonance of your own poem. I don't think this happens in any of your pieces, because what they depend on for their effect is the particular view of the moral situation you take. There is not a single one of the three that doesn't establish an independent attitude to a situation which the author has judged somewhat differently.

And now R was wrestling with the idea of the sonnet itself and arguing with Mizener about making one poem of several as Mizener had been doing and which R was (politely) critical of:

We are in thorough agreement about the sonnet form. It's a wonderful help and guide.... I can't reinforce the argument about oversimplification which I brought up. Still perhaps it is something else. The 14 line form, despite the variations you have in them, leading up to the Shakespearean sonnet at the end, with a finishing couplet — is designed for a complete poem, not a part of a poem. You know; a beginning, middle, and end. I can see no objection to writing a series of them, on subjects which are related. The objection is to the attempt to *fuse* them into ONE poem which is what you do, in effect, in number four despite the fact that you are now dispatching them separately. In other words my objection to the fourth poem is based upon its references to the others, not its intrinsic worth. Suppose I were to write a sonnet about heroines in general — after I dash off a couple more specific heroines it might work, but the danger is that the form doesn't stand extension. It stands by itself. Thus, a sonnet about heroines in general might be successful but only, I think, if it were to be complete in itself. Now what you've done is try to make each one of the 14 line poems at once self-sufficient and a part of another poem — the whole. That, it seems to me, is an awfully tough job even granting that a discussion of childhood, youth, and old age covers the possible forms of innocence and is not an oversimplification of the subject.

While R was sending his poems to Mizener as he wrote them, Mizener began sending them to literary magazines, at the same time replying with exacting criticism and encouragement: "If you can write poems in the army, then I think the gift must be safe from anything, indestructible. I shall begin pushing them around to the periodicals at once."

Mizener's efforts included trying them "on [Allen] Tate (who is now editing the *Sewanee Review* and making a first-class affair out of it), and Ransom and Delmore Schwartz (poetry editor of the *Partisan Review*) first." Then on January 30, 1945, he wrote R excitedly, "Rosemary and I could not bear the thought of your waiting till this letter got to you to know that Allen Tate has taken *all* the poems I sent him for the *Sewanee Review*.... I am already beginning to consider," he wrote near the end, "who we will allow to publish your first book."

R was stunned.

Well Jesus Christ and a few other people! I was given your letter six minutes ago and upon opening it with trembling hands (for I have been lying in wait for it since your last) I emitted a great cry and staggered to the window for air. Nothing naturally could give me more pleasure, after quietly stagnating in this army atmosphere so long, than Tate's decision.... Because I am too much disturbed to philosophize further upon the event I'll recapitulate and then go to supper. Tate has accepted White Cross, Black Cross and the three lady sonnets, making five poems.... Well I must run — I couldn't possibly walk.... And oh yes, the money. Well, first, I wish you would take out of it whatever is necessary to buy a bottle of the very finest something or other, aged in old manuscripts, and drink a toast to yourself, for me.

These and other poems produced on his pleasant Neapolitan balcony came out well and would be the core of his first book in 1946, *Heroes & Heroines*. Their chief fault was perhaps in the couplets, R feels, which displayed an ancient Puritan vice that he might as well have picked up from Jonathan Edwards, that of rushing in with a moral. Why did he feel so upright on his Neopolitan balcony in the sun at lunchtime? Why couldn't he remember that he was damned lucky to be in the world's greatest, maybe the most horrible, war without discovering that war was all hell?

He had by now been living so well in Naples — for nearly a year — that sometimes he began to feel as if he were in permanent exile from civilian life with his rich Uncle's backing. Naples and its "sumptuous balconies" persisted in R's memory and sometime in the early 50s, in Minnesota, he wrote "Naples," which made its way into *An American Takes a Walk*.

Those of you who do not narrowly explore
The Bay, the Mountain, and the Mantuan Muse
Will hate this city. It is more
Than tired tourists excuse

Where the ash from all those seethings drifts, the earth,
The richer, yet singes, what it bears,
The fresh and greenness, with the scars
Of its own hot birth.

And where the sun on sumptuous balconies engenders
Delicate destinies in pots,
Rising on the moist air grossness tenders
Its respects.

Too bad. Think what in this setting might have risen —
Eden by the sea — had not Naples.
Or think what might have been, had Naples risen
Naples as Naples is, but graced as Eden.

A month or so before D-Day in Normandy he was flown back to Algiers to be part of a mighty committee (his very first) planning an invasion of *Southern* France. Luckily the Normandy invasion came before the committee's decisions amounted to anything, and the Germans were unable to handle three fronts (the Italian front by then was north of Florence and holding, and they simply abandoned Southern France). As a result, on the Southern D-Day R flew to an airfield outside Marseilles, and there he was able to take another of his solo jeep tours — all these solos were officially against regulations — in order to check on supplies the Germans might have left behind. He drove to a big "tank farm" north of Marseilles in order to bang on the tanks with a wrench and declare to himself that they were all empty, then returned to the airfield via a street café in a suburb of Marseilles, where he drank a glass of wine and nobody even noticed that he was an invader. How French. And that very night he was amazingly back in Italy, this time in a pleasant room of his own in Siena's Grand Hotel, overlooking a soccer field.

Yes, General Beverley (George H) had a remarkable eye for finding comfortable quarters, and the tie between the quarters and the war became increasingly important as the war proceeded. In Naples the accommodations had eventually included — aside from the three handsome buildings already mentioned — a lordly mansion right up the street where an officers' "dining facility" was created, complete with a bar done over from old Italian elegance by covering the walls with tropical bamboo and installing a juke box. And in Siena the Grand Hotel — sufficiently elegant for a HQ even without bamboo trimmings — was supplemented by a fine office building near the city's famous Piazza del Campo. That edifice even had a "secure" inner court where top-secret papers could be burned every night. But R developed some contempt for the solemn paper-burning ritual — a contempt partly justified because most of the matter burned was not secret at all — and he once found himself condemned for security carelessness right in his own office, condemned for at least two weeks to be the primary nightly paper-burner down in the courtyard. He had earned his punishment, but by then it was early 1945 and the war was unsecretly winding down, at least in XII AF circles. By then he had become chiefly a keeper of records — how many bellytanks and gallons of petrol were used in 1944, and so on. For such work he had the help of a brand new PFC, Irwin Touster, the artist behind a cartoon that appeared in *Yank*. Irwin was a Brooklynite who had been extracted from a Replacement Depot in Naples where he found himself classified as an expert in charts. He was good at them but he was even better at cartoons, and after the war he would emerge as a fine artist and sculptor. He would also become the post-war *Furioso*'s art editor and did the cover art and drawings for *Heroes & Heroines*.

The cartoon in question shows R's immediate boss, Colonel Beery, on the left, then R, then R's other office mate Sgt. Sam Aquino, and then of course Touster himself, the active agent in the office's moving of a presumably top-secret document to its deserved resting place. After the war

he and R became close civilian friends, even though he claimed that R had deprived him — for reasons still unknown to R — of a good-conduct medal. As for cartoonist Touster, with no hard feelings 25 years later, he described R as follows in *Voyages*, a fine magazine William Claire began publishing in the late 60s and that featured R's work.

> We all considered him strange, and were a bit ashamed to be under his command. He didn't look like an officer, and he didn't seem to care. We were relieved to hear rumors that he had taken the general's shirt in a card game. We escalated the amount of his winnings into six figures to put him in a new light.
>
> I have a few mementos of my captain during those war years — a Yank magazine, a few samples of his "top-secret" prose later downgraded to "restricted," a letter he wrote "to whom it may concern" to enhance my chances for civilian employment, and his order revoking my Good Conduct Medal.
>
> I remember receiving those orders. I was confused and angry. I confronted him, and demanded to know why I was to be so deprived. He

shrugged his hunched shoulders, turned his boyish face to me, and said nothing. The Mona Lisa smile was too much to fathom, and I stalked off.

Later I came to sense what that smile was saying. In revoking that medal he was giving me a badge of a higher order, a commendation for action in sowing wild oats, the approval of youthful rebellion, and perhaps even the acknowledgment of his friendship.

He captained four of us in the POL (petroleum, oil, lubricants) office: a warrant officer (an old army bastard with fingers in everything not nailed down), a staff sergeant (coal mining in West Virginia, the office trigonometrical whiz), a buck sergeant (later to marry a marquise, when he asked the captain to give him away) and me, a private from Brooklyn (the captain couldn't be spared that cinematic touch). Our job, quite literally, was to help grease the gears that turned the propellers that flew the Twelfth Air Force.

Though I was trained as a chemical warfare specialist the captain "hired" me from the Repple-Depple. I considered this one of his many rash moves. He assumed that I, an artist, could make charts. His new general was big for them. The captain had me turn in my decontamination equipment for an issue of three rolls of graph paper and a box of color pencils. I walled the office with the graph paper, cutting openings only for entrance and egress, and under his direction I rendered thereupon a series of zigzag mountains and valleys in eight colors. The general, on inspection, was gravely impressed.

After breakfast we would come to the office, read *Stars and Stripes* and wait for our airfields to 'phone reports of consumption and on-hand statistics of their fuel supply. These figures were tabulated and a daily summary, in eleven copies if I remember correctly, was distributed. We did nothing else — that is, except for the captain. He was a silent man. His work was top-secret. I could only imagine why he seemed so harassed. The anxiety with which the high command awaited his reports led the rest of us to believe that the outcome of daylight bombing turned on his pencil tip. His monthly GOBO (gas, oil, bellytanks, oxygen) Report was famous for its acid attacks on our allies, for its audacious critique of our military system, for its letters to the editor (a kind of wishful fiction) and for its personal ads. During a particularly harried moment the captain placed an ad of his own. It read: "TIRED OLD CAPTAIN wants ticket — no, not that kind — to you know where. Call Gordon 114."

It was always with an utter uniqueness that he solved little problems, usually leaving the whole office nonplussed. The telephone was a great source of frustration. We either got cross-conversation or were left with the crank in our hand. When this happened to the captain, he simply threw the whole telephone into the waste basket.

As for Sgt. Sam Aquino he was a hillbilly from West Virginia with relatives all over Rome — and while he would not reappéar in R's civilian life the memory remained, of the three of them holed up, largely idle and joking, in a small back room during the war's last months. Siena was a fine place not to be warlike.

And strangely those last war months — early 1945 — even produced two old college friends who somehow discovered R's theoretically secret whereabouts and came visiting. One was *Furioso* co-editor Jim Angleton, who should have been busy with the OSS in London but was amazingly planning — after a drink with R in the Grand Hotel's lounge — to put a spy (who Jim said was waiting outside in Jim's Jeep) through the German lines north of Florence after midnight. The second visitor was Dave Jones, R's black classmate at Andover, by then a lieutenant stationed with an old-fashioned segregated military dock loading battalion at Leghorn. Unreal. In other words the war was — by this time — effectively over for R and friends.

What was not over was R's continuing correspondence with Mizener, which included numbers of poems, among them "The Lizard" that Touster would illustrate and that he was fond enough of, with all its enjambment, to include in *The Past, The Present, The Future* more than 40 years later.

How is it this green lizard
Climbs the climbless wall?
And when to where he goes he
Comes, why fall?
Surely he who crawls so
Far against the law
Can crawl a lawless minute
More. With awe
I watch the conduct of green lizards.

He also sent "The Anchor" with the following epigraph: "'About this time, however (Eighth Century B.C.), an important advance was made in seacraft by the discovery of the anchor.' J.B. Bury, *A History of Greece.*"

Son, that was progress then. The older pilots fussed
Whose moorless craft a hundred times had sailed
Safely to Cythera; who without this novelty had crossed
The Pontus, depths where only seamanship prevailed.

In contrast younger men set off insisting
Anchors held all souls aboard secure.
And finding elemental things persisting
They dropped one, and foundered miles from shore.

Only a few wise chaps at first perceived
Its useful limits. Steering through danger they
Anchored in silent harbors undeceived,
The true discoverers. And you and I,

My son, if wise, can undiscovered find
Most of the gadgets of mankind.

R was unhappy with the heavy pointedness of the poem's moral but worried, in a letter to Mizener, about how to bring in needed source material without having it take over.

> I confess I think the only way I'll write any good poetry is by drawing from a previously established situation heavily. If this poem is no good it is because the connection between the poem and its source material is too thin. That source material is awfully important. I'm tired of drawing from some past personal experience: it's much too limited. I want something in somebody else's story or history and I'm looking all over hell for suggestive subject matter, particularly when and if I get a chance to write a narrative poem or short play.... I need to give myself an assignment, saying, for instance, "Here is the story of Romulus and Remus. Now be a good chap and take this story and turn it into a one act play in galloping hectets which is a serious commentary upon the peculiar people down south called the agrarians."

In another decade a good deal of American poetry came to draw directly on personal experience — the autobiographical and confessional lyric was to establish a strong beachhead. R too would write many such poems and yet he was often uncomfortable with them, perhaps because of his New England Puritan heritage, though that heritage had no effect on Robert Lowell who rifled his life past and present as subjects for hundreds of poems. R often took on an ironic or skeptical tone (at best) and a sarcastic one (at worst).

Mizener responded to R's speculations on material for poems with a good deal of seriousness. "I'm convinced," he replied "that a really good poem is not written wholly out of the guts — if it were the romantics with all their great natural talents would have done more; there are damned few good poems among the romantics, though a good deal of fine poetry. Good poems come out of the fusion of a subject and a sensibility, out of the writer's ability to find a story, an argument, an action which seems as a whole significant to him and full of a lot of angles and then to shape this story in such a way that it says all he wants it to and also becomes satisfactory for a story." Arthur was not finished.

> This the Bard did for the theatre, Dryden for arguments, and Jane Austen for stories. I don't see anything to belittle in this and I deplore the way you go on as if you were faintly embarrassed to discover yourself wanting to write this way; it seems to me the way every really good writer has written. So give yourself the Romulus and Remus story or — as one of our candidates called it this year on her comprehensives — Browning's Horatio at the Bridge — and make it a commentary on those dreamers from the old days of the reasonable man, economic rationalism, and pleasure-pain psychology, the editors of the *Partisan Review*. This is the way good poems ought to be written.

At least the writing of poems (good or bad) and the living in Italian luxury had not kept R from collecting a superior number of "points" for three years overseas, with the result that after V-E Day in May 1945 he was shipped home almost instantly on a freighter with no freight aboard other than fifty ancient, similarly pointed heroes. These gambled in the hold — with R as adjutant holding funds — for two weeks before being landed in Virginia. Then R was shipped north to where his military life had begun, Fort Devens, and was granted three months' terminal leave. He was soon knocking on the door of the apartment on Livingston Street. His father was waiting.

~~~

Fifty years later R found himself reading a memoir by a friend and fellow poet, William Jay Smith, who had been in the Pacific for WWII but had, before that, distinguished himself by being an "army brat." (That was the title of his memoir.) He was two years older than R, and when the Japanese attacked Pearl Harbor he had just picked up an M.A. at Washington University in St. Louis. At that moment R was nominally ahead of him in wartime service, about to become a 90-day wonder at

Fort Benning. But Smith was a whole lifetime ahead of him in the traditional military world, since his father had been in the Regular Army from the time Smith was a baby. The father had been a corporal, and for a while a sergeant. He had been busted several times for drunkenness but that vice had perhaps helped make him a fine peacetime soldier. Smith had grown up in or near Jefferson Barracks in St. Louis, and by intelligence and luck he had made it into the world beyond the bootlegging poker-playing life his father lived. He was soon to be a naval officer in the Pacific, yet already he was far ahead of R in insider knowledge, knowledge for instance of snafu and its origins. His father had told him the secret, which was that the higher ranks were always the cause because they arranged that "only the sycophants, the brownnosers" got ahead. As for the apparent discipline and order to be seen on the parade ground, Smith wrote in *Army Brat* that "that was merely a cover-up for the disorder of the men leading them."

Reading his words R was much impressed by how differently they had both come to wisdom, though he was also impressed by how their differences did not remove a common warm bond for the military. After four years in uniform R was not sure how to live out of it. What did one do in a civilian place like New Haven anyway? Where was the officers' bar? Well, at least the war had given him two dozen or so poems and also the illustrator, PFC Irwin Touster, for his first book. It had also begun shaping the questions about poetry that he would be preoccupied with over the years ahead, two big ones for starters: what did it mean to be a poet and what was poetry's *use* anyway.

History & Furioso *Redux*

chapter six

In any memorable private experience there is always a kind of San Andreas Fault lying underneath, to the presence of which the young learner must accustom himself as the Fault intermittently shakes him up, telling him, Watch it, kid, the ground you walk on is not yours. R knew that in his own wartime life, even on sunny days on the Neapolitan balcony, the Fault kept speaking to the frivolity of his being where he was, doing what he was doing. And it seems clear that if there was one subject he and Arthur Mizener were really working at in their many long letters, it was the Fault: what it did, what it meant, how one reckoned with it. What the War and the Fault kept telling them was that though their correspondence was in some ways ridiculous — who cared about an infelicitous word in the first line of a tiny tiny sonnet? — still, the word was what they had and what they *could* intelligently care about.

Probably what R chiefly learned as soldier-scribbler was a little about the deceptions of self. For instance, he learned that just settling in to study self-deception needs to be a core subject, in our time, in any curriculum devoted to understanding rather than doing. A tangled subject it is. In the sciences, for example, the professional focus is on the obstacles that keep an experimenter's self from making experimental objectivity possible. In psychobiography the focus is on how a biographee leads himself and his disciples astray by mythologizing his own being. And in literary criticism the focus is on the slipperiness of textual meaning, with much heavy argument proceeding out of those who say that no literary text has meaning independent of its readers' meaning for it. Not that R was so lucky as to be an undeceived self. His mind was a smorgasbord of amateurish speculations — a bit of his father's Darwinism, a bit of Marxism, a bit of Mizener, and a large bit of a New England *I*. R learned to disapprove of

American self-glorification generally, but remained an *I* through all the disapproval, yearning, as an *I* always does, for glorification.

⁓

R came safely home immediately after the end of the European War in May, 1945, then spent two months in Father's Livingston Street apartment wondering what lay ahead (it did not yet seem time to worry about his still being in the Reserves). Of all the lessons in self-understanding that he had, none was more critical than of coming home to his lonely father. He can still remember, as he entered the apartment, his father's old bathrobe, his old voice, his telling R to sit in the old leather rocker amid the neat clutter (the neatness was his, the clutter had been his mother's). And as in a deep dream he can remember discovering that his father's self was no longer a depth to reach for. Four years earlier Big R had had "interests," but it was in the leather chair that Little R learned his father was now some-one else. So there he was, and there was R, and as they sat together pro-ducing long silences, R could see that he was the only full self in the room.

One could say that R was in the process of finding his self, while his father was in the process of losing his; but that is glibness. So is saying that he was anxious to get on with his life and that he had to make his own decisions. What about graduate school? In August with that in mind R took a train to New York, a train to Ithaca and a bus to Wells College about half way up Lake Cayuga in order to visit Arthur and Rosemary Mizener. He was there when the A-Bombs were dropped on Japan and *that* war was over.

Willard Thorp, one of Mizener's old English teachers at Princeton (and founder of the university's American Studies Program), was there too, and on the night of V-J day he climbed to the top of the Wells Chapel tower in order to ring out bells wildly. He and Mizener persuaded R that grad-uate work at Princeton — on the G.I. Bill of course — was a sensible move. After the visit he went back to Father with their suggestion, and his father of course wanted him to go. He did. Within two months Father was dead. It was much later, when R was nearly his father's age, before he could write about him in "The Feel of Rock."

My father went broke on a shaded street.
My mother drank there.
My brothers removed themselves; they were complete.
I kept to my room and slicked down my hair.

Would it not have been better
For father to have been bitter
In Switzerland, writing a weekly letter?

The ground by the house was gravel like grandmother's heart.
He had his pride
But God and he stood apart.
He slept with his radio by him as bride.

I did not know until grown how alone
In a bed in a dark room
One could be, one had been, little father clone.

After the funeral and the settlements (R's two married brothers and he dealt with the burial of their past with customary New England familial frigidity) and after sitting in the New Haven apartment (now to be abandoned) the beds, bureaus and much else was moved to storage; for the moment R had no reason to argue about furniture since he had no home to put it in.

R's inheritance was Father's aged Buick, which he soon traded in for a Ford as yet unbuilt, and about $30,000 in a breakable trust (which he soon broke). Before losing the Buick, he drove it down to Princeton's Graduate College behind the golf course and settled in again to college life and books. (It would have been a good time for him to take up golf but he never did.) He was only twenty-six but had reason to feel older. He had no friends at Princeton other than the Thorps. His army life had suddenly retreated into his childhood but would be resurrected on paper a few years later, during the Berlin Air Lift, when his supply expertise with 100 octane would be discovered in Pentagon files. (An explanation of R's clever evasion will come later.) As for friends at Yale and among New Haven townies, four years of war had simply removed them from his life, and he was as if a stranger even when walking his old home's once familiar streets. To put this differently his here-and-now had suddenly come to seem empty, and having had long experience as a military loner sitting idly in a Jeep in some foreign land trying to be (somehow) literary, he was now even tempted to go back on Active Service. But a drive for something unexplainable trumped temptation and he made it instead to Princeton.

Though still dreaming of the literary life he decided to try History there, his excuse (when he thought he needed one) being that he did not wish to become a literary *specialist*. But in addition to three history courses, he did sign up for American Lit with Thorp and right away he found himself writing a learned and dull paper on Melville's *Pierre* (*Pierre* being a graduate student's kind of book, that is, a book for scholars rather than mere minds).

Much more stimulating was sudden surprising news from New York, from a publishing connection that soon brought about a visit with a young editor at Reynal & Hitchcock, a firm briefly in chips from a best-seller during the war, Lillian Smith's anti-segregationist novel *Strange Fruit*. Soon he had a contract for a book of poetry, *Heroes & Heroines*, though he did not yet have enough poems to fill it. "This is remarkable news, of the very first order," Mizener wrote R. "Fancy, a book of poems at your tender years." And soon he had an illustrator as well, the now civilianized PFC Irwin Touster, who had drawn excellent cartoons for R in Italy to supplement solemn gasoline consumption charts (100 million gallons one year, R now thinks). Touster was back in art school and provided several fine caricatures of such subjects as Paul Revere wondering if his head is on straight, and one (for the dust jacket) of a worried Sherlock Holmes, about whom R had also written, though not well he now feels.

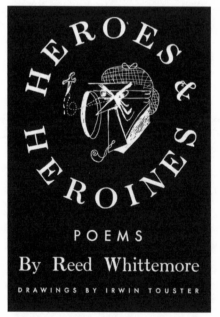

Graduate school itself was less comforting. There were just six students in history including R. They were all Vets, they were all on the G.I. Bill, and they all sat together for very long silent days around a big table in the History Seminar Room of the old Witherspoon Library — six single serious and insecure males, oppressed by thoughts of being now obliged to run their own lives, since their good Uncle was pushing them gently out (on the G.I. Bill). History was hardly new to any of them, but making it central and relevant to their lives was a dubious experiment. R would never know how many of them survived the quest for an advanced degree in History, but he managed to avoid thinking much about such a fate for himself. He tried to concentrate on simply sitting in the seminar room on a rubber cushion and reading reading. History history.

And his writing? Put aside that profession, if it is one, for a moment, and concentrate on R's reading. He did need to "do" history, having as an English major at Yale picked up little of it except literary pasts. What he remembered most convincingly was a fuzzy sophomore 20th century survey course taught by a debonair young showman instructor who one spring morning arrived in class still in a tuxedo. R's most depressingly effective history lesson had not come from that but from reading a lengthy essay on the nature of history in his father's old *Encyclopedia Britannica*, 11th Edition, 1910, another inheritance and one he has now been carrying with him for some 60 years. A young scholar from Canada had written the essays, James Shotwell, who was at that early time thoroughly sold on history as a science. Early in the article he acknowledged that history was also an art, though he soon put the art aside and annoyed R thoroughly.

The occasion for Shotwell's writing the piece was itself of historical (call it late Victorian) interest. He had been visiting London with his wife and six-month-old child, and there had met the editor-in-chief of the *Enc Brit*, 11th, Hugh Chisholm. Chisholm and other scholars were having a squabble at the time, and Chisholm, liking the 30-year-old foreigner, asked him to quiet down the Encyclopedia's offices by becoming managing editor. Shotwell declined, but wrote the history essay instead (before sailing for America to teach at Columbia) in which he advised the reader that history in the modern world had become a magnificent "tool" for human understanding. He dwelt at length on the "new machinery of research...perfected in the 19th century [the reference was to German scholarship] and set going in all the archives of Europe," noting that soon the attention of social scientists dwarfed such ancient "machinery." (R's animus towards social scientists and the increasing grip they've had on so many aspects of American education has its roots in Princeton.) He spoke of the archivists "devoting lives...cataloguing... indexing...and in general insuring that texts be as correct as they could ever be." The article reached its depressing climax with Shotwell's claim that the world's archives were now so complete that "no one need go astray who takes the trouble to make use of the mechanism that is at hand."

Of course R reading Shotwell had managed to be offended by the "mechanism" even before arriving at graduate school. And, luckily, one of the pleasures for him of Princeton pedagogy was that of finding historians there who also disliked such machinery. One of those was ancient Professor Thomas Jefferson Wertenbaker, who was in charge of Colonial History and had not thought for a single moment of archives as mechanisms. He soon had R reading pages and pages of the journals of Governor Winthrop and others of the Massachusetts Bay Colony, and facing up to the unscientific problem of how best to go astray in order to produce something of interest and consequence. R did not solve the mechanism problem then (nor would he ever). He merely turned out a fine monograph on drinking (at breakfast) in colonial New England, then moved to loftier matters. What mattered was that Prof Wertenbaker did not let R suppose that history was a profession for pushing the buttons of a mechanism.

And more to the point of making history central in a struggling scholar's thought was a seminar with Joseph Strayer, Chairman of History. Strayer wanted his students to worry unmechanically about what history was anyway — a good question that R had managed to ignore. And since Strayer was a medievalist another big question came up — what is a medievalist? Or, rather, why on earth does one become one? Apologetically, as if confessing a sin, Strayer revealed that he became one because he understood that if one read in the medieval "field" long enough one could "cover" everything extant and available *in* it.

Now there was another unShotwellian revelation. Historians put things together all by themselves by deciding in advance what was possible to "cover." But why did one have to "cover" everything anyway?

Put that cynical question aside. When not being a medievalist Strayer was really quite practical and human. He had recently edited *The Interpretation of History*, an anthology of essays in which many fields and views were covered without fear of missing a few sources. Strayer himself led off the volume with a quiet editorial selling balance rather than coverage, and he was reinforced in the lead essay by Columbia historian Jacques Barzun who recommended that a scholar develop a "sense" of history, rather than any theory or ideological position.

But it was hard to pick up the sense (and achieve the balance) without the coverage. Accordingly R, as a nearly historyless newcomer reading among these authorities, felt no temporal urgencies pressing in on him as he balanced readingly on his library air cushion. Yet he did begin to wonder how long it would take to achieve those three troublesome virtues even if one did not become a medievalist. The best estimate he could arrive at was a lifetime, and at age twenty-six that seemed too long. Didn't he need "prospects" of some sort before he settled in? Of those he could only see, glimmering ever so slightly in his crystal ball, matters literary rather than historical.

Yet history was at least putting him in the world of books again, lots of books, books other than the literary ones that his father had shipped overseas to him in small packages. Also some of the new history books brought back his undergraduate affection, theoretical at least, for socialism. Of special interest was an undergraduate course he was now auditing taught by R.R. Palmer. For it he informally wrote a piece on 19th century anarchism that achieved a climax of sorts with the Haymarket Riot in Chicago (1886). For this event he did most of his research in the basement of Princeton's Witherspoon Library, where old yellowing newspapers were then filed. (These were the days before tapes, discs and so on, and the basement air itself was challenging.) This research experience — perhaps more than the reading of scholarly tomes — moved his mind into daily 20th century crises, and into matters close to his own intellectual world, matters that kept being unbalanced and often senseless, matters on the edge of current events that little magazine editors and other anarchists (it *is* the best word for them) are tempted by. To find himself wrestling with such collegiate material again, though well protected by ivied walls and a golf course, was refreshing.

Yes, so he even found himself siding (most tentatively) with the Haymarket Riot villains — though they had indeed killed several policemen. He took their side in order to produce a poem written partly from the point of view of one of their leaders, a certain T. Lizius. The epigraph for "T. Lizius Reconsiders" came from the man himself who on Feb. 21, 1885, had written in *The Alarm*, a Chicago anarchist newspaper, "Dynamite! Of all the good stuff, this is the stuff. Stuff several pounds of this sublime stuff into an inch pipe (gas or water pipe), plug up both ends, insert a cap with a fuse attached, place this in the immediate neighborhood of a lot of rich loafers who live by the sweat of other people's brows, and light the fuse. A most cheerful and gratifying result will follow."

Comrades, times have changed.
To free the world and furl the tyrant's standard,
Sweeping all from all till all is splendidly estranged,
Once was a passion gayly squandered,
Once was the brave caprice
Of a single rebel with a strange device.

But times have changed.
Chit-chat is the stuff of revolution now,
Contention and concessions smilingly arranged,
That serve no subversion but perpetuate the foe
In his high office perched on sufferance below.

For times have changed.
The stuff of Revolution now is all unfused;
Walls are never breached nor trousers disarranged,
Wrongs never righted, rights never used;
And men with beards and bombs may come and go
Unseen, unheard from, in the heartless anonymity of General Woe.

Oh! If yet the time were only ripe
To stuff more stuff in the old lead pipe —

The poem itself — a curious exercise in adopting a persona — was not (at that pre-terrorist time) a threat to civilization, and anyway R was not planning to become a unabomber. (Nor did he think of bombers as suicide bombers since that kind of terrorism was still half a century away.) His procedure was one he had adopted in the literary sonnets he had begun writing during the war, where the poet played the role, very tentatively, of his subjects. He had been sympathetic with most of them, though he had ridiculed poor Paul Revere a bit for not remembering which signal (one or two) he was supposed to beam from the old North Church (the legend itself came not from history but Longfellow's fervid imagination), and in another poem, "Tess," he lectured Thomas Hardy overmuch about his handling of *Tess of the d'Urbervilles*. (Hardy hadn't given the poor girl a chance.)

Tess of Blackmoor Vale was what you might call
Bitched from the start. Hardy had his way
Digging early and deep the pitfall
Where she tumbled on her tumbling day.

Timing, to have the wrong tick off the right,
The right chime wrong, was all, as always, sin
Being nothing but thinking in the night
The clock strikes one when one is gone.

So Hardy hardly had to lift a spade,
The first hole dug, but dropped a wicked tear
Observing how his Tess obeyed
His ticker fixed and dingling in her ear.

And when he pushed the button reading "stop,"
Her time was whatcha might call up.

He was now learned enough to worry about T. Lizius and the range of anarchism as a ... *what?* — a political ideology? a historical phenomenon? a way of life? — and not to let the subject go after finishing the poem. And here again, remarkably, his father's *Enc Brit*, 11th, came in handy with an essay on anarchism by none other than Prince Peter Alexeivich Kropotkin. That the *Enc Brit* could move its heavy intellectual tonnage from the primitive scientism of Shotwell to the complex ideology of Kropotkin was itself an indication of the range and ambition of that remarkable 1910 edition. The Empire was still thriving then, and apparently Kropotkin himself was in London at the time (where Shotwell had just been), having settled there in order to preach the utopianly peaceful virtues of an ideology that had jailed him in both Russia and France. His essay described anarchism as "a principle of life and conduct under which society is conceived without government — harmony in such a society being obtained, not by submission to law, or by obedience to any authority, but by free agreements concluded between the various groups, territorial and professional, freely constituted for the sake of production and consumption, as also for the satisfaction of the infinite variety of needs and aspirations of a civilized being." Whew. What a liberal and liberating utopianism.

Kropotkin called his anarchist allies the leftwing of the Socialist Party and he professed to share with socialists the conviction that "private ownership and capitalist production for the sake of profits represent a monopoly which runs against both the principles of justice and the dictates of utility." Of course he *denied* that his notions were utopian, and supplied an immense bibliography of thinkers on his side from Zeno rapidly forward to the likes of Proudhon (who seems to have used the word "anarchism" first) and Bakunin. He also discussed anarchism within workers' unions — and the division resulting between the belligerents and the sensible folk. In this connection he referred to the Haymarket Affair, noting that the convictions of seven anarchists there (and subsequently the hanging of four, and the pardoning of three after seven years) had brought forth unpeaceful retaliation from Anarchists. Yet the peaceful principles of proper Anarchists seemed to him not to have been essentially betrayed.

So R found himself reading casually about Kropotkin's exploits, discovering that he had been a pretty fair scientist before moving over to governance and its problems. R had known a number of academic scientists who seemed to him to be naïve politically, but Kropotkin writing of his noble family and of growing up when Russia was passing through major upheavals — the end of Czardom, the end of serfdom — was no mere academic. To put this another way he had a way of being at once serious about anarchism and peacefully scholarly about it. Among R's most pleasing memories was an episode when Kropotkin was in a military school at eighteen and wrote an extremely private paper complaining of a number of current governmental vices. He slipped copies to three fellow students and asked them to put their remarks "behind the Scotch clock in our library." He received two replies expressing sympathy but worrying about him. So he wrote a second paper in which, more forcefully, he insisted "upon the necessity of uniting all forces in the name of liberty [from governance]." To that he received no replies at all but the two sympathizers came quietly to him, sympathizing and saying, "Your paper has done its work. Let us be friends.... If it becomes known that there is a paper of this kind the consequences will be terrible for all of us. Let us constitute a circle and talk [sic] about everything; perhaps we shall put something into the hands of a few others." How conspiratorial and yet peaceful. This had great appeal for R.

Yes, and also how comically like the affairs of a little magazine. Here was indeed a connection (one to vanish along with little magazines themselves when anarchism itself changed character). So R was charmed by Kropotkin, wrote his unrevolutionary Haymarket paper, and turned to other authors of radical literature, among these, Thorsten Veblen and Joseph Conrad. An unlikely pair. Veblen's heavy language in *The Theory of the Leisure Class* was annoying though the man did have moments of grandeur, as when he described the world's managers as barbarians. (Kropotkin would have liked that.) He was also appealing on the subject of fashionable aesthetics, and as a naïve early social scientist he preceded the age of polls and the rendering of truth thereby. He had many failings and is said to have been a terrible teacher, but the man's rebellious center still seemed (in 1946) coherent and important.

In the first few months after returning to civilian life, R moved from sonnets to several verse dramas, none of which advanced past a scene or two. His main efforts were aimed at converting two novels by Conrad, *Lord Jim* and *The Heart of Darkness*, to the stage. He even became scholarly and went off to Sterling Library to see how Conrad (and Henry James too) had fared when they attempted such conversions. He found that the process had routed them, neither being able to do anything, even in prose, but butcher stage dialogue. R marched ahead undeterred for a month but his labors on *Heart of Darkness* emerged as merely more sonnets, while his *Lord Jim* added up to just a few unrelated soliloquies.

So brief dramatizing did not work, though it was a useful failure. More than sixty years later, he still knows the immensities involved. And aside from the virtue of trying, there was the wisdom he gained from simply reckoning with Conrad's characters' complicated selves, especially Lord Jim's.

He included two fragments of this work in *Heroes & Heroines*, one being a sonnet soliloquy by Jim, in which R had ship officer Jim talking tensely about the nasty little fix he had put himself into by abandoning his ship in the middle of the Gulf of Aden (only to find out later that it didn't, with its boatload of Mecca-bound pilgrims, sink). R himself had personally abandoned no ship, had not even been able to abandon the XII AFSC — his resignation was laughed away — yet the heroic chatter he supplied Jim with in the terrible sonnet must have had something to do with himself, a modest supply-officer hero from the war who now lay abed, unshaven, feeling like a comic-strip derelict. The sonnet began with Jim crying, "Why this?" and came back again to the same tough question at the end. "Why this? Why are all my bravest plans amiss."

But the other, longer monologue went further than to have its speaker fret. The speaker was a narrator like Conrad's Marlow, and he told Jim at some length to stop moping around and do something. Do what? Do

something escapist, but *do it*. Do what Conrad's Jim did in the last half of
the novel: go to Patusan (a remote, primitive, fictional Eastern country,
where Jim recovered his self-respect and became the head man). The connection with R seems to have been that R was arranging to go to a Patusan
of his own at the time — and that Patusan was Princeton. Here's the
poem "Patusan."

> Jim, there's a land within this land
> (Of parakeets and palms)
> Where a man may partly live;
> Live and partly die; a land of whispers.
> Jungles of greenest wonder crowd the clouds.
> Creatures of zoos, flowers for fabulous gardens
> Creep to a lush and lazy end. A man,
> A man of garden talents
> (Looking for long-tailed monkeys, flying frogs)
> Might, might, might there, at last,
> Find peace.
>
> It is unlikely. Even a hundred forest days
> (Of sandalwood and fern),
> And the laced-in hazards of the covert hills
> Are not enough.
> Oozing through teatime fringes, gliding up fished-out streams
> Oddly the outside presses in.
>
> Or if that secret place
> (Of the green-crested gaper, the claret-breasted dove)
> Still somehow partly unprofaned sleeps on,
> Yet is unlikely.
>
> Even in Patusan the bright-plumed bird
> Hides in the thickest scrub;
>
> And even there —
>
> Jim, it is unlikely. Go there.

R read Conrad's *The Secret Agent*, which at first seemed a fine companion to the world of Kropotkin and all the other dissidents that R's Marxist

friend at Yale, Arnold Kettle, had recommended. While Kettle had called *The Heart of Darkness* "perhaps the most horrifying description of the effects of imperialism ever written," he had managed to avoid comment on *The Secret Agent.* R, wondering why, came on the book at Princeton for the first time and was dazzled by the opening chapter's craft. Any movie director setting out to make a thriller of the book would need no further help on how to photograph a mysterious mix of the commonplace and the ominous to be found in a seedy London shop out of which came forth the wonderfully intellectual plot to bomb the Greenwich Observatory. In it the "perfect anarchist" is known as the professor and walks about with a "sinister India-rubber ball" in his pocket. (It is attached to a bomb on his thigh that can be exploded in thirty seconds.) This professor runs casually into the chief police inspector. They discuss the troubled social scene as if in class, and the professor advises the man of law to "give it up. You'll find we are too many for you." Cut. Back to the seedy shop and to in-passing mention (in chapter four of the book) that a bomb has exploded near the Observatory. It seems not to have killed anyone resembling a professor but to have blown to bits (as soon revealed) a slight, fair-haired fellow wearing a velvet collar. Not until about chapter twelve is the failure to destroy the Observatory itself explained, and the high-falutin scheme for a vast psychological attack on all existing capitalist tyrannies (as represented by the Observatory, symbol of misdirected modern science) is dismissed in favor of producing a sentimental family tragedy. Conrad, R slowly decided, did not follow Kropotkin in being seriously committed to any anarchist faith.

But of what ingredients were *serious* commitments made? This question kept troubling R as he sat in Princeton's history seminar room. The point is he was doubting his own seriousness in just being there, and he was also wondering about literary folk in general. The subject would not go away, and his general post-war confusion was well illustrated by his suddenly going right out and buying (he was still rich from having spent nothing in the Army) an odd little cottage in the woods in Madison, Connecticut, not far from where he as a teenager had gone swimming. So when he settled in at the cabin for a short summer he at least knew he was confused.

Yes, reader, when he arrived at his new woodsy cabin for the summer he was instantly faced with what was he going to do with his life there? Or anywhere? Seriously?

The cabin could have been an excellent starting point for a peacefully anarchic career like Thoreau's — and it was much more comfortable than Henry David's hut. It had two bedrooms, a good bath with shower, a good living room with fireplace, a good porch with screens (but with no other view than dense woods), a good kitchen and a sensible small cellar with a tiny furnace that made winter living practicable. Also it was, though in the wilds, just a few miles from several beaches. It therefore quickly attracted other potential anarchists who were also fresh from wartime service and also wondering how to be serious.

For two or three weeks R still had no car and had to bicycle to Clinton for his rations. Then two old non-literary friends from New Haven arrived on four wheels and made the bicycle unnecessary but at the same time encouraged frivolity. They brought with them a fine dancer named Tibby, fine because she could tolerate R's amateurish two-step, and the summer became mainly vacation time — pleasant but not serious. When R's literary friends showed up, the frivolity continued for a bit, and might well have sent R back to Princeton in September without having advanced an inch into the realm of the serious if someone — could it have been himself? — hadn't proposed reviving *Furioso*.

Jim Angleton was not among the summer visitors since he was already in Washington as a peacetime soldier, engaged in the conversion of the wartime OSS to the Central Intelligence Agency. He would eventually rise to become chief of counterintelligence. Those who did arrive were Howard Nemerov (with a new English wife, Peggy), John Pauker (with an Ohio wife, Gini, he had married in college), and two still-unmarried Yale friends, Ambrose (Ambie) Gordon and W.R. (Bill, known as Stooge) Johnson. Soon literature supplemented dancing.

R was Yale '41, Pauker, Johnson and Gordon Yale '42. Nemerov was Harvard '42. Pauker and Nemerov were New Yorkers who had gone to school together in Manhattan before college. All were jobless, all seemed ready for literary seriousness.

Nemerov and Johnson had already experimented with collaborating on a short story about chess; it was printed in *Story* magazine where founder and editor Whit Burnett declared it to be the greatest chess story ever written. R and Johnson had also tried working together, by speaking alternate chapters of a murder mystery into a tape recorder. (That didn't work at all.) As for Pauker he was busy that summer collaborating extensively with himself by creating several pseudonyms such as Thomas Rowley and S.J. Canbrode (or was Canbrode Nemerov?), and providing each with a distinctive style. These pseudonyms were to soon appear in issues of the new *Furioso*. The key word at this time for all of them — as they dreamed of their futures — was "strategy," a word Pauker had first used literarily in an old college essay where he labeled a writer's potential audience as the enemy — and to be recognized as such. Perhaps he had really borrowed the idea from Aristotle but at any rate Johnson liked it a lot, Nemerov and R liked it a little, and Ambrose Gordon was merely amused by it since he had his more modest writing ambitions well in hand and was planning to be a straightforward Yale graduate student in English.

R no longer remembers how the first issue was assembled, typeset, and proofread, or how former PFC Irwin Touster redesigned the *Furioso* cover at the last moment. But in October the fact of their summer collaboration became visible in packages of fifty from the Central Printing Company in New Haven. The copies were then mailed to an ancient subscriber list, and sold in a pitiful few places like the Yale Co-op. In starting the magazine up again in 1947 without Jim Angleton — he and sister Carmen were listed as "absent editors," later on as "editors emeriti" — R shifted focus from the elder modernists to his contemporaries and himself. The shift was natural enough — the editors had few credentials other than having passed Shakespeare and the Romantics. But for R, the shift was also necessary psychologically. He wanted to be *in* the magazine and have the other editors in it. So they printed their own work mercilessly. The first group consisted of Nemerov, Pauker, Johnson, Gordon, and Touster (art editor).

Where *Furioso* Vol. 1, No. 1 had begun with a letter to its editors from old modernist Archibald MacLeish calling for a poetry of the people — a poetry in which its suitability for radio would be a register (literal and symbolic) of its success — *Furioso* Vol. II, No. 1 led off with a searching if not always clear manifesto by R. It was "The Continuities of Poetry," and in it he explored MacLeish's argument — that poetry be written to be heard and written to be "understood when heard once." The most vociferous critics of modern poetry, he wrote, "sit hidden behind the charges of obscurity and exclusiveness and behind the cries for a Poetry of

Democracy, a Poetry of the People. He added that it is difficult to dissoci-
ate those cries from those of public-spirited souls who wish to 'use' the
poets, to draft them into the service of a Nation or a Cause."

> We merely suggest here that the dissociation should if possible be
> made if only to demonstrate the possibility. We are not fully persuaded
> that the virtuous are always obtuse, the villainous direct, nor that
> MacLeish's precepts need be used only in conjunction with war bond
> drives, recruiting, and other immediacies of an unfortunate political, eco-
> nomic or military situation. We think that the limitations imposed upon
> a poet who is, unlike a good child, to be heard and not seen may be con-
> sidered (and will be here) as technical, not ethical.

And what did these limitations amount to in writing a poem?

> On the one hand they may influence the poet's use of language. And
> on the other they may modify or alter the order, logic or sequence of sense
> upon which the component parts of his finished statement are hung.
> The language restriction is not unlike that which Wordsworth, the
> Imagists and others have tried to impose upon their verse. It is a restric-
> tion for which the boundaries are always imprecise and therefore dis-
> putable. For our hypothetical radio poet it is a restriction which impels
> him to exclude — if he is to be assured of a one-time listener's under-
> standing — what he judges to be extraordinary and therefore difficult ver-
> bal complexities and concentrations; to exclude, for example, construc-
> tions which present the problems of a German sentence for someone
> unfamiliar with German sentence structure.... The other restriction is
> structural. The poet is obliged to provide his listeners with an immediately
> perceptive continuity to follow, like a lifeline, through.

"This provision," R concluded, "is no hardship for a narrative or dramatic poet, since his plot is his lifeline. But for the lyric poet sequences of
action are normally useless...the lyric poet has no lifeline comparable to
plot. His nearest substitute is the metaphysical conceit: unification by the
imposition of an outside logic (a figure) upon the poem's 'matter.' But for
the poet who cannot or does not choose to find the suitable, the adequate, the proper figure, even this is no help. He is left with a paltry
choice. He may borrow from the logicians and state his piece in the form
of an argument. Or he may borrow a musical formula; what we will call
Continuity by Association."

R's "Continuities" may have focused on poetry alone, but the new
Furioso now had a larger literary scope. While the first issue included
poems by younger poets — Kenneth Rexroth, Weldon Kees, Dunstan
Thompson, William Jay Smith — and the older guard, Wallace Stevens
and Richard Eberhart, its center was a thirty page collation called
"Mammon: A Gross Concert Upon Publishing," in which the editors set
out anarchically to *destroy* the New York industry. Hyperbole? Yes, but
serious hyperbole. They were not vain enough to imagine destroying even
the Book of the Month Club, and they were not opposed to thinking quietly that one or more of them might find a venal publisher for themselves
amid the enemy. Yet they were definitely serious about sitting at their
typewriters. Writers are like that.

R led off the concern with an "Overture" (below) as his own early way
of being a serious anarchist. As for the other editors they were milder but
also experimental as strategists and the result was uneven but promising
— a genuinely new beginning for *Furioso*. In 1940, the undergraduate editors had given themselves no voice. In 1946 R was trying — when not at
the beach — to be *engagée*, which is at least one meaning for "serious."

Those minor deities who whisper in my ear of the merits and virtues
of things are normally a sufferable annoyance. Even the publishing gods
— whose cunning ways I find more vexatious than the others' — can, I
think, be put up with in silence for long stretches. But there comes the
time. . . .

I listened to their offers for years. They held out High Adventure for
two bucks; Truth, Beauty, and/or Understanding for three. They offered
me Appreciation and Pleasures of The Mind. They proffered me Reality in
Stark, Earthy, Turbulent, Moving, Epic, Spiritual, Heart-Warming Tales by
the Fire in The Evening. They warned me against Injustice, Ignorance and
Isms. They were prepared to lead me out of Darkness into Light — to grab
my hand and lead me to The Light.

And for years I took their Word as Talk. What else? Nobody means all
this, I said. By "Beauty" they mean "Trees"; by "Truth" Recrimination.
What they call an Epic is any important Bore. "Adventure" is for Morons;
prospective mothers are "Moved."

So I accepted their deceptions as deceptions and established between
us (deceivers and deceived) a kind of silent compact, as I thought, by
which I took a certain percentage of their Word and by which they were
bound to take my discount.

- MAMMON: A Gross Concert Upon Publishing
  (In Four Parts)

- POETRY by Wallace Stevens, Kenneth Rexroth,
  Weldon Kees, Lindley Williams Hubbell,
  Howard Nemerov, Richard Eberhart, William
  R. Johnson, Reed Whittemore, Dunstan
  Thompson, William Jay Smith and Arthur
  Mizener

- THE CONTINUITIES OF POETRY — an ESSAY

- REVIEWS

FURIOSO

FALL 1946

CONTENTS

Editorial Board: Reed Whittemore, Howard Nemerov, William R.
Johnson, John Pauker and Ambrose Gordon, Jr.
Absent Editors: James J. Angleton, Carmen M. Angleton.
The original design for the cover, by Graham Peck,
has been revised by Irwin Touster, Art Editor.

Furioso, VOL. II, NUMBER TWO (Or Whole Number 6).
Address: RFD 1, MADISON, CONNECTICUT
Copyright, 1946, by Reed Whittemore.

First post-war issue of Furioso.

I failed, however, to consider the cumulative effect, on both sides, of perpetual dissembling. I failed to observe that a disguise worn long enough becomes a....

So. There comes the time when I must write a little stinker for *Furioso*; when here I am, and here they are, with our accumulated lie. I look at them. They look at me. We scratch around a bit; talk about the weather, old times. And suddenly we see that our touching but tenuous relationship has changed. They've lost their old cunning, my immortals, and they mean *all* they say. I've lost my old judgment, faithless fool, and I discount everything. We've lost each other, too....

Among those *Furioso* editors, John Pauker was closest to the New York publishing scene — his father was a literary agent who trafficked in movie scripts. Writing under a stiff pseudonym, Robert Lloyd Griffith, he was able to supply what he claimed was a true story of a bad writer with a bad story who had it doctored up (by dozens of others) until it made a pile of money as a bad movie. Solid Southerner Ambrose Gordon took the critical high road and gave many examples of commercial book-review conformity, especially in the businesslike hands of the *Saturday Review of Literature*, the *New York Times*, Henry Seidel Canby and J. Donald Adams, commercial literary big shots of the period. As for Nemerov he — with help from Bill Johnson — made the Swiftian proposal that all the New York book publishers get together, settle down to no-nonsense business and concentrate all their efforts on just *one* big super profitable Book every six months.

Thorsten Veblen might well have approved the irony in such prose though the *Furioso* editors tried not to be funny. As for Kropotkin he might have been amused but might also have noticed the oddly narrow focus of the editors' rebellion. They seemed only interested in destroying institutions possibly useful for their own advancement. And into what were they planning to venture? In that summer R was the only literary creature present with a (small) book, *Heroes & Heroines*, which would soon creep into print, and not one of them was yet a teacher. They were still Vets, not rebels. They were less concerned with straightening out the world than with printing themselves and seeing what happened.

After *Furioso* Vol. II, No. 1, the editors, though dispersing to different parts of the country, went at their mixed mission for six more issues with the RFD 1, Madison, Conn., address. R and his editors had become portentously editorial; they tried to be objective and judicious about what should be accepted, and what not. They passed manuscripts around in grocery-store bags, they mailed them to each other, argued, took votes, and argued more. Sometimes they agreed, though what impressed them most was how much disagreement they could arrive at. Put an innocent poem in front of them and they would come up with two yes's, two no's, and a maybe.

In the issues that followed over the next two years, Nemerov led the way with 28 contributions of poems, stories, reviews and essays. Pauker and R were close behind, and Pauker even held the magazine together by spending a winter in the woodsy cabin, performing as managing editor. Years later, after *Furioso* had disappeared, he wrote that during this "incumbency" his editorial objective was "to seek and develop new writing talent. I pursued this policy, with the result that three out of every five contributors were newcomers, many of whom went on to establish themselves as seasoned writers."

Contributions began to include regular bulletins from the semi-political "Department of Culture and Civilization" that took on the pretensions of American literary culture wherever the editors happened to spot them. They could not be easily ignored. Take one example. Bulletin No. 5, "Gift Horses, White Elephants": it examined *"The Readers Encyclopedia*, [which] according to a legend on the front of the flap, contains 18,499 articles within the compass of more than 1242 pages...it is asserted that the *Encyclopedia* is Easy to Read, Easy to Use, Accurate and Authoritative, Complete and Unique." Pedro *Furioso* noted, however, that among the 18,499 articles, there was "none on (for example) the Alcazar of Toledo, Spain." Istvan *Furioso* asked how it was that "the many estimable works of Ferenc Kormendi (for example) and of Lajos Zilahy (for example) and Frigyes Karinthy (for example)...are omitted," while Francois *Furioso* raised his objections. Another bulletin from the Department offered an "Introduction to Your Career as an Author."

> Here are coffee, cigarettes, a quantity (sufficient? Oh, yes) of white paper, and the typewriter, the machine which is to reduce my incredible thoughts to intelligible size, starting them on the first lap of that journey whereby they are to be multiplied into a large number of misunderstood commonplaces in a number of minds which will provide these suitable housing. Like so many jelly beans, my thoughts will be clearly differentiated as to color....

Clearly *Furioso*'s radicalism — if it was that — was directed locally, at institutions within the ken of a few Vets new to civilization as practiced in their neighborhood. Whether they were or were not serious was not a question to be answered simply — and R would worry that word "serious" for some years, even reaching the point of writing an essay in the mid-50s, "But Seriously," in which he argued about how to be serious his way — that is, as a social-political satirist — and not merely clever. Though this is getting a little ahead of his story, it may be worthwhile to get at where his thinking, and his poetry, were heading.

His proper hero was Jonathan Swift and among moderns he gave Auden cautious praise, Ogden Nash limited brickbats. He undertook the essay as an exercise in helping himself understand a basic psychic problem in his own head. Two quotes he began with give some indication of how serious he was. The first is by Dryden, the second from R. Garnett in the *Century*.

Satire has always shone among the rest,
And is the boldest way, if not the best,
To tell men freely of their foulest faults,
To laugh at their vain deeds and vainer thoughts.

…without humor, satire is invective; without literary form, it is mere clownish jeering.

"I have in my mind's eye," R wrote, "an ideal satirist who is happy in his work (taking it 'seriously') and who, though perhaps stuffed to the gills with subconscious aggressions, has also a sense of justice, truth, all that." No doubt, he was justifying himself. After all, he wrote:

I am one of those who, when I look at history, literary and social, find that I side pretty steadily with history's eccentrics. I don't mean all the mad astrologists and mystics — the best satirists have not, I think, gravitated toward exotic ideals and idealisms — but simply the mundane eccentrics who have stood on the sidelines with the game in progress, and made frosty remarks instead of cheering. The kings and noblemen and high churchmen, the generals and senators and big-league pundits — all these responsible gentlemen who have had and continue to have the burdens of the world upon their shoulders make less of an impression upon me than the fools (like Lear's fool) and the Hamlets and the Falstaffs, the Sancho Panzas and Huck Finns and Holden Caulfields.

"The best satire," he went on to say, "has to be 'informed with pity' or it is inhuman."

As the years went on, R's sometimes uncertain balancing between pity and invective showed up in such poems as "Mr. and Mrs." where a hopefully serious social complaint somehow dwindled into a not very funny joke. To wit:

> They'd charge a bit less, of course, in the off season.
> The Mrs. would do for the maid, and they'd close up the snack bar,
> And if they filled three of the rooms in a night they'd break even,
> Which, as the Mr. said, was all right, wasn't it? since,
> When the rush season came, they'd make a good thousand
> A week (before taxes)
> Easy,
> Which, as they both said, would make them financial
> In no time, at which time,
> They'd sell the damn place, buy a yacht and go someplace decent.
>
> So they bought it.
> But since a new cut-off took all the arterial traffic,
> Somehow the off season stayed through the on, and nobody
> Lived in the break-even rooms but a brother
> Of Mr.'s, and surly letters
> From stores and utility people
> Arrived by each sad, sad post, and Mr. and Mrs.
> Sat by the desk in their lobby thinking
> Deep,
>
> until one day the Mrs.
> Said to the Mr., Don't you
> Think, Mr., we'd be more financial and all
> If we bought a nice orange-juice stand on U.S. 1?

Unlike R, his good friend Pauker was more extravagantly comic though sometimes more serious too. An issue in 1950, for example, carried a detailed exploration of Wallace Steven's "Sea Surface Full of Clouds." While Allen Swallow published a first book in 1949, *Yoked by Violence* (it included poems under two of his pseudonyms, Jethro Somes and Thomas Rowley), somehow his verse never caught on. It should have. A small collection of his work, *Angry Candy*, was printed in 1976. He was indeed a serious man about his own work, with the odd result that as a substitute he often turned to translation, real or pretended. He translated an immense 800-page Hungarian novel, *The Dukays*, by Lajos Zilahy, which a New York house published (it's still in print). There was an introduction to it said to be by Zilahy, that though not published in the book did appear in *Furioso*. Pauker may well have written it. A bit of hocus-pocus was a necessary part of his life, as was a part of *Furioso*.

The other editors during the Madison years, though less determined to confuse the world, seemed to enjoy such antics. When R sold the place, the editorial board lost its woodsy core, Ambrose Gordon going to teach at the University of Texas, Nemerov to teach first at Hamilton, then Bennington, then Brandeis, and finally at Washington University at St. Louis, and Pauker moving from New York to Washington to work at the Voice of America. A new editorial board moved to the masthead in 1950 that included Charles Shain, Jack Lucas, Edwin Pettet, and both Arthur and Rosemary Mizener. A little later two other writers who had retreated into academia joined up — Wayne Carver and Erling Larsen. By then the new editors were at Carleton College in Northfield, Minnesota — but this is looking ahead. First, there is Princeton to finish off.

In fall 1947, R was back on his History Seminar Room cushion wondering if he would be "balanced" enough in the new term even to make it through. At least he now did have the new Ford he had ordered, and with that temptingly sitting at the Graduate College behind the Princeton golf course, and with grim testing sessions ahead at which he would be asked to show his reading skill with heavy German and French texts, he found the Fall term dragging. He was of course still reading History and still picking up useful data that Shotwell for all his archives would have neglected — such as the suggestion from Strayer that the migration of herring from the Baltic to the North Sea in the 13th century may have had as much to do with the rise of the British Empire as anything the British themselves ever did. But like almost any graduate student who has been reading reading for long enough to doubt that his mind would survive, R — wondering why he had gone into History anyway — began to doubt he could last another year-and-a-half of the course grind plus of course the eternity of producing a thesis. He worried about the possibility of adequate coverage and began to fear that his sense was fading. As for balance, well, he secretly decided that he favored unbalance and wished to tip. He noted that there were many normal but undesirable (for a historian) activities that encouraged tippage and with which he might find himself involved at any moment. For as Barzun had pointed out in his essay "History Popular and Unpopular" there were the schemes of hopefully popular historians, journalists and biographers who could be tipped by the lure of sensationalism and money. There were the plans of ambitious textbook historians who could be tipped by the artificiality of talking down to students. There were the polite strategies of bureaucratically minded "white paper" historians who could be tipped by the demands of officialdom. And there were even the plots of miserable thesis-writing history graduate students who could be tipped by the prejudices of their teachers. R began to feel that his own tippage might show up at any time of the day or night and, worse, that it might be a good thing if it did. Yes, the more he thought about tippage the more attractive it seemed, especially when he thought of little magazines. All the good ones seemed truly inspired creations for tippage.

Meanwhile, he had continued corresponding with Arthur Mizener, writing about his dissatisfactions, not only with history but also with poetry itself. For instance, this in January 1946:

> I am trying to consider seriously the use of historical symbols as subjects. The situation boils down to looking for a person or an incident or a thing about whom or which there is (somehow or other) an immediacy making them at least potentially whatcha might call significant symbols in our time. But a graduate course in history is the worst place in the world to find them. There the symbols are dissected to a degree that deprives them of their possible whole significance.

R's letter was accompanied by "Only the Dead" that was to be included in *Heroes & Heroines*.

Only the dead have manners; they alone
Are never trapped between The Lady and The Door,
Never drop The Spoon and never need be shown
How to slice The Blanc-Mange, or what The Sauce is for.

Only the dead are nice. Where they go
They never pass the careful line that cuts

Good Taste from Show
Nothing from Too Much.

Only the dead are heroes; they alone
Achieve that final Elegance, that last
Umpty of grim Gallantry unknown
To those who must exonerate their past.

Wiser than the living, they have shown
How true Nobility is bred in The Bone.

Mizener, who was now the chair of the English Department at Carleton College, wrote back, perhaps with some exasperation at R's indecisiveness. "For god's sake don't hang on at Princeton if it doesn't interest you, but do something. Come out here and teach, for example, or go some place else — fairly far away from the big city — & do some job that will leave you time to write. I take it that it goes without my saying so that anytime you want to you can teach here." This letter was dated Oct. 16, 1946. In December he received a letter from friend Bill Weaver:

Received the shocking news that you are seeking employment as a teacher.

ARE YOU BEREFT OF YOUR SENSES

Why in the world do you feel impelled to take up a life of drudgery? Are you afraid to live or something? For God's sake, why don't you just be a poet and let who will be teachers. If you do take such a job you will find yourself enslaved and enervated and unable to write anything, even rejections.

I am being completely serious, trying to save you from the great mistake. Let my experience be your text. Please…please.…

DON'T DO IT.

He did, writing Mizener about a teaching position that would begin in the spring. "There are hitches," he wrote, then asked rhetorically what they were.

One: poor old R thinks that he has no very solid reason for telling himself that he likes English Departments and procedures any better than History departments and procedures. Two: poor old R doesn't think he would like Teaching — even Chaucer. He hears too much from the practitioners about correcting papers, heavy schedules, in short, teaching — and he can only see himself liking a teaching job which is not a teaching job at all, the idiot. Three: he has floating around in his so-called mind the theory that teaching English might, as he will not quite say, destroy him, or destroy the remnants still standing.

Yes R did need to leave Princeton and, with no other prospects, took Mizener up on his offer. Mizener, for his part, was caught off guard by the suddenness of R wanting to come teach for the upcoming spring semester — he had been thinking about the fall when he could readily find a place. Nevertheless he did manage to make room, and R took on what was going to be a temporary teaching job in English right after Christmas. As things turned out, he kept it for nearly twenty years. It gave him much, including many poems, among them "A Teacher" which takes its epigraph from Chaucer, "And gladly wolde he lerne, and gladly teche."

> He hated them all one by one but wanted to show them
> What was Important and Vital and by God if
> They thought they'd never have use for it he was
> Sorry as hell for them, that's all, with their genteel
> Mercantile Main Street Babbitt
> Bourgeois-barbaric faces, they were beyond
> Saving, clearly, quite out of reach, and so he
> G-rrr
> Got up every morning and g-rrr ate his breakfast
> And g-rrr lumbered off to his eight o'clock
> Gladly to teach.

Out in Minnesota

Rfound the following letter in an old file. Perhaps he was planning to use it in a story, but at any rate, the money mentioned in it was not fictional.

Dear Aunt Alice:

You turned out to be an excellent aunt and I could kick myself for not having written you to this effect before your death. I now want you to know that I spent the $28,000 you willed to me wisely on a plane and a magazine, not hoarding it as your lawyer said you did. Of course he was the one who wrote me of your bequest, and when I visited him by plane (not the one I later bought) in Haverhill, Mass., he did not — I feel I shd advise you — speak kindly of your "usage" (his word) of the biddy who worked for you for decades, with the result that she ended her days in the "poorhouse" (his word). So he left me with the impression that you were an old New England "skinflint" (my word) — but the odd thing is that I don't even remember meeting you. Could you have been at the Thanksgiving dinner in Dedham at my Great Aunt Gertrude's house, where I sat in a corner with other "small fry" (my father's words) safely removed from the grown-up's table? I don't remember more than three or four grown-ups at the meal but I *had* heard your name often from Mother when she talked relatives. She said you were an old spinster, so I felt pretty good about spending the money.

Your Grateful Nephew,
Little R

Any explanation of R's life at Carleton College when Aunt Alice died must begin in Northfield, Minn. What was to come over the nearly 20 years there was teaching, a pilot's license, marriage, children, poetry, essays and reviews, *Furioso*, its dissolution, books, visiting lectureships,

The Carleton Miscellany, and more (even for pete's sake chair of the English Dept and a very brief stint at the CIA in Jim Angleton's outer office). It all began, however, with *Haus Nuttink*. That was a mansion two blocks from campus. It had a main entrance and a side entrance. In 1947, 27-year old R was one of its three lodgers — all new teachers and all using the side entrance. To reach the back stairs to their second floor rooms they had to pass Uncle Clem's room. His door was open when he was awake, and then he could be seen sitting, unmoving, in a straight-backed chair beside his one window. Then one January day his niece, Mrs. Nutting, was embarrassed to ask R for help because Uncle Clem had amazingly risen, wandered down into the cellar, and was now lost down there with no clothes on. Not that Mrs. Nutting (Elizabeth) needed help often, being a fine specimen of New England womanhood who had gone to Smith College and then been taken west by her bank-president husband. John Nutting was not incompetent either, though as a true Vermonter he seemed to believe that all words in a sentence should be run together at high speed in order to be correct English. How these two originally found each other back East is another matter, but there they were in Northfield caring for poor Uncle Clem and renting out rooms to three new loner teachers: R in English, Gene in music, and Hans in German.

R of course is the hero of this work. Gene was small and silent and will not be heard from here. But Hans, who was large and noisy, will be, briefly at least — he was the one who called their residence Haus Nuttink and was an instant disciple of R, or at least of R's car. He had noticed the car before he noticed R, and as soon as he made the connection — the car was parked in the snow at the Nutting's side entrance — he concluded that car and person had appeared in his life in order to take him to Dundas. A (speculative) momentary aside: Hans' voice may have had something to do with the "shaggies" R was to become addicted to years later. "The Sad Committee Shaggy" is an example.

In good ole day ze king need no committee.
Was nize.
Him says, them does; him sells, them buys.
Good system.
But then come big push make king one of guys.

So king buy chairs, say me no king me chairman.
So knocked off paradize.

Dundas was three miles south, smaller than Northfield but with two bars. Northfield was at the time dry. Soon R and Hans were making evening visits to Dundas where Hans, a bear in a sweatshirt, showed that he could indeed be a fierce bear on any political/sociological/ideological subject. He could also be in quick succession a communist, a socialist, a democrat, a Freudian and a spiritualist — but he could never be a moderate. Luckily he could convert his enthusiasms to comedy, and one day when he was down the hall from his own messy room talking and talking to R in R's tidy room, he happened to see Mrs. Nutting pass the messy room. He saw her look right into that room, stare amazed at it for a few seconds, and then say — to herself of course — "Well I never." So that very evening, seated on a Dundas barstool, Hans toasted Missez Nuttink, crying out, "Vell I neffer!"

Dundas was good for shouted toasts. If some dutiful social scientist were to have wandered through the Midwest in mid-20th century looking for a representatively dull seedy backcountry burg he'd have settled for Dundas on the spot. Hans and R simply settled for it two or three times a week for a little vodka (R's) and bourbon (Hans'), though they soon found that other Carleton people disapproved. At least most of the new teachers, being learned Easterners, thought of Dundas as a primitive place, which it was, and a poor intellectual environment, which it was. And for Arthur and Rosemary Mizener the Dundas slumming evil was magnified by R wandering down there with the primitive Hans. Arthur was quickly direct, if not blunt (he liked to be blunt), commenting at an early lunch in the Carleton Tea Room with R, other lofty English teachers and the Dean of Men, "Well there, R, what did you booze hounds do for the world down in Dundas last night?"

But there was no serious malice in Arthur except when speaking of a few despicable literary critics such as antique romantics like Chauncey Tinker whom he had served with before the war. He was simply educating R, having been at this academic game ever since Yale. He and Rosemary remained parental about him. Even before R went overseas, Mizener and he had been exchanging detailed views about each others' poems. Arthur had himself been a regular contributor to its pre-war issues, with poems like "What Humpty Dumpty Didn't Mention."

"Dear me," said Alice
A matter dark indeed to comprehension,
Written on no wall, even in dreams, for wisemen,
But growing unobtrusively among
The breakfast dishes and the ringing of the telephone.
At first unnoticed, only gradually catching the attention,
Then hovering at the edges of conversation
Like a name not quite recalled.
Remembered,
A ship's anchor, it comes up encumbered
With the refuse of a busy harbor-bottom —
Old tunes, seaweed, girls' voices and rusty tin —
By shoving all its rubbish down the manholes,
And everyone's embarrassed to discover
What a state things do get into down below.

A nice poem, not stickily personal. R had a difficult time with any stickily personal poem and though he was to write them, they often came slant-wise. "Mrs. Benedict," about his mother's drinking, is one example. Another are these lines from the mock epic "The Odyssey of a B**t" that draws on his father's loathing of FDR, Franklin Delano Roosevelt. The narrator, ruminating on who his B**t hero's enemy could be,

remembered the choice of his father: FDR,
Who made a perfectly dandy *bête noir.*
His father would open the paper at breakfast, and lo!
The day had begun, the bile had begun to flow.
And mother? His father's mother had made her unstable,
Given her traumas, and pills on her bedside table.

Arthur kept his own life off to the side of his poetry, but his feelings were never missing. They were steadily addressed to the sad state down below of the moral, political, aesthetic world he was born to. Shakespeare had helped here. He had taught the plays for years, and had brought their wonderful dealings with the down-below state to R, in and out of class. He was full of quotes from the plays, with the quotes tending to be messages that recommended *Looking Below* and *Not Faking It.* When he took on his biography of Scott Fitzgerald, *The Far Side of Paradise*, his steady theme about the man was that he was knowing about himself and, though a thorough romantic, was *not* a faker. And partly because of Arthur's influence R's wartime literary sonnets broadcast, in their ironic way, such a credo. So, eventually, did R's performance in class.

Shakespeare's help here was particularly strong in *As You Like It* where much good advice appears for soft Easterners in Minnesota's winter wilderness. Arthur had gone to Princeton and his pedagogy was not helpful when trying to start a car at 20 below; the same could be said for his English Department, which was heavily citified. A proper literary person could call the scene pastoral and remark, rubbing together frozen hands, that the "penalty of Adam" was right in Northfield; but Shakespeare would want him also to remember that the good duke in his play's woods was a softy from the city himself. Further, that the woods were full of fakers, that is, lovers under the influence of each other's dreams who had to be put straight by realist Rosalind. She looked at the sick romancers as they professed to be dying of love, and remarked that the world had been going for six thousand years and nobody had died so yet.

In contrast the woods of Wordsworth always seemed to have for R the light of the urban shining through them, together with persistent worry over what poetry was trying to bring out from those woods. R's "The Departure," which was to come later on after a three-week sojourn in a writer's colony, is one instance of his skeptical romantic view.

The artist must leave these woods now.
He must put his books and files back in the car,
And stuff his bags with shirts and shorts and sweaters,
And clean his room and take a load to the dump, wherever the dump is,
And go the rounds and say goodbye to the artists — goodbye —
And the trees — goodbye —
And cash a check and fill up with gas and set out
For the world again, the world, to talk up art.

The world likes that.
It likes to get news of the spirit fresh from the woods,
What birds are saying and frogs. It sits in its cities,
Thirsty. The artist will fix that.
He will bring in a carload of essences quick on the thruway,
Mists for everyone's parlor, sunsets, done up nice.
Cities want their essences done up nice.

So the artist must leave these woods now. For that.
He takes a last walk in the woods: what is the news, woods?
And the woods reply in their woodsy way that the news
Is woods, woods.
He hears the news, notes it down and walks back
To his shirts and sweaters while out of the sky
Art in its arty way keeps saying: goodbye.

But now the reader should put aside poems, put aside Dundas and drinking, and think of the work at hand. On a cold Monday in January 1947, R walked out of Haus Nuttink into Minnesota's snow to learn to teach.

∿

His first class in Northfield was Sophomore Lit, and his students, having already made it through a term that raced them from Chaucer to perhaps Thomas Gray, were suddenly sitting in front of him in a classroom on the second floor of Willis Hall (directly opposite Mizener's office) waiting for the Romantics. Yes there his first students really were, two fine sexes of them (including three male Vets) chatting and giggling. They seemed large, handsome and intelligent (mostly). They also seemed to be chatting and giggling at having a new teacher, which made R also feel like giggling. How, oh Lord, how was he going to take on this pedant business? He knew perfectly well that he didn't know how, so he looked blankly at them, nervously for perhaps a minute, and then said "hello." They giggled. Then he said that he had just come from the East in a snowstorm and they giggled further. It was only when he said that for Wednesday he wanted them to read six poems by William Blake as well as Wordsworth's preface to Wordsworth and Coleridge's volume, *Lyrical Ballads*, that they knew that he was, beyond giggling, a pedant. Or maybe he was looking at himself.

But when he informed them that first he was going to tell them about the French Revolution the giggling was over and the notebooks were out. If he had been more experienced he might have prefaced his lecture by asking if one of them could describe the French Revolution. That would have produced new giggles, but since he had too many lecture notes in hand to be sensible he now proceeded with his prepared verbiage at a good clip, bringing in absolutely everything that he, fresh from History, knew about the French Revolution, especially what he knew from having written a paper at Princeton on Thomas Carlyle's account of it. He spoke long and well — or so he felt — into a steady, slightly ominous class silence until about 9:45 (by his watch), and he remained nervously hopeful that he was being rather eloquent until there was a rustling of books and papers and shoes in front of him. Why was the class disturbed?

Yes his watch was wrong — he was running over — so he apologized, said that he would never do *that* again, and they rushed out giggling. So R walked across the hall to Arthur's office, annoyed at his watch but thinking that at least he had done the French Revolution well and that the class *did* need the French Revolution. He also felt that he had an obligation to tell Arthur how he had handled his first class — that obligation vanished, however, when Arthur spoke first, telling him he had "surely done the French Revolution up brown." It became apparent that R had filled the whole second floor with the French Revolution for fifty minutes and Arthur had not been able to miss a word. First pedagogical lesson: a small class of intelligent gigglers is not a squad on a drill field.

If there was a lesson No. 2 it soon came from the students themselves who liked to be treated as knowledgeable humans even when they weren't. He was not long in adjusting his new pedagogy to conversational classes rather than 50-minute lectures, though conversations had their drawbacks too. The giggling slowed down, R's nervousness lowered, and he began even to think that yes he could be a teacher for a year or two without losing his mind. After all Sophomore Lit was easy since he had plenty of high and low opinions to express about Romantics, Victorians and the great American yawper. (*Furioso* was about to print a boxed note regretfully announcing, "to certain unprinted contributors, the death of Walt Whitman.") His section of Freshman Comp was much harder to handle than the Sophomore Survey and solutions seemed missing. He hadn't quite understood Freshman Comp when he took it at Yale, and even Maynard Mack had never been able to teach him a thing about writing in the course, except to be brief. As for the military, well, it had only taught him a way of writing that no one should ever learn. Yet there he was at 27 — and in a teaching job — stuck with teaching what seemed unteachable.

Luckily the old-fashioned class text, then being used by all the Freshman Comp sections, was sensible. It was *Problems in Prose* (editor, Paul Haines) and was filled with intelligent questions and exercises, for instance, in referring to a passage from Mark Twain's *Life on the Mississippi*, this: "Why are the pigs before the town drunk rather than after?" Or starting with the word "homespun" in "early American Types" by John Bach McMaster, "How can one explain *linsey-woolsey, Christmas, blacksmith* and *curtsies?*" Furthermore the text also contained many good short pieces encouraging students to feel giggly, especially one describing a classical scholar, Walter Headlam, who couldn't find his coffee cup amidst his scrambled books and notes. Absent-minded professors could always be entertaining, so R made Headlam a hero for his freshmen, on a par with other comical scholars and writers such as those who had written whole novels without punctuation or had simply become druggies. (R began several novels but never brought them to conclusions that satisfied him.)

But at night back in his Nutting room, with the piled-up 300-word papers on his bed, joking came hard. When could he leave off marking faulty continuity ("Coh," for coheherence, was his favorite scribble) and say something worth saying. After all, the Haines text, though helpful, couldn't begin to reduce the course teacher's immense obligation to talk forever and ever in individual student conferences, worrying about why such-and-such a sentence lacked Coh. Yet all the teachers in Arthur's department — except Ed Pettet who had Carleton's little theater to worry about — had to teach Comp, and if there ever was a course designed   to make clear how hard it is to be a teacher at all, Freshman Comp was (and is) it.

And then came February. The temperature was below zero and R's car had failed to start twice. But R was becoming car-wise, and for three mornings running it had started. Better yet there had been no snow for a week and the Dundas road was dry. By this time his young teacher-neighbor Hans and he had ridden down it eight or ten times and had tested both bars, in each of which they had discussed snow, Mrs. Nuttink, Carleton President Larry Gould, President Truman ("he ees ein hick"), Communism ("mebbe vee hafta haf it") and Tiny's Smoke Shop. It was there also that the subject of Jesse James robbing the Northfield Bank came up, about which Hans had a learned request. To present it he pulled from his pocket a paperback copy of Voltaire's *Philosophical Dictionary*, rolled his large head around, and said, "Effryboddy in Yurop reads Voltaire, ok? Let me read you." And he read this passage:

If we compose a history of France we are under no necessity to describe the course of the Seine and the Loire, but if we publish a history of the conquests of the Portuguese in Asia, a topographical description of the recently explored country is required. It is desirable that we should, as it were, conduct the reader by the hand around Africa and along the coasts of Persia and India; and it is expected that we should treat, with information and judgment, of manners, laws and customs new to Europe.

So R listened and wondered: could it be that Hans was thinking of himself — as with the subject of Jesse James — now rounding the Cape of Good Hope, and hoping that R, as a historian on home territory way out there, would put Hans straight about his new cultural location?

Something like that, but R's trouble — which was hard to explain to Hans — was that R himself was not yet clear where he was. How long had Hans been in America? Two years. Where in America? Brooklyn. Well then clearly Hans knew nothing about America and needed to be told that Brooklyn was a place where no knowledge of the true America existed since Brooklyn was an isolated place where only ignorance of the true America prevailed.

"Vare is you come?"

R explained he was from the oldest part of America, excepting Virginia, Mexico and Peru. He wished Hans to understand that the melting pot was a late and insignificant manifestation of democracy and had little bearing upon the exact place on the planet where America — as represented by Northfield — was.

"I sink you fib me."

R acknowledged that this was the case but found it amusing that Hans should be asking R to explain the Midwest since R had just arrived too. But Hans, ordering another drink, yust vanted to know vere de hell he, Hans, was, and R admitted that Northfield was troublesome in this respect, being a two-culture town with Lutherans sitting over on the west side at St. Olaf College, and New Englanders on the East side running (sometimes) Carleton. Also of course Northfield had been the site, though it was now a seemingly academic and settled site, of a curious manifestation of what was known as the Wild West, in the form of the personage Jesse James and his....

"Ach, yes, now vee come home. Tell me heem."

"But you should understand that he did not rob the Nutting bank. He robbed the other bank."

"C'est dommage."

"Don't you like the Nuttinks?"

⁓

R did like the Nuttings but soon tired of both Hans and Dundas. He had begun liking the Midwest too, what little he knew of it, since he had brought with him from childhood a wish list and Northfield had many of the important items on it. The list favored easy access to life's necessities, and Northfield's main street had a food store, a drug store, a doctors' building, a clothing store, and a sedately uncomfortable hotel. Just off the main street it also had an old-fashioned movie house that showed at least one Jesse James film a year. And no matter which way one left town — north, south, east or west — there was always corn, wheat and big sky. Its isolation from most of the major 20th century ills seemed, when R's mind was idling, almost complete. He could (theoretically) agree with a remark by Southern Agrarian Andrew Lytle — Lytle was a poet, novelist and editor of *The Sewanee Review* through the 1960s — that a cornfield was not a place to make money but to grow corn. Lytle had himself in his time grown a little corn (though he had also gone to Yale Drama School and lived in New York) whereas R had no farmer background.

The strength of Carleton life for R lay in the relatively relaxed life for a few males who saw each other several times a week over a pool table after a chatty lunch, Bill Johnson and Arthur Mizener among them — with the Dean of Men presiding (and usually winning). His basic life mission seemed to have become one of sitting angrily reading 300-word themes while the true citizenry of the Great Plains wondered what he was doing there. When his first Midwest spring came — in late May — he walked east one day on Fourth Street to the point where suddenly the town was over and done with and the street became a dirt road. He walked the road for a quarter mile and reached a graveyard with fine old trees, but then he found the road stretching before him treeless and straight into what a city boy could only call infinity. On the spot he gave up his country constitutional, turned back, and for his next walk tried only a small civilized patch of woods just off campus called the Carleton Arboretum. The endlessness of the Plains unnerved him and he was to wait three years before travel-

Seasons in Northfield, Minnesota.

ing the graveyard road again in order to take flying lessons seven miles east at the Stanton airport.

In the meantime there he was, in a country that seemed no more his than Hans's. His memory went back to his Andover days of reciting Housman, and his still lonely soul brayed that he was lonely and afraid in a land he had never made. But who had made the land they lived in anyway? Whom should he include in his sophomore survey course? Sinclair Lewis managed to sneak in with a collection of stories *I'm a Stranger Here Myself*. But Lewis wasn't a stranger to Sauk Center and the Midwest, which R definitely was. *Heroes & Heroines* showed this, having for "basic" subjects the lives of numbers of self-centered literary folk. He came to the end of the term trying hard to ignore the most obvious fact about himself — that he was emotionally as if "in solitary" at Andover again. There was nothing wrong with his Nutting room and nothing wrong with his Madison cottage, but he was largely an unsettled loner in both, commuting between them. At the end of the term he was sure that he didn't want to come back, "certainly not to teach Freshman or Sophomore English," he wrote to Mizener who had gone off to Cornell for a term. What he would do was uncertain — perhaps return East to a publishing job, or to work on a novel. He wasn't sure. Yet that unsureness — and his proposal to teach only a seminar course — led to a "change of heart."

"May I come back," R asked, proposing that he "come back as yr visiting poet." Why this change, he asked for Mizener's benefit, then answered. "The alternatives which have presented themselves so far have been unsatisfactory."

> I remain a renegade from the English Dept system and shall spend most of my time next year, if I come back, telling you what's wrong with you guys. I shall also, if I do what I idly think of as what I *should* do, try to become as ignorant as possible as soon as possible of all standard works of literature. There is in me (and has been growing) a fundamental dissatisfaction with the basis upon which the English Dept. rests its main plank, which is, as I see it, Appreciation (though no respectable member of this dept will use the term); but its chief merit is not in this direction (metaphor) at all. I think you will agree that primarily we are concerned with the problem of dealing critically with facts. No other department does so. All other departments are concerned with the rendering of facts.

But it is not consistent to conduct a sophomore Survey course as we are conducting it, or a Shakespeare course, and at the same time to investigate (which means to undermine) the values of the course. And it is certainly difficult to investigate values which have already received the blessing of the Pope, Professor Tinker, etc. What I am driving at is that within the Dept. we are chiefly concerned with destroying or revaluing our own creations — and this is too much for our undergraduates to understand.

R was just warming to his subject.

For myself, having had to reckon with these revaluations with an intensity no undergraduate needs to, the problem is the same. I think the energy that has been expended (by me for example) in trying to relate my work to the grand tradition and to evaluate it in those terms is important. But the second step, which is to change the tradition and its values to accommodate first the peculiar talents of the individual and second the peculiar banalities of our decade, has not been made. *Furioso*'s groping indicates this failure — but the *Furioso* editors are at least more aware of the problem than any people I know. It was thus something of a shock (and one of the reasons why I decided in the middle of last night to write this letter) to receive 17 poems from [Howard] Nemerov which either

a. dealt with the old issues of the artist's isolation in this modern world and gloomed, in heavily ironic phrases, about the future — thus telling me that Howard might as well not write at all, or join the *Partisan Review* crowd, unless he snaps out of it. Or

b. turned out to be pure Donne. I just can't see what future for Howard, or anybody, lies in going back 300 years when Poetry, etc., is so clearly facing opposition which undermines even the best standards of our own century. Much more than an institution like the Catholic Church (which might well be our model in this instance) must we *conform* to what's around us. Or if conform is an ugly word, say *adjust*. Howard's poems (do not tell him this. I do not yet know how I will deal with him diplomatically) are nothing more than a confession of proud isolation intellectually from everything — and while I can sympathize with this I cannot write this way. I will rather (much rather) not write at all.

R ended with a semi-apology for "being much more 'serious' here than I should be." At the same time, he included "In Memory of an English Professor," a poem he never published.

Our dear soul

Might have lived longer if someone had sent it away
On somebody's yacht,
Telling it gently not to let anything fray
Its nerves, no matter what.

But since of all possible luxuries most it deplored
Getting packed,
It decided to stay with the mob and be cured
Or cracked.

So though it took to asking its students to carry
It out to its car,
It was healthily sickly for months and might still be if Harry
Hadn't been there.

But Harry, good Harry, Harry of Hapless Hall,
Sat in its class at the back.
And Harry, brave Harry, manliest man of them all,
Was a yak.

Yak as he was, a yare yokel, pride of the breed,
Yaklike he bore
The burden of Lycidas, Lucy, Endymion, Lucy, Lucy and Ganymede
With ever increasing yakor.

And heavier, heavier loads still more yakly he tamed
Until yak and the spirit of yak
In the minds of all men massively was sustained,
And our dear soul, not Harry, broke.

If R was a loner, so too was *Furioso* — in the overcrowded literary world. The subversive "Mammon" issue (Fall, 1946) announced that the magazine had become a quarterly — but then no winter issue followed. And the spring issue, though late, was remarkable for appearing at all. It was printed back in New Haven and mailed — but to whom? An excessively cute preface (possibly by R) reported that the number of copies sold "exceeded the number of contributions received by a slight margin," though the wonder was that it had any subscribers at all since its subscription list had been pulled from a four-year-old file of mildewed 3" x 5" cards.

As for the 1947 issues themselves (three in all), R's now aged assessment is that they weren't bad. There was an odd but genuine story, "Little Red Riding Hood in Yoknapatawpha County" by William Faulkner, though listed as by C. G. Lumbard. (It had only been printed abroad — in French; Faulkner's translator living in Princeton, Maurice Coindreau, supplied it). Then there was a "new" story by Scott

Fitzgerald, one discovered by Arthur Mizener, his about-to-be biographer. There were contributions from a number of talented young writer-vets, friends of the editors who were also groping for their futures. There was even a groping for happy amity between the magazine and the New York publishing world it had tried to destroy, in the form of an announcement of a poetry book club. John Pauker was instrumental here in contacting publishers and making arrangements. The amity began with Reynal & Hitchcock Inc., which had published R's *Heroes & Heroines* and a volume by another *Furioso* contributor, Weldon Kees. Joining the club was a cinch: "simply fill out the coupon below (or any reasonable facsimile); or even a coupon which does not look very much like the coupon below," plus $1.30 for Kees' book, *The Fall of the Magicians*, plus $2.00 for a year of *Furioso*. The club offered a Nemerov volume, *The Image and the Law* (Henry Holt) for $1.30 in the fall issue, and a volume by William Meredith, *Ships and Other Figures* (Princeton) for $1.30 in winter. The book club then lapsed as most business enterprises connected with little magazines do, though the magazine itself was able to proceed for four more years largely because of R's inheritance from Aunt Alice.

The sale of the Madison cottage in Connecticut inaugurated *Furioso*'s third age, a campus one. By this time several of the editors were already in their teacher roles. Had Pound known of the switch (by now he was in St. Elizabeth's) he would have disapproved, though he would have blessed the magazine's frequent annoyance with academic minds. Here is a sample of Pound's anti-teacher verbiage in high satiric register.

> The teacher or lecturer is a danger. He very seldom recognizes his nature or his position. The lecturer is a man who must talk for an hour. France may possibly have acquired the intellectual leadership of Europe when their academic period was cut to forty minutes.

The magazine's most effective move against the educators surrounding it (but not of course inhabiting Carleton itself) was the pertly polemical Department of Culture and Civilization. "*Furioso* took arms against the academic world, the new criticism, the writing world, the advertising world, General MacArthur, and the production of H-bombs," R later wrote in "The History of a Little Magazine and Other Matters," which appeared in *New World Writing* #15.

> We had a long series of short pieces on how to write a novel, which doubt-less convinced many people, until they read our pieces, that *Furioso* was a kind of writers' handbook…we covered the writers' conferences and sug-gested the clothing to be worn, the liquor to be brought, and so forth.… And once we had a crossword puzzle for the puzzlers of the world, though the people who bought the magazine for that feature soon discovered that our notion of a crossword puzzle was not theirs.

The satire on the academic world and the new criticism took various forms. A whole section of the magazine was entitled "PFLA, or Publica-tions-of-the-Furioso-Language-Association," which had as its target var-ious kinds of minute historical criticism. Mizener's "Four Elements of Good Teaching," for instance, blasted away at professional educators infesting our teaching minds with pompous formulae. *Furioso* also man-aged to be annoyed by the then new Creative Writing forces starting to flood colleges and universities. R himself took this issue on in a number of essays that attacked the self-congratulatory separation of American poets from the culture out of which their poems derived. (More about this later.) The *Furioso* editors also produced funny how-to bulletins for writers looking for big money, while taking on the little magazine world as a target — and though much of this material is now dated, one result of criticizing academic and literary pretension was that *Furioso* attracted talented writers living in scholarly danger spots such as Chicago, notably Walter Scott and Wayne Booth, who became regulars and took on pretentiousness of all kinds.

Booth, who is best known to English department graduate students for his *The Rhetoric of Fiction*, was a first-rate satirist and joined *Furioso* as Department of American Editor. He had completed a scholarly work on Laurence Sterne, and in The Department of Culture and Civilization he set out to prove that "all modern literature...has one source and fountainhead: *Tristram Shandy*." Meanwhile, Scott conducted a fictitious survey of critics in which a roving reporter by the name of Jack Churchmouse asked various critics a number of questions, such as:

1) Roughly speaking, how did you happen to "go in" for criticism?

2) Are you inclined to feel (a) hurt, (b) angry, (c,d) scornful or indulgently amused when someone appears to be insufficiently serious about the things that you are sufficiently serious about? For instance, Original Sin. Hot Jazz. The Devil. Criticism itself.

3) Do you make any special preparations for engaging in the act of criticism: i.e., lying down for a few minutes beforehand, beef tea, prayer, mental fantasies, raw eggs, whiskey?

In another piece, Scott gave advice on how to live a writerly life, e.g., "The novelist must have been, by the time of his first big success as a Novelist, at least eleven of the following: in any order: (1) an all-night counterman; (2) a bodyguard (politician's or gangsters); (3) a carnival wrestler; (4) a deckhand; (5) a dishwasher, etcetera."

Jokestering this may have been and, in retrospect, R sometimes felt the magazine was indulging itself too much. "By doing so it was doing what it objected to others doing. It was being provincial in a bad sense, taking as its province a subject, literature, rather than some social unit into which the subject fitted." It was, he said, more than self-deprecatingly, "being professional." And yet, it provoked some response, if only by other litterateurs. Edmund Wilson, for example.

In far off Cape Cod Wilson was trying to be out of it but found himself surrounded with solemn literary types starting new solemnities on summer beaches. For such writers out in the big world *Furioso* proved to be a good place to send a little dissonance. After Paul Goodman reviewed *The Oasis*, a novel by Wilson's then-wife Mary McCarthy — its opening sentence: "This is a weak and disappointing satire, toothless, only moderately pleasant" — Wilson sent a caustic letter to "Dear Furioso," which Dear Furioso then published.

> I congratulate you on your brilliant winter number, with only one reservation in connection with the "Paul Goodman" review…it was fun to discover that Paul Goodman had been all along simply the most elaborate of the *Furioso* hoaxes. It was audacious of you to pull the legs of the other minority magazines by putting over on them the woozy avant-garde fables and the befuddling speculations on Kafka of the fictitious Mr. Goodman. But the joke was on your readers, too. I confess to having been disquieted when I found the preposterous Goodman cropping up in *Furioso*. But this review gives the imposture away…. I do think it rather unfair that a book by Miss McCarthy should be sacrificed to create "Paul Goodman," amusing though he certainly is.

Along with its seeming hoaxes — Isaac Rosenfield's "An Experiment with Tropical Fish" (in *Furioso*'s Research Laboratories), its how-to's (e.g., "How to Start the Novel," "The Novelist as Human Being," "How to Review a Movie," "How to Read a College Catalog") — the magazine had poems by Weldon Kees, W.S. Merwin (who went from William to W.S. in *Furioso*'s pages), John Ashbery, Kenneth Koch, Anthony Hecht, Josephine Miles, Kenneth Rexroth, Donald Justice, and others who were just getting started in the poetry business. It also carried a good deal of work — poetry, essays and fiction by — Howard Nemerov.

This may be a place to pause and speak of Howard Nemerov. For nearly 40 years, he and R were in constant touch with each other — first, as editors of *Furioso*, and soon after as confiding friends. They complimented each other's books — on R's pamphlet *Little Magazines*, "very somber as befits a tragicall editor" — and criticized each other's work, from line breaks to images to form and purpose. R to Nemerov on the latter's poem "Cybernetics": "I do think it is uneven and this concerns me some because basically I admire it so much. I've already mentioned my doubts about some of the line breaks; there is also the switch in tone and statement in the last stanza. It seems to me that the switch shd either be more or less obtrusive." And in the same letter, on "Lot Later": "The second line with the image about the fabric of a dream — it seems not in character with our colloquial narrator, though a nice line. What think ye?" Nemerov replied to R on "The Odyssey of a B**t."

> I think it is not serious enough to take the weight. This goes especially for the character of the hero, but not much less for the success story which is yr tragedy.... Many points of mockery are well-taken and finely accomplished, esp. the ones about epic devices, which you parody so happily — and yet. And yet. There is about the poem a kind of petulance which sometimes overcomes the tragic disillusion that (as I conceive) is the true subject. Your disillusion is of wrong expectations, as though you were being disappointed, really, at the failure to find a model the mechanical imitation of which would be sufficient for the production of a masterpiece. Agreeing, as I unforcedly do, that much about letters as about life at present is mere folly when it is not mere viciousness, don't you in part become the victim of your own attack?

Their letters covered literary affairs and sometimes literary gossip. In 1960, for instance, R replaced Delmore Schwartz, who after a week walked out of a writers conference in Utah. R wrote, "Schwartz left most of his students annoyed with him and improved things no whit after his departure by writing a stern note complaining that he had not been paid enough money." In another, "Had dinner last week with Robt Frost at the [Allen] Tates, and found it most pleasurable till John Berryman entered and began to ridicule the old boy. I am thinking of a return to the golden age when there was — so I've heard — only grace and gentility in wit and the newfangled slobs hadn't arrived yet. But I've also heard that the golden age was a bit of a fraud too; at any rate, for about two hours I really felt I was in it; then Frost began to repeat himself and Berryman came in. Still, it was quite a fine evening." They commiserated on literary miseries

Howard Nemerov and R in the living room on Elm Street, North-field, Minnesota. Arthur Mizener signing a copy of The Far Side of Paradise *for Carleton College President Lawrence Gould. R before a Carleton class in 1959.*

and poor reviews — Nemerov admitted, "I've got to confront the fact that after twelve books that didn't sell I don't sell. (I wasn't really full of self-pity about my sales figures. I thought them pathetic in a way complete enough to be funny, hence to be spoken about.")

Then R wrote that "it wd be nice if we were to publish a book of literary letters," and went on to speculate what such a book might be. "Of course they should be a little more formal than these have been. Unhappily he then added, "I feel my prose tightening up here at the mere mention of Print — I will be posturing from here on in." Nemerov replied with characteristic irony, "As to literary letters: as a solution, I am keeping a carbon of this, and will continue keeping carbons of mine, interleaved with your originals, in a new folder appropriately labeled. It embarrasses me somewhat to do this, but less, I think, than it would embarrass you. This way, also, we need not plan, but can simply wait to see if some theme develops, without feeling under any formal pressure to develop it." Nor was Nemerov finished:

> As for this book of ours. My idea is, to begin with, one of informal remi-
> niscence tending to center around how we got into letters, if indeed we are
> in, and with what view; how this view has been changing; whether some
> sort of limit has not lately seemed to be reached; what are the choices
> open; how does one generalize from the experience. It has seemed to me
> as though the valuable criticism now might consist in a kind of
> Biographia, a history not of taste but of one's own relations with it; and
> that two such informal histories, or memoirs, might at the least be criti-
> cally useful one to another, and might work up some sort of dialogue at
> last.

Well, such a book never developed. Finally, R didn't have much interest in going back over the past in that way, though in glancing through these years and years of letters, he was somewhat astonished by how many hours they spent speaking to each other in front of their respective typewriters.

A number of those hours were spent in 1961, when Kenneth Rexroth started a small storm in *The New York Times Book Review* with a review of three books of poems: Weldon Kees' posthumous *Collected Poems, Possible Laughter* by James Michie, and Howard's *New and Selected Poems.* Three years before, Kees' car was found abandoned on the approach to the Golden Gate Bridge in San Francisco — the police concluded that Kees had drowned himself in San Francisco Bay. In his praise of Kees' book, Rexroth slighted Michie and Nemerov's books, concluding, "[it is] curious that both these books of light verse should be about the same things as Weldon Kees' and even in a sense say the same things. It's a little frightening. In fact, it frightened Weldon Kees."

Nemerov and R were outraged at the imputation of the last sentence, that Rexroth, as Nemerov wrote to the *Times*, was holding up his work "as a sample of the sort of thing that made society intolerable to Weldon Kees and occasioned his disappearance or death." R and Nemerov were in constant touch in deciding how best to reply — R felt his "warrior blood seething," he wrote Nemerov, and in the next issue of *The Carleton Miscellany*, he published an essay in which he referred to "Rexroth's history of similar accusations": "he long ago told us who killed Hart Crane, E.A. Robinson, Dylan Thomas and a number of other poets, in his poem, 'Thou Shalt Not Kill.'" Given the temper of Rexroth's outbursts, R concluded by quoting from an essay that Rexroth wrote about the virtues of the Chinese classic novel: "It is not a term we usually think of as part of the jargon of literary criticism. The word is magnanimity." There is an end to the story: Rexroth published a letter of apology in the *Times*, writing that he was "sorry indeed to have given Howard Nemerov the impression that I was insinuating that his work was the sort of thing that made life and society intolerable to Weldon Kees."

R closed *Furioso* down in 1953, partly because he felt its intensity had been softening and also because of a lack of money. The editors began returning all manuscripts with a mimeographed notice of the end. Among the receivers was Weldon Kees. *Furioso* had printed 14 poems by Kees, in seven different issues; it had also made *The Fall of the Magicians* a selection of its tiny Poetry Book Club. Kees wrote, "Dear R":

> Today I had a manuscript back from *Furioso*, and attached to it was a somewhat ambiguous mimeographed note, along with a message: "Sorry. This is it." My first thought was a blank, my second that *Furioso* is folding. I hope that this is not the case; I hope so very much indeed. For the mag-

azine is the only literary organ that I have been able to read with pleasure and admiration during the last few years; and it is also the only one where one's own work appears in non-shameful hospitality the magazine has shown to my poems right along, and to poetry.

Say it isn't so. Tell me what's going on. Is there anything I can do? Please write.

Faithfully, Weldon

Furioso's demise had an upside for R. While he had been publishing his own work there and in other literary journals since arriving at Carleton — in 1948, for instance, a review of Pound's *Pisan Cantos* in *Poetry* — he now had more time, in between teaching and beginning a family, to write poems, and think through ideas in essays. It would be seven years before he started *The Carleton Miscellany*. During that time he was writing reviews and articles that appeared in the *Yale Review* — "Churchill and the Limitations of Myth," "The Modern Idiom of Poetry and All That" — *The Sewanee Review, American Scholar, The New Republic,* and *Poetry* magazine. In 1954, *Poetry* awarded him the Harriet Monroe Memorial Prize — these were works that would begin appearing regularly in books a decade after *Heroes & Heroines*. This first book had a mixed reception from reviewers. It ranged from characterizing R's work as "unusual [and] distinguished for its readability...a talent that is lyric, critical and dramatic" (R.L. Lowe in *Poetry* magazine) to an impolite dismissal from Mr. or Ms. Anonymous at *Kirkus Review*: "This is not serious poetry but as satire or even comic poetry it is not brilliant enough." In the *Saturday Review of Literature* Jean Untermeyer — wife of the prolific poetry anthologist Louis — damned him, while critics from the *New York Herald Tribune, New Yorker* and *San Francisco Chronicle* had a go at R as well. There will be more about R's literary affairs in the Fifties and *The Carleton Miscellany,* but first back to Aunt Alice.

Poetry & The Miscellany

Yes, Aunt Alice's money helped bring on R's flying career. Taking off was simple, landing less so — it was like getting rejection slips back with one's work, though it had an edge on the rejections since each rough landing encouraged (in good weather) a new try on the same field. In a Piper Cub trainer on a windy day — and most days in Minnesota were windy — the problem was chiefly one of getting the machine down at all. And even with his own first plane, an old two-seater Cessna 120, he kept finding himself near the end of runways and still flying. Just staying up in the air seemed safer (usually) (in daytime) (with no clouds). On a clear quiet morning, flying out of the Stanton airport east of Northfield he could climb way up — to perhaps 6000 feet — and practice stalls high over St. Olaf without endangering either St. Olaf or himself. Soon he was so expert that when he really wished to fly places he did. Then he was able to tell friends very casually that in two easy flying days he had made it to Seaside, Oregon. But what he was less likely to tell them was that in trying to land on a miserable 1100-foot runway at Seaside he was about to hit a house at the end when he managed to pull the plane up — to the amazement of his waiting brother Dick and wife — and miss the house in order to fly north ten miles to a big airport.

Not much later, when flying to the East Coast with a Carleton senior as passenger, he was also embarrassed by the size of Princeton's field, where he did get the wheels on the ground but was only able to stop them a foot or so from a fence at runway's end. Otherwise he had much fine flying time on such trips. From Princeton for instance, leaving the shattered student as planned, he had flown brilliantly to Cape Cod, visiting Howard and Peggy Nemerov at Wellfleet and then taking them — one Nemerov at a time — to Martha's Vineyard.

Then there had also been the fine occasion when he flew first to Jacksonville and then to Savannah, where he visited Ambie Gordon at

Christmas. Yes, this was definitely his most sustained period of loner whenting (to recall Bill Williams' letter to his father William Carlos) and in retrospect he could at least say that it had cost relatively little. The aged Cessna two-seater 120 was $2500, and then the relatively new four-seater 170, $8000 — figures that later seemed, even in accounting for inflation, ridiculously low. Yet the mere fact that he was *whenting* in such style was a bit hard on his leftist (or anarchical, Kropotkin-like) political ethics. Luckily this bachelor style was to change, though not before he participated in several cross-country races with a friend Carolyn Pettet serving as navigator.

In early 1952 Helen Lundeen was a Carleton student though not taking any class of R's. Then at a student-faculty party she stole R's pork-pie hat. Soon R gave her a ride in his Cessna 170, and when spring came he flew her northwest for an hour and a half to Fergus Falls, her Minnesota hometown, and landed there, only to decide that the time was not (yet) right for him to meet her parents. He fueled the plane, took off with her again, and following her instructions flew over nearby Otter Tail Lake where the Lundeens had a cottage, then back to Stanton. A week or two later R and Helen declared themselves engaged, returned by car to Fergus Falls with the news — which Helen's father received calmly though commenting privately to R that Helen was a bit wild — and then unexpectedly spent an afternoon at the family's lake cottage before driving back to Northfield. That summer R flew off East alone, notified a few friends of this new development and returned to Carleton to teach more Fresh-

R and Helen on their wedding day, October 3, 1952.

man Comp. Later that year, in October, they were married.

Helen was twelve years younger than R. She was more impulsive than wild and did enjoy stealing hats. Unlike R she was thoroughly familied.

She was not fond of the Cessna and R was suddenly not fond of it either. He sold it and they moved into a reformed farmhouse on the edge of Northfield that for two years R had shared with Thurlo Thomas, a colleague in the Zoology Department. That farmhouse made its way into "The Farmhouse" some years later — by that time, it was filled with three children, Cate, Ned and Jack; Daisy had to wait until 1967 when R and Co. were living in Washington.

Our house is an old farmhouse, whose properties
The town has gradually purchased, leaving it
Only a city lot and a few trees
Of all that wood and busheldom and breeze
It once served. It is high and square,
And its lines, such as they are, have been muddled by several
Conflicting remodellers, whose care
In widening, lengthening, adding on, letting in air
Has left it with four kinds of windows, three porches
And a door that leads to a closet that is not there.

The city houses around us have borrowed from verse
And the Old Dominion; their cosmopolitan
Muddle is elegant next to ours.
We think of moving, and say we'll add no more dollars
To those already spent making a box
Of what was, is and will be, forever a box,
When there's land, empty and unboxed, down a few blocks
Waiting.
We say this as we pull down, pull up, push out
And generally persevere with our renovating —

That is, making new again — knowing
That houses like our house are not made new again
Any more than a man is. All that growing
Up and away from the land, that bowing
To impersonal social forces that transform
Wheat fields into rows of two-bedroom ramblers
Must be acknowledged; but the warm
Part of our country boy will not conform.
It remains, behind new windows, doors and porches,
Hugging its childhood, staying down on the farm.

Once an easterner, R *seemed* to have left everything eastern behind. In marrying Helen Lundeen he had married into Minnesota. This was especially so in spring and summer — and in a number of poems. A short, exuberant one with the hint of Chaucer and Shakespeare is "Spring, etc."

> And now at last I come to it: spring,
> Spring with his shoures sote,
> Shoures of snowe stille in Minnesota
> But spring all the same, starting all over
> All of those worthy projects in grass and clover
> That somehow got tabled last October.
>
> Spring in the trees and gardens, spring in the mind,
> Spring in the fields and rivers, springing the blood,
> Spring, spring, spring, and then again spring.
> Wet, warm, bright, green, good.
>
> So now at last I come to it,
> Long long overdue,
> Come to it late by bobsled and skate, but come
> To it, by golly and gum!
> To it! Tu-whit, tu-who!

Otter Tail Lake was Lundeenland. Helen's parents and their five children — plus many relatives — had a notion that summer was Otter Tail season. Many of these children and relatives had their own cottages on the lake, many of them ate two or three meals a week at the main Lundeen cottage on the lake, and all of them always knew what all the others on the lake were doing. At dinner on a small screened-in back porch not overlooking the lake R was apt to be one of nine to thirteen bodies squeezed next to each other. The meal itself would be long and complicated, as would the post-dinner clean up. Naturally R was the official greenhorn. He could not escape drying, was obliged to ask where each dish went, and then had to stand foolishly in line with small children for the next dish to dry. This was tiring, as was the playing of a card game called "99" next door after dinner with even more Lundeens. R was frowned on (but not grimly) for calling such heavy socializing "Lundeening" — but for all his faults he remained welcome in the family though not as a native. As for the children they simply were native. Even their youngest, Daisy, though born in Washington, thought more

Helen with Ned and Cate at Otter Tail Lake.

warmly of lake life than R did; and as for Helen she knew and felt at home with the whole lake community, family by family and house by house.

R's problem was — at least partly — his preference for ocean. He snobbishly put ocean and summer together rather than lake and summer, though his own family had never owned even a summer tent on dirty Long Island Sound. His mindless late-night dream of Really Living remained a self-centered, melancholy fantasy of a wide and empty beach of fine-grained sand that he could walk along and be alone on — and properly miserable. Those fantasies lived somewhere on the page. Years later, he set "Clamming" there, a poem that found its way into *The New Yorker* and numerous anthologies.

> I go digging for clams once every two or three years
> Just to keep my hand in (I usually cut it),
> And whenever I do so I tell the same story
> Of how at the age of four I was trapped by the tide
> As I clammed a sandbar. It's no story at all
> But I tell it and tell it; it serves my small lust
> To be thought of as someone who's lived.
> I've a war too to fall back on, and some years of flying,
> As well as a high quota of drunken parties,
> A wife and children; but somehow the clamming thing
> Gives me an image of me that soothes my psyche

Like none of the louder events: me helpless
Alone with my sandpail,
As fate in the form of soupy Long Island Sound
Comes stalking me.

I've a son now at that age.
He's spoiled, he's been sickly.
He's handsome and bright, affectionate and demanding.
I think of the tides when I look at him.
I'd have him alone and sea-girt, poor little boy.

The self, what a brute it is. It wants, wants.
It will not let go of its even most fictional grandeur
But must grope, grope down in the muck of its past
For some little squirting life and bring it up tenderly
To the lo and behold of death, that it may weep
And pass on the weeping, keep the thing going.

                    Son, when you clam,
Watch out for the tides and take care of yourself,
Yet no great care,
Lest you care too much and brag of the caring
And bore your best friends and inhibit your children and sicken
At last into opera on somebody's sandbar. Son, when you clam,
Clam.

Helen had definitely not married a domesticated Lundeen character — as she would keep discovering for fifty years. R carried over into family life an advanced case of self-absorption. He also carried an Eastern, maybe an old New England, sullenness that often broke into his poems and was at odds with the New England idealism that was his as well. When this trouble was upon him he was a poor bet as husband, father, and even teacher of Freshman Comp, yet without it he probably would not have thought himself a poet at all. Poets after all are by definition troubled — and when that mood was on, R often couldn't help but write dark, angry poems; yet in another moment, with the same mood, he could write comic poems, genial *and* biting, in which he "the poet" was the object of the poem's caustic wit. One such poem is "The Bad Daddy," which came later when the children had advanced into teenagehood. Still, the poem is not autobiographical in the manner which came to be called Confessional.

The bad daddy who has been angry with the whole family, one by one
Now retires to his study to be sullen and think of death.
He has aches in his neck and stomach that he is afraid to see the doctor
    about.
He has a sense of his mind's slopping off into fuzz.
He feels that he is becoming allergic to cigarettes,
That he can't digest steak, that he needs glasses, that he is impotent.
He knows he is bored by his friends, bored by novels, Shakespeare, youth.
He thinks that if it rains one more day he will kill himself.
He lies on the cot in his study covered by a child's security blanket too short
    to sleep under,
And he improvises idly, a few two-minute commercials for a different life,
    thus:

Dear Son: In the war between the Earthmen and the Martians,
Keep your feet dry, your messkit clean, your weapons oiled.
Get plenty of sleep, drink not nor fornicate, speak
When spoken to, write home once a week, get to know your chaplain.
If upon your return I should be wandering amid the shades of the departed,
Call the president of the bank who will deliver to you
A sealed manila envelope containing three French hens, two turtle doves
And your further instructions. Vale. Your sire.

Dear Mathilda: Though we have not spoken a word to each other for
    thirteen years,
We are simpatico, you and I. We commune across the miles; we yearn;
    we dote.
I watch you drive away in your furs in the Rolls to the shoe shop,
I hear you banging pots and pans in the bunker,
And my heart, woman, twitches and the salt tears come,
Tum-te-tum. Your Daddy-o.

Dear Daughter: It was good, awfully good to have that nice little note
    from you.
Jimmy danced up and down, Mamma had tears in her eyes.
We pulled out the scrapbook
And found that the last time you wrote was your fifteenth birthday,
When you were pregnant. Remember?
And now you write that you've won the Insurgents' Prize.
And at Berkeley! Of course we're terribly proud.
But as old-fashioned moralists we doubt the wisdom of compliments,

And anyway you should know that your mother and I
Really think you're a frightful bitch. Love, Dad

So now the bad Daddy feels much much more like himself.
His typewriter pants pleasantly in its shed; the beast is fed.
Down the long waste of his years he sees, suddenly, violets.
He picks them and crushes them gently, and is at peace.
Get 'em all, bad daddy, and sleep now.

Nearly ten years passed between *Heroes & Heroines* and *An American Takes a Walk* in 1956; three years later Macmillan published *The Self-Made Man*. R had moved in on the dubious merit of lonely selfness as an obsessive necessary subject for a writer. For instance in the book's title poem he decided he had to play single-handedly at being Adam, and to wrestle with the nagging American trouble of being both an individual and a representative of the "divine average" (E.E. Cummings's phrase?) as he rode about singly in roadster or Cessna, meanwhile noting that his divinity was becoming more precisely measured yearly by Gallup and the social-science hordes. He just couldn't get around the fact that he loved himself and that his being a poet/thinker/little mag editor/reformer and singer depended on his being his one-and-only me. Was that not — despite Eve — *his* sin? Yup. And he wanted to be a socialist too. Thus, "An American Takes a Walk" with occasionally irregular end-rhymes, but rhymes nonetheless.

In the middle of this life's journey
He came, like Dante, on a wood
The notes said stood for error
But in his case stood for good,
Where his art and prowess left him
And left him become a child
To whom the wild seemed milder
Than his old neighborhood.

Had he, with those abandoned
Sons of fatal decrees,
Then been found by a shepherd
And bred up to shepherdese,

The Oxford Choral Songs

OXFORD UNIVERSITY PRESS · MUSIC DEPARTMENT · 44 CONDUIT STREET · LONDON, WIR ODE

X 238
S.S.A.T.B. (S. Solo)
(unacc.)

20p

The High School Band

Poem by
Reed Whittemore

Music by
John Paynter

PIANO
(for rehearsal only)

Duration 4 minutes

The High School Band

On warm days in September the high school band
Is up with the birds and marches along our street,
Boom boom,
To a field where it goes boom boom until eight forty-five
When it marches, as in the old rhyme, back, boom boom,
To its study halls, leaving our street
Empty except for the leaves that descend to no drum
And lie still
In September
A great many high school bands beat a great many drums,
And the silences after their partings are very deep.

"The High School Band," which first appeared in The Self-Made
Man, *was set to music by John Paynter, for more than forty years
the director of bands at Northwestern University.*

Or retrieved, like Dante, by Virgil
And led through circles and seas
To some brighter country beyond
His annotated trees,

He could not have been more cared for.
Nature was awfully kind.
Hell in that motherly habit
Put hell quite out of mind.

How in that Arden could human
Frailty be but glossed?
How in that Eden could Adam
Really be lost?

What was poetry for in American culture and what were its subjects
and who was its audience and why was it so marginalized, and why
shouldn't it be? Herewith, "A Tale of a Poem and a Squash."

Let me take this acorn squash, grown in my garden,
And place beside it a poem grown in a hot house.
You will note the difference at once; the former is jolly
And fat, self-contained, the latter anaemic,
Colorless, tasteless, the clearest evidence
That a poem does not make a squash. But now take the squash,
And shoving its roundness into a lyric book,
Look!
How those covers squinch, being quashed, to elucidate
Something or other...
                    where was I?
                         Of late
I have been reading too much on this subject.
Art is not life, I am told, and thus in my garden
(Which as a matter of fact has no squashes,
just toads), I find myself gathering
Wool mostly, a few old tomatoes of rhymes,
And a mythical rosebud or two in the hope that these items
Will store well against winter, my chosen season,
When nothing from nature is blooming except my
Dog, a few plants on a windowsill, and of course people,
Most of whom,

Like myself,
Are not of the soil, the good earth, and in winter look
More like a poem than a…
                         but, as I say,
The subject unnerves me.
Where,
Where does one go — into war? poverty? —
To keep those squashes and poems from preening and posing
For any nitwitted author who has mouths
To feed and a ballpoint pen
And some paper
And thinks that if he could settle, once and for all,
Life and art, art and life, and how they are
Knit, he (that nit)
Could stake himself some sort of claim on our cultural garden
And be forever in squ…
                         but, as I say,
I have been thinking of going away.

―――

It was about such subjects he had been writing Arthur Mizener early on in their correspondence during the war. (They were issues, too, that his Yale teacher and friend Andrews Wanning had taken up in the pre-war *Furioso*, e.g., "The Function of Poetry in Wartime.") That central matter could be all consuming. He worried about being Don Quixote reveling in his apartness from society while at the same time claiming, like Shelley, that poetry is the unacknowledged legislator of the world. He went at this anomaly steadily and tried to examine it in "The Alienated Poet Insists," a wide-ranging essay that was originally a lecture at Iowa State in 1962, where R looked at "a few things" about modern poetry "that haven't crept into the courses," particularly the "assumption that poetry at its best deals with the whole range of human thought." Such assumptions were "pretentious," he wrote, and took a quote from Conrad Aiken as a starting place.

> Poetry has always kept easily abreast with the utmost man can do in extending the horizon of his consciousness, whether outward or inward. It has always been the most flexible, the most comprehensive, the most farseeing, and hence the most successful of the modes by which he has accepted the new in experience, realized it, and adjusted himself to it.

Shades of Wordsworth's "Preface" to *Lyrical Ballads* more than 150 years before, where Wordsworth claimed that poetry "binds together by passion and knowledge the vast empire of human society" and that it "is the breath and finer spirit of all knowledge." That statement was "eloquent, " R wrote, "but wrong."

> Poetry has not been flexible, comprehensive, and farseeing, though poets have wanted it to be. Mr. Aiken has expressed the ideal, not the fact of our art, and this is a distinction that poets and institutions have collaborated upon in our time to blur. Our benevolent institutions have created a refuge from comprehensiveness, farseeingness; and the artists have jumped at it. Only the rare poet nowadays thinks of his art as an adjunct to anything; it is the whole hog. And the institutions with which he allies himself either agree with him or are willing to go along with him by providing conditions under which he can think it is the whole hog. The critics, meanwhile, safely ensconced in their halls of graduate studies, strengthen the poet's notion of self-sufficiency by churning out grand new doctrines of self-sufficiency.... It is also easier for the poet than for the playwright or the novelist to ply his trade in the isolation of Yale and Yaddo without ever thinking about anything but his art. Perhaps this very ease has been the chief cause of the present conspiracy between critics and poets, a conspiracy to kill poetry by making it free, free of the culture, the world.

These themes — the poet's isolation from culture, and the complicity of institutions that give safe harbor to poets and critics where they can live apart from, rather than be *a part of*, the American culture — were ones that R sounded in poems and in essays and reviews. Cleanth Brooks and Robert Penn Warren set out with good purpose in their work *Understanding Poetry*, he wrote, to change the "softheaded view of poetry's function," namely that a poem was merely an occasion for introspection, "or, if not that, it was an occasion for browsing about in the lives of the poets." But the result was the autotelic poem, which "stands alone; it establishes its own conditions for being and can be judged only by them." He kept coming back to these issues in working out a voice for his own poems that could accommodate his being a loner but a loner who lived in the world, one who "is frequently dissatisfied with certain conventional kinds of knowledge." While a bit of alienation goes with the territory of being a poet, "real alienation isn't worth much," he concluded.

The impulse to achieve it may be one of the good impulses, and any poet who doesn't have the impulse and doesn't want to be saintly a few hours a week is probably not a poet at all. But after that, no. He has to join the lunacy — at least some other than his own — do *something,* something communal or institutional, something unalienated no matter how mad it may be, or he just can't live.

Doing one of those "somethings" meant doing more than just writing poetry or writing about poetry — it meant going against the current of conventional ideas intellectual and otherwise, often in writing and even in the publishing of his work.

For several years, R had been experimenting with narrative and voice in rhymed couplets. The results were "The Boy From Iowa," "The Odyssey of a B**T," and "Ebenezer and His Eight-Man Rocket." They differed from anything else he had tried or that his contemporaries were writing. His editor M.L. Rosenthal at Macmillan, which published *The Boy from Iowa* in 1962, was skeptical and wrote R two years earlier that he was "really against the sort of thing you're doing with these mock-epics."

> I think you force your wonderful wit the wrong way in them, & the form doesn't — can't — avoid a certain tedium no matter how hilarious and telling the satire often is — However, I've convinced myself that's all some-what beside the point. You are doing these poems, and very well, and there's a special exuberance in them. I feel these satires still settle for too little. You are capable of doing something more shattering, more *extreme* — something that *The New Yorker,* for instance would not like or even agree with.

R replied a few days later: "I disagree in part with yr feelings about the epics. I know it to be shared by a couple of good friends [among them, Howard Nemerov], and I know that they (the poems) have plenty of weaknesses.... The form fascinates me; I think I'm getting a little better at it." What their form owes to Byron R no longer remembers, though he had been through Byron's epical works and wrote an extended essay-review, "Childe Byron," for *Poetry* magazine around that time on *His Very Self and Voice: Collected Conversations of Lord Byron* (edited by Ernest J. Lovell, Jr.).

"While I despise *Childe Harold, Manfred,* and most of the oriental tales," he wrote, "I like the satirical Byron, particularly *A Vision of Judgement* and the early cantos of *Don Juan.*" Byron was "a poet moving indiscriminately between tragedy and comedy, epic and burlesque, drama and melodrama, and in doing so describing primarily his own moody self." How close a self-description this was, R can't say at this remove, though he did write, "I find solace in the fact that toward the end of his career the satirist in him was clearly ascendant, for this might mean that he understood himself and his true medium then as he did not when he was writing *Manfred.*"

Just as Byron had a boy protagonist in *Don Juan,* so too did R in Teddy, his boy from Iowa:

And now let me present my story's hero,
One who carries on at ceiling zero,
Brave, strong humble, not low — but *right;*
In short, he who has made me pen up pick,
An earnest, honest, American epic hick.
Born on a big old farm, he grew up with the notion
That land was a good thing for man, even better than ocean.
There, if everything went well, you lived your life through
In a pleasant pastoral haze with a farm girl or two,
Working and earning your bread in biblical fashion
Except for a tractor and combine to increase your ration.
And everything *did* go well for Teddy (his name),
A wholesome lad with a hoe who clambered to fame
When he was thirteen or fourteen by winning a mare
For showing a prize acorn squash at the county fair.

Through eight cantos and more than 400 lines, R sent Teddy away from his parents farm in "Ioway" through a circuitous route into the big city where he experiences the bottom of utter degradation and the high of being saved by an elderly woman, who dies leaving him a million, that he squanders on women and high living. Was he down and out?

In him was yet
Enough Iowa left to help him reset
His sails and start over, so that his flaw
Might not be left with no tragic subject to gnaw.
Seeing himself in a glass, with creases, dark pouches,

And a future of mornings of headaches, nausea, and grouches,
He bleated, "How sunk! how soon! oh mirror, mirror,
Must thou then make the obvious even clearer?
No! Not by all that is good in Dubuque or Des Moines.
What is writ on a wall may be unwrit" — Girding his loins,
That resolute lad, unresigned to declines and decreases,
Shattered the glass, swore fiercely, picked up the pieces,
Started all over, rose up next morning at seven,
Did pushups and kneebends, had breakfast, and left at eleven
To find a good job, as he did (of all things) and began
To work (of all things indeed) as a customers' man
For a very important brokerage house on the Street,
Where his innocent Iowa smile soon made more than ends meet.
In a trice he was married, childrened, and living in Rye...

The American dream? Not quite. R brings Teddy slowly to a realization of
what he has become:

"Here I am now in my middle years," he did rage
(He was in fact twenty-six, but old for his age),
"With all things a man could e'er want in this life, so attest
Such magazines as the *Post* and *Reader's Digest*,
To both of which, now that I think of it, I subscribe
(And may I be damned for it, I and my tribe) —
Here, then, am I in my little red rambler with wife,
Children, magazines, all — what a stupid life!
How has this happened? Gol darn it. How can it be
That after all I have learned I still am me?
In other words, how has (gol darn it) it come to pass
That I am, still and forever, so middle class?"
....
So Ted was revealed to himself, and did mightily rue it.
His flaw, then? Not what he was, but that he knew it.

So mock epic turns mock tragic, as the epic hick makes an end: "My
Teddy, Teddy, Teddy, all alone/ In a world that he, a child yet, had out-
grown,/ Tore off coat, pants, shoes, bared chest and flank,/ Waded into
the deep, held nose, and sank."

If R was satirizing middle-class life there and the pretensions of middle-class poets, he was also satirizing all the claims for poetry and poets.
Thus in "The Odyssey of a B**t," an even longer cantoed piece, he had

his hero discover "that he was a hack like the rest of us." From there he went on to put scientists in their proper place in "Ebenezer and his Eight-Man Rocket."

In 1962, Macmillan published *The Boy from Iowa* and the next year, *The Fascination of the Abomination*, both these books bringing together a mix of genres, poems, essays, reviews and even stories. R won't summarize their receptivity except to say that one fine poet-reviewer X.J. Kennedy, while characterizing *The Boy from Iowa* as "one of the most devastating and compassionate attacks on two-car-owning America" also had his reservations. "It is too bad [the mock epics] aren't more painstakingly written and more consistently funny."

In the second collection, R included the longish essay from 1953, referred to earlier, "Churchill and the Limitations of Myth." Written soon after Churchill had been awarded the Nobel Prize for Literature for *The Second World War*, R had been annoyed with Churchill's self-mythologizing.

> His documentary evidence was in large measure written by himself. And while the governmental position he held was so weighty as to fill his files with matters of indisputable historical importance, the assembling of material in *The Second World War* inevitably makes the war a Churchill war. I do not happen to think it was a Churchill war (though I'm prepared to acknowledge he played an important role in it), and so I am especially struck, from a literary point of view, with the achievement of Churchill in making it appear so. It seems to me — and I say this without malice — that Churchill is something of a myth-maker.

R then cited examples of Churchill's particular forms of self-mythologizing, the beginning of the prime minister's legend and how it grew, the author making himself a legend in his own time.

> I think the difficulty arises partly from Churchill's writing about himself. Mythologizing seems not just egotistical under such circumstances; it seems also delusive. "Human kind," says Eliot, "cannot bear very much reality." One reality, however, that seems to me must be borne is the smallness, the limited scope of self. One may in imagination lend a great deal of authority and virtue and prowess to others without being personally deluded; it is not just an act of faith; it is an act of creation like sculpturing an enormous figure for some garden. When complete the piece exists in its own right outside the self, an ideal if you will, or a projection of pos-

sibilities. But to let the imagination go to work on oneself, to lend the self
all the authority and virtue and prowess that imagination can conceive —
this, it seems to me, is a real evasion of the reality of self. To put it grossly,
how can poor Churchill, as he pulls on his trousers in the morning, say
that he secured North Africa?

In the meantime R wrote poems that gave voice to what might be called
the numinous, as in this first stanza of "Still Life":

I must explain why it is that at night, in my own house,
Even when no one's asleep, I feel I must whisper.
Thoreau and Wordsworth would call it an act of devotion,
I think; others would call it fright; it is probably
Something of both. In my living room there are matters I'd rather not
     meddle with
Late at night.

Still, such poems didn't prevent him from deflating the pompous and
pietistic. One example is "Wordsworth and the Woman," which began
with these offending lines from the *Prelude*:

"...travelling southward from
our pastoral hills, I heard, and
for the first time in my life,
The voice of woman utter blasphemy....
I shuddered...." — *The Prelude*, Book VII

Old shuddering Wordsworth, I'm in your country.
I've got rocks, trees, little hedgerows, and a big sky
Under which I too can be solemn, godly, portentous
When I'm angry. You make me angry.
I'm reading you near a simple pastoral fire
One hundred and sixty years after you shuddered,
And I say that by god an honest woman or man
Who'd fit god's scheme
Has a duty to blaspheme.

For when I see what an honest woman or man
puts up with in the name of god and the son
And the holy ghost and a thousand other pieties

Including those of yours out in the hedgerows,
I don't even need to think that god gives a damn
To know that if he has pleasures he'd have pleasure
In seeing you shudder.

An honest woman or man has a moral duty,
Man, to use god's name in vain when the establishments
Which put his name on their doors are vain,
Including that temple or rocks and fastidious naturals
Of yours, man.
So, from the other ranks,
I send to the girl who defiled that temple: thanks.

"Alfred Lord Tennyson," is another example. It is comedic yes and as R
well knows the comedic in poetry runs the risk — if only a literary one —
of being taken as simply funny and therefore inconsequential. Yet even
the funnily comedic can have heft (so much depends...) — whether
"Tennyson" does or not, R can't say. It begins with an epigraph that started
the poem off in the first place:

> *That is all that you will ever make from poetry.*
> — the Reverend George Tennyson, upon giving 16-year-old Alfred
>   half a guinea for some verses

Alfred was a ninny
With his father's half guinea.
He didn't make more
Till he was thirty-four,
And what he got then
Was a gift from the Queen
For having a bit
Of a deficit.

But at fifty, ah,
He lived like a shah,
And said to himself,
My name is pelf.
He took a big bite
Of the Isle of Wight,
And though his publisher failed
Fred's fortunes sailed

Up, up
With Morgan and Krupp.

So when he died
He had gratified
His heart's dear itch
To be rich, to be rich.
With considerable bother
He had shown his father
You never can tell
What will sell.

The comic and satiric are often the outsider's role and R's outsidership is one he kept questioning privately and in public. In "An Exercise in Criticism," for example, which first appeared in *The New Republic*, he began with a poem that he proposed to use "as a whipping post."

June comes, the end of a kind of year,
And the thought of starting again with a new set of points
And a full tank of whatever it is that makes
Our own cranky old crate rattle on toward the scrapheap —
This seedy thought
Hobbles our way on its endless circuit, bearing
Its regular summer line of beaches, parks,
Mountains, canyons and islands with and without
Bath.

        We are charmed.
We read the brochures.

At all the resorts the proprietors pretty their cabins,
Fatten their calves and rates, and look to the weather,
God and the Chamber of Commerce to send them
A better season than last, and to make us
Quiet tenants who don't drink.

Makers of boats and mosquito repellent,
Owners of drive-ins and fruitstands,
These persons too await us, as do
Jellyfish, horseflies and oilers of highways, all
Biding their time as we with our children,
Luggage, golf clubs and travellers' checks

Turn off the juice, lock doors and fussily set forth
On what will no doubt turn out to be like the last
Several brochure summers, which we remember
Now were delightful but couldn't, we're sure,
Possibly match the one we're about to endure.

R criticized himself therefore for failing to carry out his original intentions. "As I see it," he wrote, "the poem should be at least twice its present size. I should have a second narrator who would come in just as the
present speaker leaves off and deny some of the latter's *clever* but intemperate slurs upon the unfortunate 'we' of the poem. By so doing this new
character would undermine the present easy indulgence of the poem's
'we,' the facile dismissal of anything but mauve ironies from 'we's' reper-
toire. I should then have a pleasant agon going between the two opposed
points of view; and in the stress and strain and, yes, tension existing
between them the totality or complex that I apparently originally envi-
sioned might emerge."

In the '60s R, like many other poets, was appearing in occasional performances trying to "sell" the fading genre of poetry. Of course even Pound
had had sales in mind as part of a poet's job. But Pound had mixed salesmanship with so much political-aesthetic doctrine that the simple business of standing on a platform and getting the audience below the platform to stay there for fifty minutes seemed irrelevant. MacLeish in his
inaugural letter to Jim Angleton for *Furioso*'s first issue had complained
that poets always seemed to be up in the stratosphere addressing only critics and other poets. He had proposed that they try to talk to ordinary folk
instead, persons who "understand the sun on the side of a wall...and the
feel of things, naturally and simply with the hands and the mouth and
the eyes." R liked that idea well enough but he began to wonder how one
went about actually talking the idea — without of course making the poet
all-knowing.

His wondering became serious to the point that he committed himself to a series of performances on a small-college lecture circuit. The great
platform poet at the time was Dylan Thomas but Dylan Thomas was
Dylan Thomas. He had resonance somehow even when whispering, and
he could do what he did when he could hardly stand up — until he killed

himself by his doing. Of course MacLeish's injunction — which was really
absurd coming from the pen of such an elegant rhetorician — did not
have its modern-world start with Thomas, but no matter the source. The
problem of speaking as if informally to an audience just did not jibe with
a poet's obligation to recite. Recitation was not ordinary speech; it was
performance speech. Also, the poet had the duty of prefacing each prefab-
ricated poetic item with a conventional announcement (preferably short)
of the subject or at least a title. R in setting forth with such an act in front
of strange student audiences naturally had many cynical thoughts. For
instance, he recalled Shakespeare's frivolous gambit in *Love's Labours Lost*,
when the play's demented poet-lovers pin sweet sonnets to trees where
they are found and understood to *be* sweet. A possibly better idea, at least
for R, was R's own, this being to merge his explanatory prefaces with the
poems themselves, doing this so terribly cleverly that a poor helpless
audience would not know when the poem had arrived. For instance,

It is tiresome always to talk about weather, or think about it.
We ought to be able to rise (always rise) above it
By dedication
To our jobs, wives, children, even our art. Thus this poem,
If it is a poem,
Ought (always ought)
Not to be written.
                    — from "The Self and the Weather"

"What has he been taught (and taught and taught)
at all academies? — there is really
more than one way, lad, to skin a cat.
                    — from "The Negator"

There's a section, with sketches and text, in an Army field manual,
About it: how to take cover. Some basic refuges —
Cellars, foxholes, ditches, trees, bushes —
Are first described at some length in good Army prose…
                    — from "Cover"

Thomas McGrath once wrote a fine political poem, "You Can Start the
Poetry Now," with this notion roughly in mind, but his intent differed
from R's in that he was trying to get a listless audience hyped up, feeling
revolutionary (or at least involved) rather than just beauty-prone. R's

intent at the time was to sleepify listeners about poetry with a capital "P," lull them into thinking that a dull reciter was about to tell them at great length how much trouble he had had composing the great work he would eventually read, only to find that the trouble had already happened. Of course this theory worked poorly but at least it led him to reach for an unpretentious recitative mode. He knew that he was neither Thomas McGrath nor Allen Ginsberg but a mild man, uneasy in the role of rhetorician who had once been so ineffectual in training at Fort Benning that he had trouble making a helpless awkward squad start and stop at his command. Also he was starting to realize, now that he and Helen were raising a family, that he was a dreadful disciplinarian (and of course for better or worse the children kept liking him best that way).

Yet underneath his apparent speaking-and-writing mildness he did have a Poundian JOBBING principle still at work in his head, steadily urging him to some sort of action. The JOBBING principle kept pushing him to confront and express his ethical/ideological literary intentions — and to do so even in poetry despite that genre's addiction to truth and beauty.

———

It was the late 50s and after a nearly seven year hiatus, R had been feeling the little magazine itch. The costs were too great to finance it himself, as he had done with *Furioso,* so he went to Carleton College President Larry Gould asking for the college's support. Though the name settled on was *The Carleton Miscellany,* its antecedent was *Furioso,* as R wrote in the first issue.

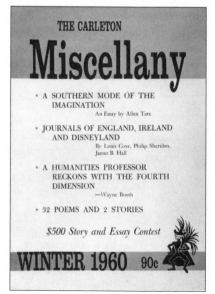

The Carleton Miscellany will be modeled in part after *Furioso....* To affirm the connection, the old *Furioso* symbol (a sort of chimney sweep) has been planted here and there. The symbol has not aged (still looks about 25), but this editor has aged, which is one reason for the change in the magazine's name. As for the name — sufficient controversy has been achieved on the subject that we may, for a year or two, change the name each issue.

The magazine not only had Carleton backing, it had as fellow editors two other writers in the English Department, Wayne Carver and Erling Larsen. It was a fine new opportunity — and the magazine was destined to proceed for many years after R had left Carleton in 1966 — but for R, while editing it, the question of intent remained: what was his game anyway? And to that question was now added a supplement: was the game now any different from the one when the magazine had been his without institutional backing? His interests remained large— poetry yes, but poetry in a broader cultural context.

In late 1959, for instance, before the first issue went to press, he returned a poem to James Dickey with detailed criticism, adding that though the magazine is "being sponsored by, and ultimately responsible to, an institution...I am bound and determined to make it not another literary quarterly." He then asked Dickey for other work:

> If you have satirical matter, or reportorial matter that you think wd fit the bill, I'd certainly like to see it. I'm especially interested in personal experience when that experience reflects upon the customs and patterns of the two worlds I suppose the magazine will be directed at, the academic and the literary (but I'd rather what you wrote were not expressed in such crummy sociological terms).

A year so later, he was writing Dwight Macdonald (social and political critic, an early editor of *The Partisan Review* and later editor and publisher of *Politics*) about contributing to the *Miscellany*, suggesting potential subjects, which "may indicate the kind of thing that I think we can and should make our continuing province." Among those subjects, (1) the world of the periodicals — the general intellectual decline of some big magazines; (2) manners — "my position is that the connection that ought to exist between cultural traditions or conventions and manners is missing; our manners exist in a vacuum, as does our morality, which doesn't proceed from any given set of principles or even precedents, but is simply given us by fiat, as it were (so that it is no wonder that in literature, for example, the first move of a good many intellectuals is to reject the manners and 'make it new')." His aim, he wrote Howard Nemerov,

Editor: Reed Whittemore
Associate Editors: Wayne Carver and Erling Larsen
Business Manager: Helen Lundeen
Editor, Dept. of American: Wayne Booth

THE CARLETON MISCELLANY, Volume I, Number 1, Carleton College, Northfield,
Minnesota. Published by Carleton College.
The Carleton Miscellany is published in January, March, May and October. Rates are as
follows: 90c a copy; $2.50 a year; $6.00 for two years. It is distributed to newsstands
and bookstores by B. De Boer, 102 Beverly Rd., Bloomfield, New Jersey. Manuscripts
are submitted at the author's risk; further, they will not be returned unless they are
accompanied by stamped self-addressed envelopes.
Copyright by Carleton College
Entered as second-class matter at the post office at Northfield, Minnesota

3

Contents of The Carleton Miscellany's *first issue.*

The Carleton Miscellany *editors conferring prior to the first issue:*
Wayne Carver, Erling Larsen, and R.

"is the obligation not to be alienated like a good poet but committed to the world's affairs...I don't think it's a matter of being political, but merely of being involved."

And so R was stirring up cultural issues to put his ideas into practice. Over the next several years he organized several "symposia," for *The Miscellany*, inviting contributors to respond to particular issues. Thus for a discussion of "Foundations & Magazines," he set out a number of propositions that had 12 respondents, among them Dwight Macdonald, Henry Rago of *Poetry*, Robie Macauley (*The Kenyon Review*), Paul Carroll (of the defunct *Big Table*) as well as several foundation reps. Then he had one on "What to do with or about *The New York Times Book Review*," i.e., how to increase its range and quality. For that he brought together Emile Capouya of Macmillan, Larry Bensky of Random House, Robert Bly (*The Sixties*), Robert Sward (*Epoch*), Wayne Booth and himself — "all of whom take a stern line" — as well as those with more moderate views, John Ervin, Director of the University of Minnesota Press, Bernard Perry (Indiana University Press), and John Leggett (Harper & Row).

Robert Bly may have been the most provocative by calling for the outright removal of Francis Brown and Lester Markel from the *Times*. Until that happens, Bly wrote, all plans or suggestions for improvement "remain mere talk.... The discussion here can be reduced to personalities." Bly was drawing on a pamphlet he published a year or so before, "A Broadsheet Against the *New York Times Book Review*." Bad manners (so Arthur Mizener wrote R) or not, R agreed with Bly's call for removing the editors, but he came at it in a different way, casting his contribution as a conversation that was slant and comic.

> Q. Suppose that the publishers of the *Times* were suddenly to aspire to take the state of literature rather than publishing as their province. What would they do?
> A. First they would be wise to take most of their present book editors and give them a page in the business section of the paper.

If editing, writing, teaching and fathering in themselves were not enough, R now complicated his life even more by committing himself to a ridiculous organizational anomaly, a union of anarchic little magazine editors. As he wrote Nemerov in June, 1962, "I have had little time in the last few months to worry about the frivolity of art, poetry, etc., having been almost completely submerged in either college or ALMA [the Association of Literary Magazines of America] politics. The politics of both, I shd add, stink very noisily right now."

~~~

ALMA, which was the forerunner of the Coordinating Council of Literary Magazines, seems to have come out of the blue, over breakfast in Salt Lake City at a writers conference R was participating in. The breakfasters were R, Andrew Lytle of *The Sewanee Review* and Robie Macaulay of *The Kenyon Review*. Who it was who first complained about the sad ununified state of literary magazines in America is not recorded, but at any rate R then went back to Minnesota, talked with a friendly official of the McKnight Foundation in St. Paul and, lo, soon had a grant, through Carleton College, for a meeting of little mag editors — to improve their sad state.

The meeting was held in St. Paul on November 11, 1961. It was attended by "representatives of 19 magazines and certain other publishing organizations." R was acting chairman of the meeting. Allen Tate (then a professor at the University of Minnesota) was elected president of the new organization. And a summary of the all-day proceedings that took place was printed in the *Miscellany* for Winter, 1962. These proceedings included a "statement of principles" devised at great labor by a fiery principles committee in a smoky hotel room several floors above the main battle. R was a member of that committee and the challenge of committee-composition was new to him. Afterwards he also thought — very briefly — of writing a three-act play dramatizing the committee's creation of a single paragraph. Here is a small piece of the created paragraph.

> It is a well-known historical fact that American Literature since 1910 would not have survived in its present variety and vigor without these magazines. Almost without exception, all the distinguished modern writers in America started their careers in them — writers such as Faulkner, Frost, Sandburg, Eliot, Hemingway, Saroyan, Tennessee Williams and Robert Lowell, as well as scores of writers now emerging into prominence…. The literary magazines of the present generation are continuing this indispensable tradition.

Anyone reading this should imagine the committee's turmoil as it composed its little listing of "all the distinguished modern writers," and should also imagine its steadily disgruntled bickering about such phrases as "a well-known historical fact." And he or she should further imagine the all-day squabbling down in the main meeting hall about such matters as who should be admitted to ALMA and who blackballed. After the meeting no one could deny that the meeting had occurred, that the organization could now tell itself that it existed, and that it had even resolved to have a second meeting in New York in six months. Yet few were able to walk away unscarred, and as for R he now knew even less about the game to be played than he had before going to Salt Lake City. He would attend a number of future ALMA meetings, including one that he arranged for at the Library of Congress in 1965 — there will be more on that in the next chapter of this saga — but he would keep wondering what God, not he or anyone else at the orgies, had wrought.

Meanwhile *The Carleton Miscellany* in taking over *Furioso*'s old functions found time and occasion to ridicule the many new forms of promotional creativity blossoming around the country in the 50s and 60s — writers workshops and the like. One issue offered, for instance, suggestions about the equipment a seriously moronic literary creator should take to his carefully selected summer creation retreat, as well as what he/she should expect there: "The siren blows every morning at 1 a.m. A mechanism connecting all the berths with the laundry chute immediately dumps all the members of the Retreat into the waters of the lake where," etc. R and his associate editors Wayne Carver and Erling Larsen also had a fine time drawing a map that showed where the best retreats were, while composing travel schedules for an earnest creator wishing to cover a few writers conferences on the run. Thus they proposed a modest Eastern tour that included the University of Vermont, the University of Connecticut, Breadloaf and the University of Maine. And they had similar plans for the Midwest and the Rockies as well as for a Grand Tour in which the "approximate mileage traveled" was to be 6800.

Yes, and somewhere in the midst of such doings the hard-to-define creation game behind it all was clarified — or at least put in bold type — by a large gathering of English teachers in Texas.

What the literary agenda *actually* was in Texas no person still alive can be expected to remember, but it must have had something to do with creativity on campus, since a number of editors and writers were actually there. After a day or two of conventionally dry sessions in hotel rooms a conclusive cocktail party took place where dissident creators were loudly to be heard, and where — late in the party — an unpleasant, surly anar-chic enemy editor-writer came up to R, drink in hand, and said "Are you serious?" R just stared at him. Then other unacademic editors came up, also with drinks in hand, and began to sing a crazy Beatles song, "Yellow Submarine." So R didn't have to answer the question put to him at all. Instead he simply sang with the enemy about sailing off to the sun to live beneath the waves of the sun's green sea.

Poet as Bureaucrat

chapter nine

In 1963-64 Howard Nemerov served as Poetry Consultant for the Library of Congress, so he was more than partly responsible R knew for his appointment the next year. R feels that Allen Tate probably put in a plug as well — Tate was Consultant 1943-44. Off to Washington, then, went R (with a year's leave from Carleton) in the summer of 1964. Robert Bly, who had been on the ALMA board, sent him a congratulatory note with a crack on his becoming the "woosy-whoose in Washington! That will be a great change from Northfield," Bly wrote, "and now you'll have to give up writing those poems about feeling isolated out in the garage." And of course his family did more than tag along. It was a great moment.

R and Helen packed up and packed the three children — Minnesotans Cate, Ned and Jack grew up knowing that Minnesota is a big place with two major centers of humanity: Northfield in the winter and Otter Tail Lake two hundred miles northwest in the summer. Daisy who was not born until 1967, and then in Washington, grew up knowing that in most summers one took an infinitely long trip northwest to Otter Tail Lake while being jammed in the back of a VW bus or Checker for two or three days. The point is that all four children grew up as travelers.

Helen had not traveled widely before marriage and had homebody notions of how to move from one place to another. Of course R's wartime life had given him different views, and when he was safely out of uniform he was able to count (sleeplessly at night in conversation with himself) over one hundred beds or floors or orchards he had warriorly slept on or in before landing at Princeton's Graduate College. And after Princeton came his flying years, which were also driving years, with Minnesota conveniently located between the two coasts. At marriage time he was an old hand at moving about, but since he had (while solo) only moved with a barracks bag or two, or the civilian equivalent, he had absolutely no idea what family travel was like. And he was still innocent until second child Ned was born. At that time a Ford station wagon came on the scene and R noticed that it was always full. Then came the real and true start of the family travel era, the first Whittemore-Lundeen trip to Washington, carried out with the aid of a moving van. The family knew it was going to Washington merely temporarily yet it took *everything* anyway — except a playhouse. The amazed owner of the moving van said the load was the largest he had ever moved out of Northfield. R could never after understand how, originally, he had moved from the East to Minnesota in a mere car. End of family and travel notes.

Though he thoroughly expected to return to Northfield, for several years R had been looking out for other possibilities, teaching and otherwise. There was a tentative offer from Macmillan in the early 60s, though that didn't pan out. Midway through his year at the Library, he wrote Howard Nemerov, "I'm perhaps in a better position to make some grand switch than I was in the past — partly of course because of Washington." Nemerov replied, "I'd like to think about getting out of teaching too," but added, "I am by this time untrained for anything else." For R, his year in Washington turned out to provide the impetus, though I'll get to that in the next chapter.

⁓

Now, as for the playhouse left behind, that was a sad loss but at least R had been able to plan ahead and move it to a friendly family's Northfield backyard while there was still snow on the ground. He did so by simply towing it behind the VW for six blocks — it slid well and it remained in the recipients' backyard for years until *they* left Northfield. R doesn't know where it now resides but feels sure it is still alive and well, being a fine indestructible edifice with a Dutch door and a little window beside the door that could be raised, as at a fast-food drive-in, and customers served through it — that is, served tea as in "The Party" (with a touch of Keats at the end).

They served tea in the sandpile, together with
Mudpies baked on the sidewalk.
After tea
The youngest said that he had had a good dinner,
The oldest dressed for a dance,

And they sallied forth together with watering pots
To moisten a rusted fire truck on account of it
Might rain.

I watched from my study,
Thought of my part in these contributions to world
Gaiety, and resolved
That the very least acknowledgment I could make
Would be to join them;
           so we
All took our watering pots (filled with pies)
And poured tea on our dog. Then I kissed the children
And told them that when they grew up we would have
Real tea parties.
"That did be fun!" the youngest shouted, and ate pies
With wild surmise.

R had built the amazing playhouse much more solidly than he was ever
able to build his own life, doing so by basing it on four five-foot 4 x 4s.
Its presence seemed to make him a good family man briefly and the children did like it. If it had traveled to Washington it would have been
insulted by placement in the tiny backyard of their rented Georgetown
townhouse on 28th Street, NW.

And the Georgetown house had no front yard at all, just sidewalk. And
a driveway? No. And a parking place? Seldom. So Washington with its city
faults was hard for a country family with tons of luggage to squeeze into.
Also, though a pleasant town, its unforgivable fault was that it had no
center. Surely its endless government buildings were not a center. And the
White House with its big fences was not a (civilian) center. And where
were the stores?

Well, there was Wisconsin Avenue, which began right in Georgetown
and wandered north past a Safeway before becoming impassable
because of traffic. (One of R's foreigner remarks about it that made the
papers was that hell was simply Wisconsin Avenue forever.) And there
were also little clusters of civilization to travel to, like Arlington (across
the river) and Baltimore (on the way to New York), but as for a plain old
Main Street where everything of importance was supposed to happen,
well, no.

Luckily the Library of Congress where R settled in for a year was excellently central for R's professional work. He could park in a reserved place

at the Jefferson Building opposite the Capitol, take an elevator to the third floor, walk thirty steps to the Poetry Consultant's private office looking out on the Supreme Court, or walk another ten steps to the comfortably official Poetry Room with couches and a balcony. And from the balcony he could watch with impunity important government ceremonies on the Capitol grounds (if the FBI happened not to take the balcony over, as at Lyndon Johnson's inaugural in January 1965).

His arrival was duly announced as he assumes most were, and still are, in the newspaper of record, *The Washington Post*, which sent a reporter to interview him in the Consultant's office. The quotations that distilled the interview into 11 column inches are the kind that can leave one embarrassed on the day they appear in print. "There will be no poem for his 45th birthday," wrote the reporter, followed by this from R: "I wrote a poem for my 30th birthday [and] I wrote one for my 40th, but that didn't get done until I was 41. I think I'll wait until I'm 50." (He didn't then either.) "He writes poetry in spurts, in cycles as he put it," reported the reporter, "and nurtures a poem in his mind until it jells. He is always writing something, however, and ascribes to the late William Carlos Williams' statement, 'When I can't write, I'm a sick man.'"

Some of his Consultant activities were also reported in the paper, R was surprised to discover: a talk at the D.C. Teacher's College, a performance with classical guitarist Charlie Byrd where R was to "read a new poem, 'Useful Art,'" a meeting with engineers at Goddard Space Flight Center, "various groups of school children…a group of Cardozo High School students." Less than a month after the inauguration, *Newsweek* saw fit to do a story on the Consultant's role — "a public-relations job, really," it quoted R. "I suppose I'm a cultural attaché for the Library of Congress; and if I have a function, it's evangelical." While he spoke of visiting schools in D.C. to speak about poetry, the magazine titled the article "Poetry and Power," which gave R a chance to speak about the "uselessness" of poetry in American culture, at least in the ordinary utilitarian sense, though he did say writers could be used by government — "and the government had better."

> The poet is the great conservator and replenisher of language; and when language is debased, the nation's thought and quality of life are debased. What are the sources of public language these days? They're bureaucracy and public relations. The first is mechanical and depersonal-

ized, the second is dishonest, and they're both splendid ways of destroying the language. It would be a great thing if the language — the statements — of government could be made by people — not machines, not
bureaus or committees or offices or departments — but people. You know
— *people*!

Also looking down three floors, inside, to the building's entrance hall
he could watch the ant-people coming and going. Could not the distance
between the third floor and the ant-people be inspiring for a professed
poet? Something like looking at the Pacific perhaps? From a peak in, was
it Darien? — Well a little like.

The practical work-a-day distance between the Library of Congress and
the Library's Congressmen was also impressive, and in a good sense. No
Congressmen were apt to consult the annual Library Poet since they could
always call the Library's immense Reference Division staff instead. Also
they had a financial reason to respect the Poetry Consultant's independence, since his job as well as the Poetry Room (at least the furniture in it)
had been endowed by a Washington widow, Gertrude Clarke Whittall,
who in R's year as Consultant could regularly be seen seated in a reserved
aisle seat in the Coolidge Auditorium for readings and lectures. So though
the Consultant's independence had obvious limits they were not often
visible. R just parked his car out front, rode up to the third floor and sat
down at his desk in order to wonder what he was expected to do. Howard
Nemerov as R's predecessor had already described the duties well, noting
that the Consultant was expected to cope with questions from the
American public like who is the heroine of *Jane Eyre* and "What is an I
am?" Nemerov had also noted a tie between the Consultant and leaders
in American industry, with the "real work" of both being usually done
elsewhere. And he had further observed that the Consultant, when not off
telling local classrooms about poetry's wonders, could just ask Phyllis
Armstrong what his job was. R thought of it as mostly an honor but with
a few tasks attached — mostly teaching moments plus Library of
Congress arrangements for visiting folk. Some years later the job became
exclusively honorary and the honored one — now called U.S. Poet
Laureate — seldom even appeared in Washington.

Phyllis Armstrong was English, born in South Africa but removed to
the United States by unknown forces in the 1940s. She had been hired by
the 1946-7 Consultant, Karl Shapiro, who referred to her as the Colonel

or General. In R's time she was assisted by a first-year appointment, Nancy Galbraith, who was a mere PFC under Armstrong but became the Colonel or General when Armstrong retired in 1970. These two wise women sat at two overloaded desks in a tiny entry room to the ceremonial Poetry Room. Where all their papers came from was not clear but the business of the office proceeded well without disturbing the papers, which may well still be at rest there today. In 1964 the office staff had little to do but welcome and explicate the office's function to visitors — who were rare. If in R's year for instance a visitor such as Helen with three children should come visiting, Phyllis and Nancy would be a welcoming committee, seat them all in the Poetry Room, properly worrying about the children getting out on the balcony. They would also apologize for the absence of food and drink, for there was normally little to guzzle there. It was a room for couches, memories and silence. It did not even contain books, other than a guest book to be signed and a few leather-bound volumes behind glass belonging to Mrs. Whittall. Its most interesting asset, other than the view, was a collection of photographs showing previous Consultants seated on the room's couches and chatting with other poets, or perhaps just posing singly with the Capitol's dome in the background.

But yes there were also candelabra and silver trophy cups to be looked at in an alcove — did they belong to Mrs. Whittall? — plus a number of anonymous wall hangings. Otherwise the room performed its minimal duties without fuss as a kind of museum, the kind the city of Washington has always fostered, a retreat where the air is always unmoving out of respect for past presences to be seen in photographs albums. There was a fine photo, for instance, of Robert Frost and Carl Sandburg — who despised each other — seated together chatting on Mrs. Whittall's best couch. And there was a group photograph of several Consultants standing with English dignitaries, all being unnaturally jovial with apparently real drinks in hand.

In the Consultant's own private office the scene was simply boring for R. His desk arrangement obligated him to sit with his back to the roof of the Supreme Court and to stare at his very plain door to the very plain outer hall. In early morning that hall was crowded with young Congressional pages, for there was a one-room page school on that floor teaching page duties. But when these students went off to real work at ten, even the hall was dull. And as for the couch in R's office it was too short to stretch out on, so that his job kept being reduced to sitting at the desk and thinking of things to say about what a poetry consultant thinks about. The idleness was perhaps a form of minimalism.

But R was in no position to be critical. To have been hired to be largely idle for a whole year ($15,000 worth) was not a bad fate. He did have a few public obligations such as introducing visiting poets who came to read in the Library's Coolidge Auditorium. During his tenure, they included Philip Booth, James Dickey, Howard Moss, and Melvin B. Tolson. Also he was expected, just twice in the year, to put on a show himself. Further — and more importantly — he soon found a large shadowy cultural mission lurking behind his idleness and whispering to him, begging to be fulfilled.

That mission had been stirred up in him by many Washington issues and problems but perhaps most urgently by an odd book that oddly appeared on his Library desk one morning. It was a book called *The Congressional Anthology*, a collection of "Poems Selected by Senators and Representatives, edited by the Legislative Reference Service of the Library of Congress," and put together in 1958 by a "sponsoring committee" for members of the 85th Congress who had been invited to submit their favorite poems for the work. Fifty-two poets were printed therein, including four Congressmen. And aside from the Congressmen's work the poems chosen were by a fine assortment of poets ranging from Cadoc the Wise (his piece selected by Eugene McCarthy) to Shakespeare (works chosen by four), Wordsworth (three), Kipling (five), Longfellow (two), Tennyson (four), General Douglas MacArthur (one), and Frost (three), with all the selections — except perhaps Sandburg's "Fog" — being loaded with Moral Messages. On the cover of the volume was "the official picture of the Capitol Prayer Room" showing an altar with a stained glass window flanked by an American flag and candelabra. And on the inside pages there was no escaping the drift to piety. R was not stupid enough to have expected the volume to agitate for sin and communism, but he was a little disturbed to find that the poet's role in the world — as dreamed on Capitol Hill — was so insistently uplifting. After all, his own literary friends were a troubled mix of largely secular dissidents who, by the 1960s, were accustomed to living with 57 varieties of impiety. By then Karl Shapiro for instance — who had been one of the earliest Consultants — was making radical pronouncements by the dozen if only to keep his spirits up. Here was one:

> Almost to a man, American artists are in full-fledged opposition to the American Way of Life — that is, life according to Business, Politics, Journalism, Advertising, Religion, Patriotism and Morality...and almost to a man [what about women?] they revere the primitive America which claimed freedom of action for all men.

R was more cautious than Shapiro and not inclined to make "full-fledged" statements on the 3rd floor of the Jefferson building.

⸻

A brief aside about Karl Shapiro. R had become friendly with him after reviewing, in *Poetry* (1960), *In Defense of Ignorance*, Shapiro's attack on certain Modernist poets — Yeats, Pound and Eliot in particular — as ideological and anti-democratic. In "A Letter to Karl Shapiro" R took issue not so much with Shapiro's observations but his "fulsome praise of ignorance" as well as his intemperate tone.

> You are not...suggesting that we destroy our universities and kindergartens, or abandon our grammars and our various acquired rhetorical skills like, say, rime and reason — but if you think the neighbors hearing you will hear those "nots" you're sadly misled. They hear your curses, not your qualifications. You assert that you "believe in Blake's proverb that 'the road of excess leads to the palace of wisdom'" — would you not agree that this wisdom, if it is wisdom, is like all wisdom, something to be absorbed in the closeness, not over the back fence? Well, then, why blatantly distort it, why broadcast it loosely, why give noisy demonstrations of it.... I do think that...you might at least be civil.

Shapiro responded with a 15-page essay that he said was the unpublished coda to his book. Here he proclaimed himself "on the side of the Ignoramuses, at least if we have to make a choice between the connoisseur and the Ignu — to use a Beatnik term ...I am bored with all the old nonsense about High Culture, Middle Class Culture, and Mass Culture." "To be a poet," Shapiro went on, "one must return to the state of poet, which is a natural state of being, the childlike state in which we see and sense everything in the full light of consciousness and without having to think our way to the truth. Thinking about art, intellectualizing it, is the chief disease of art in our day."

R had one last go in a Postscript, addressing Shapiro once more.

On the one hand you say that "the great poems and other works of art are all part of a common effort, and are never the product of a single man," and on the other you say that "history can teach us nothing." Well, history, history, history. I could quote some of the modern poets of the Establishment (Stevens: "all history is modern history"; Eliot: long sections from the essays and the *Four Quartets*). . . it's enough to say here that I can't imagine a poet thinking of himself as a part of a "common effort" without history. I would be the first to grant our tremendous education failings, but I can't see that the preservation of ignorance is the solution. The ignorance that worries me most is ignorance of the fact that "the great poems and other works of art are all part of a common effort."

R was long familiar with the history of William Carlos Williams and the Library — of his being turned down in 1953 for the Consultant job after having been selected for it. Significantly, the turndown had occurred just a year before *The Congressional Anthology's* first edition, though "turned down" was not how the Library described his rejection. (One weasel phrase was that his "appointment had been deferred.") The immediate cause of the deferment was the appearance of two, perhaps three, public statements declaring him a communist. The most telling of these slurs came from a malicious poet-editor of a little poetry magazine who simply misread a Williams poem about Russia in order to make her point. (The episode is described at length in William McGuire's *Poetry's Catbird Seat.*)

Of course the early 1950s had been the urgent days of the Cold War and the McCarthy hearings. They had also been the dark days for the "mentally unfit" fascist Ezra Pound who was then penned up in St. Elizabeth's. And definitely contributing to the 1948 hullabaloo about Pound was his being given the Bollingen Award in that very year by a committee of Fellows of the Library of Congress, no less. The hullabaloo over Pound was enough to cancel the award and remove the site of future Bollingen awards to the Yale Library — all this is the background of Williams's case, since Librarian Luther Evans was at the time feeling much pressure to be a conspicuously loyal American. The basic trouble of course was that Williams was not a communist and became full of anger at the Library of Congress for taking the charge seriously. He hired a lawyer and the lawyer angered Evans. As a result the Williams appointment was not only definitively cancelled but no substitute appointment was made for four years.

With such matters in mind R, finding *The Congressional Anthology* on his desk, could have taken the book's pieties as a dark signal. Yet the Library officials he was housed with (including Quincy Mumford, the Librarian who had replaced Evans) were not nearly as holy as the anthology's politicians. So R could at least see that he had much to learn about the American Way as practiced rather than preached in government circles. And the complexities of his job were confirmed for him when he proposed that the Library host a meeting of anarchic little magazine editors in the Coolidge Auditorium at the end of R's year. All librarydom thought that was just fine, perhaps because R was able to land a Carnegie Grant of $14,500 for it. The grant-getting had some help from Peter Caws, a philosophy professor at the University of Kansas who was on leave to work at Carnegie — Caws, who's now at George Washington University, would also participate in the symposium.

Eighty or so editors did come for two days at the beginning of April, and they did rage against the American Way as well as against other editors. There were three sessions and R chaired each of them. Each involved papers by two speakers followed by a panel, each of which was followed by a general discussion. William Phillips, a founding editor of *Partisan Review*, spoke about the state of literary publishing. Karl Shapiro talked about campus literary magazines, noting that "Institutions, whether the newspaper, the university, the foundation, or the government, can only deaden or paralyze art.... No academy should ever be put in the position of having to arbitrate and establish the values of works of art." Then Allen Tate warned against subsidized publications and their legislative powers, while R followed by taking "the gloomiest possible view of the state of our literature and literary publications." One editor whose name is lost proved that liberty was alive by raging down an aisle shouting "bullshit, bullshit." And most contenders managed to speak at least a few words against the U.S. It was 1965 and the anti-war movement was accelerating.

R opened up the second day's session with "Two by Two," in which he spoke about the narrowness of so many poetry magazines and recommended that each might join with another, wholly different, e.g., *The Carleton Miscellany* with the *Bulletin of Modern Physics*. While he exaggerated in order to make his point, some little mag editors didn't take the hyperbole with equanimity. George Hitchcock of *Kayak* was outraged. "You guys have all been talking as if you were tired salesmen and boon dogglers. My own feeling about editing is if you don't get any joy out of it, if you don't feel it, if your blood doesn't flow when you do it, then get the hell out of it."

A fine meeting it was, since everybody including R survived. Geoffrey Wolff, then book review editor of *The Washington Post Book World*, reported on the gathering under the headline, "Little Mag Editors in Dither."

> Participants argued with panel members and with themselves, often yelling their frequently scornful opinions above the protests of Whittemore. The arguments went to the touchstone of art: Is its function to join society in a hope of leading and instructing it? The answer, for the most part, seemed to be an aghast NO! The little magazine must, most panelists agreed, remain aloof from the restrictive requirements of the big financial foundations and from Government subsidy.
>
> Dissenters Phillips, Henry Rago and Victor Navasky, editor of the satirical magazine *Monocle*, suggested "with a not-very-straight face" that the little magazines get all the support possible from the Government. And Whittemore changed the subject by pointing to what he felt to be a more basic problem: "mannerless poetry," innocent of syntax, logic and rhetorical structure.

In the symposium proceedings later published for the Library of Congress by the Modern Language Association of America — *The Little Magazine and Contemporary Literature* — R summarized his impressions of the gathering this way:

> It was hoped that from this group some worthwhile proposals would float forth for redeeming or restoring to health a kind of publishing now, it seems evident, in real trouble. This hope was not realized. Though a number of proposals were in fact made — I, for example, made a perfectly magnificent one — none seemed to take hold. Most participants left the conference persuaded of the difficulties of joint efforts at restoration and mightily impressed by the extraordinary absence of agreement.
>
> It was an exciting meeting. Maybe the disagreements are in themselves instructive. "Back to the drawing boards," cry the world's architects when their roofs leak, their bridges fall down. The architects of little magazines

can now go back to their drawing boards too — and perhaps project another conference.

In the interest of what today is called "Full Disclosure," R should acknowledge Frederick Hoffman's sour review of the proceedings in *The Modern Language Journal*. Though Hoffman, himself the author of *The Little Magazine in America: A History and Bibliography* (1947), found it to be chaotic, "in short, the history of one occasion of intellectual eccentricity," he also saw the argument as "a genuine exchange between one generation and another of the *avant-garde*."

The meeting was not the end of R's national involvement with organizing little magazines — when he returned to Washington two years later as a "thinker" for the National Institute of Public Affairs, he took the lead in helping to organize the Coordinating Council of Literary Magazines (CCLM), which replaced ALMA (Association of Literary Magazines of America), and became its secretary. There's much to this story, though others have taken it up with various points of view, among them, Jules Chametzky in *The Massachusetts Review* and Richard Kostelanetz on his website. R will leave it to them, which is not to say that he didn't reflect — in print — on CCLM.

~

R's one solo Coolidge performance — other than a poetry reading near the end of his tenure — came not too long after his arrival, in October 1964, in a lecture he called "Ways of Misunderstanding Poetry." The title took its lead from a report that Nemerov made on the Library's archive of recorded poetry (in it he mentioned the "appalling misunderstanding of the nature of poetry"). While R's lecture was genial in its tone, its target was the evil of positivism in America, that is, specialization, departmentalization, and "their effect upon our arts and our artists." He would become increasingly irritated by American positivism over the years. In the back of his head the complaint of MacLeish in *Furioso's* first issue 25 years before began to simmer again, that poets were always just speaking to other poets, and their critics. They too were specialists, but specialists in claiming a wise ignorance, "bellowing against the full purse and the empty spirit" of America. Along the way, R launched a waspish bit of sarcasm with quotes that journalists could report on the next day, to whit: "One of the chief qualifications for admission to some of our creative writing classes and schools would seem to be an inability to pass freshman English."

R began his talk with "Today," a poem recommending humility, especially in Minnesota

> Today is one of those days when I wish I knew everything, like the critics,
> I need a bit of self-confidence, like the critics.
> I wish I knew about Coptic, for example, and Shakti-yoga.
> The critics I read know them, and they say so. I wish I could say so.
> I want to climb up some big publishing mountain and wear a little skullcap
>   and say so: I know.
>
> Confidence, that's what I need — to know —
> And would have if I came from California or New York. Or France.
> If I came from France I could say such things as, "Art opened its eyes on
>   itself at the time of the Renaissance."
> If I came from California I could say "Christianity was short-circuited by
>   Constantine."
> If I came from New York I could say anything.
>
> I come from Minnesota.
> I must get a great big book with all the critics in it
> And eat it. One gets so hungry and stupid in Minnesota.

He took up arms against the poet as alienated critic and denied "(1) that poetry must be pure; (2) that poetry must take man back to the simple natural world around him; and (3) that poetry must oppose, deny, subvert the whole culture and somehow salvage the individual." (*The Washington Post* duly reported these views.) While he acknowledged that "American culture has done its bit to alienate its artists," he was persuaded that the artists share at least part of the responsibility: "In a way, the poets have sold themselves on their own positivism — poets from Ezra Pound to Allen Ginsberg — and now that they've got it they've also got an art that is about as central to our world as stamp collecting."

Given his polemical view, what reforms could he offer? R threw out some Swift-like proposals, e.g., advocating "the abandonment of literary quarterlies as now conceived and executed or the abandonment of literature departments of our colleges, on the grounds that these distinctive activities merely serve to enforce the deadly positivism of literary exclusion." Finally, he declared there were no solutions to the problem of the poet's irrelevance, though that didn't keep him from ending on an upbeat note. He quoted physicist Cyril Stanley Smith, a professor at MIT, who observed that the need in science now is for concern with systems of greater complexity and methods to deal with complicated nature — Smith added that "The artist has long been making meaningful and communicable statements, if not always precise ones, about complex things." And perhaps somewhat confusingly, Smith added, "If new methods, which will surely owe something to aesthetics, should enable the scientist to move into more complex fields, his area of interest will approach that of the humanist, and science may even once more blend into the whole range of human activity."

What struck R about Smith's statement was its reminder "that the arts have at least a *reputation* for ranginess." Why then, he asked, "can we not say that ranginess is *already* a part of the poetic organism, a now submerged part? If we do, our problem becomes not one of trying to change the organism, or trying to persuade or force the poetic organism to change itself, but merely to encourage it to come out of the bushes and remember to *be* itself."

His talk was seemingly a success — at least a few good friends said so — and the audience's approval of his public performance was encouraging since it was a new kind of audience for him, large and seemingly diverse. The morning after his lecture he sat at his library desk with the Supreme Court behind him and decided that he now had a new mission. He would not just read poems and explicate literary depths but he would also move himself out into the world of Washington bureaucracy in order to give it aid and comfort, especially aid about language and how to write it down intelligibly. Surely, the bureaucracy needed help there.

He went at it. His first gig was at the Department of Agriculture where, over lunch in its cafeteria, he spoke to dozens of clerks and administrators eating salads and drinking colas. He began by ridiculing the heavy military prose he had suffered in WWII, then reminded the eaters that they were now suffering as he had. They needed to *do* something about this. They needed to look critically at the bulletins and guidelines and official correspondence passing sullenly over their desks. They needed to make suggestions, take steps, recommend revisions of annoying sentences and paragraphs (and all of them were annoying). He didn't talk long. He read only one poem. He was apparently amusing. The cafeteria clapped.

His next stop was the Department of the Interior's Park Service, where his audience was smaller but more directly concerned with editing and revising. In fact the Park Service people were ideal for his purposes since they were charged with churning out dozens of pamphlets for national monuments like the Lincoln Memorial. Clearly they needed a shake-up, so R waded in and made instant if temporary converts to a spur-of-the-moment pamphlet gospel. Yes, he recommended that any government pamphlet about a memorial should be signed by the author.

They were curious and amused, but asked R to be specific. He thought fast and suggested that they let him write a pamphlet and sign it, not because he was world-famous and would make the pamphlet sell like hotcakes but because his signing it would indicate it was written by a real and single breathing human — as bureaucratic prose is designed not to indicate.

The Park Service was agreeable. R then wrote a two-page pamphlet for the Jefferson Memorial, and to the best of his knowledge it was published with his name on it and made available within the precincts of the Memorial. How long it was made available, and how many other pamphlets were composed and signed by singular real humans inside or outside the Park Service is not an answerable question here, but R was happy with the experiment.

He made further idly reformist remarks at the Smithsonian and in two churches. He also had lunch with Justice Arthur Goldberg next door to the Library in the basement of the Supreme Court where they pleasantly reformed the legal profession. And since 1965 had become designated as International Cooperation Year, R successfully recommended that the English poet Stephen Spender succeed him as the Library's Consultant — not without controversy.

In 1965 he was also on radio reflecting about the life and the death of T.S. Eliot. "It is difficult to meditate in silence about this poet's death," he said, "without employing some of the poet's own 'terms.'"

He now lives on, for his admirers, in the quotation-ridden thoughts they entertain about his death, they having learned a good deal of what they know and feel about death from him, learned of growing old with their trousers rolled, of dying with a little patience, of shoring fragments against their ruins, of dancers gone under the sea, of captains, bankers and eminent men of letters fading off into dark.

But 1965 was not otherwise a good year for international cooperation from literary folk and other born dissenters. The Vietnam War was on. The U.S. was already conducting air raids and preparing to escalate the number of U.S. troops. Robert Lowell had written an angry anti-war letter and been widely supported. The Administration was looking for remedies, and White House strategist Eric Goldman came up with a scheme "to quiet opposition" to the War by sponsoring a Festival of the Arts. He consulted R, among many others, for lists of "the most familiar front-men for the Arts." Soon a Rose Garden party at the White House to promote the festival took place (not attended by Lowell) at which Dwight Macdonald, *Partisan Review* maverick, circulated a letter approving of Lowell's stance and asking for signatures. R and eight others signed. *Time* and *Newsweek* both took up the Rose Garden story and consigned the names of Macdonald's signatories to a footnote. At the party R also indiscreetly described Goldman's welcoming speech as "canned" — and was overheard by a Washington reporter. The reporter reported. R then apologized to Goldman but made further dissenting remarks in his apology. Thus the Rose Garden party largely served to make opposition to the war more conspicuous than the White House's "backing" of the festival.

Washington is of course our nation's center for crises. Old Washingtonians accept them as normal. So do the reporters who live by them. And the real politicians — those who have the wit or ignorance and (in both cases) stamina to persist in that trade — look on them with affection as moments of seemingly moral opportunity, moments in which to display uprightness or at least orate about it. Most of the poems in *The Congressional Anthology* must have been chosen with the subject of "character" guiding the chooser. Yet in Washington in times of crisis it has oddly become conventional for character also to be displayed by dissidents, perhaps by speaking against the whole culture as Shapiro did, or by signing letters in the Rose Garden or, when really steamed, by marching about with placards. The Poetry Consultant in such times has a number of options, and he may well decide to perform like Herman Melville's Bartleby and "prefer not to."

Yes, so R later was able to find dark amusement in speculating about Bartleby in the Consultant's role. After parking in his reserved spot he could take the elevator up to the third floor each morning and become morally upright in his best negative way by sitting quietly at his desk all day playing perhaps solitaire, and then descending to the first floor, poking his head into the Librarian's office to show that he had been present in preferring not to, and then driving home in his car. Of course there is no record of Bartleby's having ever thought of himself as a poetry consultant, so the thought is ridiculous and yet....

Nemerov, preceding R, was no Bartleby but he had many fine moments of preferring not to. For example, he preferred (in a poem of his own, "On Being Asked for a Peace Poem") not to oblige a certain fervent poet who had been pleading — in an advertisement in the *Times* — for more and bigger peace poems.

> Here is Joe Blow the poet
> Sitting before the console of the giant instrument
> That mediates his spirit to the world.
> He flexes his fingers nervously.
> He ripples off a few scale passages
> (Shall I compare thee to a summer's day?)
> And resolutely readies himself to begin
> His poem about the War in Vietnam.
> This poem, he figures, is
> A sacred obligation: all by himself,
> Applying the immense leverage of art
> He is about to stop this senseless war.
> So Homer stopped the dreadful thing at Troy
> By giving the troops the *Iliad* to read instead.
> So Wordsworth stopped the Revolution when
> He felt that Robespierre had gone too far.
> So Yevtuchenko was invited in the *Times*
> To keep the Arabs out of Israel;
> By smiting once again his mighty lyre.

Of course, Bartleby would never have written a poem like that, and would not have speculated like that in prose either. He was not an imaginative speculator but a simple unredeemable negator. The quality of Nemerov's poem that seems relevant here is the anger in it, and contempt. Nemerov was normally reserved. He didn't blow up readily, and if he did he could be monosyllabic. Yet when a Joe Blow poet came across his bow he had to fire a salvo or two, since poetry and where it came from in a

poet's thinking was his life's obsession. Most of his best work was specu-
latively inward in this respect, a focus not brought on by any wish to be
shut off from the world but merely by a contempt for impractical schemes
to change it. He found steady ironic solace in knowing what the world
was always miserably (without his help) doing.

R could agree with his aloofness part of the time, but he kept being
troubled by activist urges telling him what poetry might modestly at least
try to do and be. Accordingly he wrote an essay "But Seriously" late in his
Consultant year. In it he wrestled for pages with the problem of how a
poet on the third floor of the Jefferson Building could be serious about
the world's constant mess without having ridiculous expectations like
Nemerov's Joe Blow. Though he was still full of the problem forty years
later (2005) he had by then at last learned that poetry's practical worldly
functions, never great, had been so drastically reduced by power-hungry
modern entities such as social science, Madison Avenue, radio and TV,
that any poor versifying fool who thought to use his art for world-saving
purposes was out of date, unless....

Unless? There seemed to be no other than frivolous exceptions, yet
frivolity might — he thought in 1965 — at least be useful right in the
LC's Jefferson Building. It was a 19th century architectural triumph
whose controllers had, or then seemed to have, successfully mixed the
anomaly of high culture with highly disciplined democratic "perception management." The mixture was pure Washington, with tourist
herds as the imperceptive sheep to be managed. They entered the
Jefferson Building on the ground floor in carefully herded groups and
were marched up to floor two on marble stairs where two great traditional fixtures of Western piety were lodged, they being the Gutenberg
Bible in one glass case and a distinguished medieval competitor in
another glass case. Here the tourists were halted in order to be lectured
at by guides. Then they were simply led back down and out, since they
were forbidden — by a sign directly to the East of the Bibles — to move
a step nearer the building's chief architectural wonder, its magnificent
Reading Room.

All in all the Library's tourist control, though presumably necessary,
seemed to R an ironic form of the "democratic process," worthy of a
movie satire preferably by the Marx Brothers. At the start of the needed
film Groucho might be seen leering at a gorgeous girl-tourist approach-

ing the Gutenberg while the tourist-group guide, preparing to lecture on the Bible's origins, happens to notice that both Bible and case are missing. He blows a whistle and troops arrive as Harpo runs up to Groucho wildly pointing. For Harpo has just rolled the case with Bible through a forbidden hall to the forbidden Reading Room balcony and needs help lowering it by a rope to the Reading Room floor where brother Chico — who wishes to read let us say Psalm 23 — is waiting.

And for many of the third floor Poetry Room functions the Marx Brothers tactics would also have been useful — to bring high drama down to low democratic earth. There was for instance the Pound melodrama in 1948, then the Williams tragedy of 1953, then the slapstick of R's little magazine-editorial meeting in 1965, and then — but enough. For several decades the Consultantship appointment somehow contained and yet resisted Washington's bureaucratic culture; so a brief summary of its origins is in order here, though McGuire's *Poetry's Catbird Seat* is a fulsome source.

In the beginning there were three donors and a sympathetic Librarian, Herbert Putnam. The first donor was the moneyed musician Elizabeth Sprague Coolidge who, back in 1924, gave sums to support chamber-music concerts and to "construct and equip" an auditorium for them. The second figure, closely tied to poetry, was a scholar, a translator of Spanish literature and a fan of Don Quixote. (He rode around Spain on a donkey and named his yacht Rocinante.) He was Archer Huntington, one of the founding angels of the Academy of Arts and Letters and, not incidentally, a friend of both Librarian Putnam and a poet by the name of Joseph Auslander. In 1936 a grant from Huntington to the Library provided for a Hispanic Society Room as well as the maintenance of "a Chair of Poetry in the English language" for which Huntington recommended Auslander. Thirdly there was Gertrude Clarke Whittall, herself not a musician but an admirer and collector of musical items. In the 1920s she had scraped together funds for "a set of Stradivari stringed instruments and Tourte Bows" and in 1936 her enthusiasm for chamber music and poetry drove her to part with the violins and bows. (They are to be seen in a glass case of the Whittall Pavilion next to the Coolidge Auditorium.) In the next year her enthusiasm produced two new money gifts, with the one on Constitution Day, September 17, causing Librarian Putnam to jot down a happy memo (quoted by McGuire): "Constitution Day: Leading events at the L.C.... Mrs. Whittall drops in with a check for $50,000 as an addition to her Endowment. God save the Constitution."

What needs to be added here is that her enthusiasm in 1936-7 was partly brought on by the Auslander appointment, though all Library personnel did not share the enthusiasm. Auslander went ahead for four years on the assumption that his tenure was permanent. He arranged for his wife, Audrey Wurtema, to be on the payroll as his secretary. He proposed all sorts of plans, including one for an annual series of poetry readings in the Coolidge. And he even went out on a lecture-bureau tour with Audrey, since she was a poet too and had even won a Pulitzer Prize. A flyer promoted their tour with their photo on top and with the information below that they were available to audiences for talks on four different subjects. Just one of those deserves mention here — "Poetry Comes of Age in America" — since the come-on for it reads (irritatingly for poets like R) "Let the Auslanders tell you the fascinating story of the Poetry Treasure House they are building in the Library of the Nation."

During all this activity Librarian Putnam retired and was replaced by Archibald MacLeish who soon schemed with Library officialdom to take Auslander's Chair away from him. This was done with bureaucratic wile by simply having him renamed the Library's "gift officer" and putting his treasure chest elsewhere in the Library. Soon MacLeish, laboring with Allen Tate, set up the Consultantship's role and tenure quite differently, their changes leading to the series of 26 poets who then served, from Tate himself forward to Gwendolyn Brooks in the 1980s.

The change proved to be also a change in the "mode" of poetry that the Consultantship was programmed to sell, since Auslander had been rather belligerently behind the poetic times, as R discovered many years later by reading an anthology he had edited and published (together with Frank Ernest Hill) in 1929. It was called *The Winged Horse Anthology* and was remarkable for simply not representing major Modernist figures such as Pound, Eliot, Stevens, Cummings, Williams and (of course) MacLeish himself. Not that any of these figures was ever to become the Consultant. The Auslander omissions were notable since they suggested where Auslander stood in relation to the poetry world that MacLeish and Tate lived with. When MacLeish was made the LC Librarian he had been busily modernist for years, and in 1939 had been satirized venomously by Edmund Wilson for being so, that is, for always being up-to-date, "A clean and clever lad/ who is doing/ his best/ to get on." Yet the promotional intent of Auslander's poetry tour may have troubled MacLeish and Tate more than his *Winged Horse Anthology.* Auslander was clearly playing salesman for the genre, and neither MacLeish nor Tate — though salesmen of sorts themselves — would have talked of a "treasure house." The mention of treasure-house poetry suggested treasures such as "the best loved poems of the American people." It suggested sweetness and light, plus of course the genteel pieties of *The Congressional Anthology.* MacLeish and Tate had been brought up with all the dissidence of 1920s modernism, so were looking for something tougher.

But they were hardly similar. MacLeish had been damning the social irresponsibility of American writers for some time. The first issue of *Furioso* in 1939, the year he became Consultant, opened with (if you remember) "My dear Mr. Angleton" in which MacLeish took off against most poetry magazines as "completely sterile" — poets were speaking to other poets, not "an audience of men like other men who understand the sun on the side of a wall, and the shadow in the shade of a tree, and the feel of things, and the thinking of things." In *The Irresponsible: A Declaration,* he argued that writers needed to become engaged. But at that time Tate was engaged about being disengaged and disagreed with MacLeish in the quarterlies in an essay "To Whom Is the Poet Responsible?" There he wrote the poet is responsible "to his conscience, in the French sense of the word: the joint action of knowledge and judgment." Yet it was MacLeish and Tate together who concocted the *non*-working, privately funded Consultantship. That non-federal funding gave the Poetry Consultant the right to be irresponsible in the way that Tate insisted a responsible poet sometimes had to be. In fact, he was full of engagement principles and as the first Consultant, he delighted in it. The poets who came after him took on their "responsibilities" in different ways.

R was younger than they but in editing *Furioso* while at college he had been supplied with the tastes of his elders. Aside from harkening to the work of MacLeish himself, and of the difficult Pound with his JOBBING plans, and of other poets who were not sweet, he had been much attracted by the satires of Dudley Fitts whose "Proletarian Poem" for instance would never have been found in the saddlebags of any winged horse. Here are its opening stanzas:

When Poppa came home from work Momma was waiting.
Momma was waiting. When Poppa came home from work
Momma said *Poppa I'm going to do it. — I wouldn't care if you
Did* said Poppa. Poppa was always forthright. When

Poppa came home from work Momma was gone. Momma
Was gone when Poppa came home from. Momma
Was *Where's Momma?* Poppa asked me politely.
Poppa was always the gentleman. *Where's Momma? —* I

Answered gently so as not to hurt his feelings. I
Answered. I said *Momma has taken the Ford and
Gone west. —* How often must I ask you
Poppa asked me *not to indulge yr taste for worn-*

Out euphemisms? Say "died."

To use a tiresome word R had been "conditioned" against genteel
poetic sweetness and light for twenty years or so before he found himself
in the Consultant's job at the Library. In his mind the sweetness-and-light
problem went far beyond poetry, touching on all the persistent demands
of a conformist culture. Yet at the LC in 1964-5 he happened to be stuck
with the poetry problem culturally, stuck with it as if he were supposed to
do something healthy and helpful about it. To be the Consultant — and
in the Congress's own Library — was like that.

Out of his year there came some Washington poems, among them
"Washington Interregnum," which *The Washington Post* first published
and then *The New York Times* took up again in 1984:

When politicos of the old life have departed,
Movers enter,
And painters
And sometimes fumigators,
To help get the new life started.

In the halls there are boxes and echoes.
There is rain on windows.
Inside windows,
Framed by taxpayers' marble,
An occasional lingering face in its lostness mellows.

Newcomers straggle up and down in the wet,
Waiting in elegant duds on alien corners,
Calling for taxis,
Searching out parties,
Questing for something obscure, unnamed, unmet.

The something decided not to attend the Ball,
Nor grace the Parade.
It failed to appear and perform in the grandstand charade
On the Hill.
Maybe it hides in an old box in a hall?

Maybe not. Anyway, there are offices, empty.
There is rain.
There is marble.
There is also the rust and ruin of parting pleasantry —
There is also the new paint, in all the empty.

So despite many cynical thoughts R had a fine time for a wonderful year! And when the year was over he and his family headed back to Minnesota with many more pleasant feelings than a serious responsible reformist should have. Yes, the whole family had liked Washington and was due to come back soon.

The Return East

In the 1960s the Whittemores' basic dog was Blackie, a cross between a golden retriever and a poodle. Blackie was large, strong and kind. He went on many trips with them — first in a Ford station wagon, then in a VW bus — but he was left behind with a neighborly Carleton family for the whole year of R's job at the Library. Early one summer morning after that year the returning VW groaned up Northfield's 2nd Street hill and passed just a block from the house where Blackie had been billeted, then continued down 2nd Street to Nevada Street where it turned left to the college house newly assigned to the Whittemores. The bus found its new home, several Whittemores opened its doors, and there was Blackie, now revealed as a genius, in the street wagging and dancing.

He was not a barking dog, and he only ran after birds and large cats. Neighbors — except cats — did not seem offended that he made regular unleashed rounds of his neighborhood. Yet soon after the W's had settled in on Nevada Street Blackie came home one morning after breakfast and lay down on the front stoop with a dog catcher's dart deep in the bone of his left thigh. It wouldn't come out. Dr. Rysgaard, the G.P. who had attended to the birth of the three children, was naturally called. He came. Pliers were needed but Blackie was saved — and of course went along on the second Washington trip.

The first year in Washington, or out of the Midwest, confirmed for R that it was time, long past due, for something else. He had been teaching since 1947 and, except for invitations to lecture at other colleges, summer school teaching in Minneapolis at the University of Minnesota, poetry workshops such as the one in Utah, and several months at the Agency in Washington in 1951, these years were all in Northfield. Still, what that something would be, he didn't yet know. First, there was the year in Carleton to fulfill, where he arrived in time to give the opening convocation — the talk, "Washington, Northfield, Government, Art, Freedom, Service, Etc.," was one he was to deliver, as he wrote in a footnote on its publication in *The Carleton Miscellany*, at San Francisco State College, Southwest Louisiana University, Emory and Henry College and Beloit College. In the same footnote, he promised that "with this publication I will let it rest." R opened his talk with a summary of his year as a poet bureaucrat, then got to the paradox of the artist-poet's position *in* government: on the one hand, the Poetry Consultant has obligations to the Library, a government institution; at the same time, an American poet — at least by modernist definition — could hardly be conceived of as a bureaucrat, when poets are supposed to be renegades from the system, any system. "The Consultantship is really a Washington freak," he said. "It's hard to be recognized as a poet at all if he is not an anarchist, verbally, intellectually, socially and — if a teacher — pedagogically. In some quarters he is expected to make a career of denying the going systems.... The poet — as collectively thought — is a rebel against old literary forms and old pieties, against patriots and prudes, against bourgeois sweetness and light and against bureaucratic darkness and red tape."

But the Kennedy Administration changed all that — art was suddenly *in* in Washington as were artists. "The bad boy of the culture, art, was suddenly put at the head of the class, though no mention at all was made of his being a bad boy." "One can argue," said R, "that to patronize art as the present government programs do is a way to avoid exploiting art." But appearances are not necessarily so.

> One gives the artist money or artistic opportunity or a pass to the White House lawn without demanding anything of him in return — hence no exploitation. But if the patron's commitment is not more than a commitment of money and facilities — that is, if there is no substantial intellectual or spiritual link between the patron and what he is patronizing, then the chances that the art will be exploited are great. Then the art can become as we all know merely a pretentious showcase for Veblen's leisure class, or, in the case of Washington, merely a show case for democracy, vague high mindedness, what-all.

R's (tentative) conclusion? *Service.* Though there may be a great danger of exploitation of artists who are asked to serve, "I see no way to avoid the

conclusion that an engaged artist, an involved artist, a serving, function-
ing artist is potentially the least exploited artist. He has been let in; he is
a member of, not just a performer for, his culture." Using his one year of
service as an example, R pointed to the brochure he wrote and signed for
the Park Service on the Jefferson Monument, his meetings at the
Department of Agriculture, which "was as ripe as the Park Service for, say,
a consultant in prose or a consultant in design," his meetings at NASA,
which already had an arts program. The big catch, he asked, was the
artists: were there enough to fill out the programs?

R ended his lecture with a long discursive ("meaning talky, meditative,
prosaic") poem, 140 lines or so that may have seemed even longer
because of the very long lines. The setting is an artists' colony in the New
Hampshire woods, where R had gone for several weeks at a time in recent
summers and where "the self gets pushed away in a little studio, all alone
in the woods, with nothing but a blank wall and a few birds and trees to
look at." The poem is a verse letter, "Dear God," and he placed it after
"Return, Alpheus: — another long-lined discursive poem, this one for
"the Literary Elders of Phi Beta Kappa" — a few years later in *Poems, New
and Selected*. There's one not inconsiderable difference between the version he read and the one he published.

> Though I know you're a bad correspondent I've decided to write you.
> (original)
>
> ....
>
> Though I don't believe in you,
> And though if I did I would believe you believed in the efficacy of letters,
> I've decided to write you. (*Poems, New and Selected*)

The poem is in part a self-conscious conversation about the artist going
off to a writers colony in the woods. His job, to be arty.

> Get away and get to it; write, paint, sculpt, create, create.
> And of course he does get to it, like mad. Who wouldn't? The woods are
>   lovely,
> Dark, deep, just dandy in every respect except that the life in them
> Becomes a kind of irrelevance or aside.
> The patient is well, perhaps even happy, but just barely breathing.
> He's art, all art, and his art is all art, and looks it.
> Sometimes, fed up, he thinks he'd be better off, though he wouldn't be,

If he set up shop in the middle of some city sidewalk.
At least he'd be looking at people, other people. The self gets tiresome,
As your son and a number of other religious leaders have pointed out.

R's theme, or one of them at least, is the artists' free ride out in the woods
— their job: "produce"

What if there had been no woods, no ready refuge
For our artists — if the chance for seclusion, separation, removal had never
  been dangled —
Then we wouldn't be stuck with our god-myth, our art would be different.
We'd be happily adjusted little social slaves busily creating
Lovely works of engagement (like a good slave should) rather than woods
  work.
....

               I look around me, and inside,
And am ashamed, mostly,
Not by country or freedom, not by Congressmen
(Them I'll put in a book),
But by the spectacle of the self, the pompous self,
The minuscule godlet strutting behind the wall,
And with unmitigated gall
Surviving, thriving, bragging, beating his chest, despite all.

While back at Carleton for the rest of the year, teaching, working on *The Miscellany*, traveling to other schools to give his "Washington, Northfield, Etc." talk, R was also looking for work back east.

In 1966, he and Helen became Washingtonians once more, this time for good, despite the lack of a permanent job. From the distance of decades the move away from tenure and so on seems daring; but aside from the attractions of big-city living to call them back there was a sound medical reason: son Jack's illness that he had from the time he was a baby. The medicos in Minneapolis had diagnosed his disease as cyclic neutropenia, a rarity that was under study at the National Institutes of Health in Washington. Jack was now seven and plagued with serious recurrent infections — though outwardly healthy between attacks, he would soon be a regular NIH patient. The neutropenia then seemingly vanished (it did not) and he was able to go to school and live and travel normally for many years. But suddenly some years later he was down with leukemia, and after many more hospital rooms and a blood marrow transplant Jack died, in 1997, age thirty-seven.

The second journey from Northfield — for which another moving van was needed — was hard on the family. Cate was beginning eighth grade, Ned fifth and Jack first. But at least they were able to rent a large old stucco house in Washington's Cleveland Park. There had been the possibility of a full-time job at Princeton, though that turned out to be just a one-semester turn as the first Bain-Swiggett lecturer for the spring semester.

R had only limited credentials for the kind of steady Washington position that at the time he favored, something truly Washingtonian, a job in a think tank. He had tried out that world in a 1966 weekend session in Williamsburg sponsored by the National Institute of Public Affairs (NIPA), a non-profit, but he hurt his lower back while diving into a motel swimming pool and had to depart for Minneapolis for what turned out to be a back operation. But his participation in the Williamsburg gathering made it possible for him to take a steady job with NIPA.

NIPA had been reconceived by a young political scientist from California, Carl Stover, a liberal with a respect for money. Originally chartered in 1934 to help bring college students into public service, the Institute became inactive when the U.S. Civil Service took this activity over. But Stover came in and attracted a goodly sum from the Ford Foundation to conduct a variety of education programs for government officials, public leaders and educators. He established headquarters in a sixth floor office on K Street just a block from Farragut Square, picking up a staff of perhaps half-a-dozen reformers on the loose like R. Their work was to help rescue all of America's cities, though Stover settled for concentrating on a mere eight. R had never thought about saving a city but was willing. His credentials were that he "wrote" and that he was "in" the Humanities. It seemed obvious that cities needed the Humanities since the cities needed everything. And as for what R stood for, what he did and what he knew, such matters could be put aside since help was help. So R was NIPA's Humanities man.

When later asked to name the eight cities then needing his talent, he mustered up four, Nashville, Seattle, Detroit and Washington. And when he actually sat in his comfortable small office looking north toward the Washington Cathedral R was in nearly the same predicament as he had been at the Library of Congress. That is, he had to think of things he might do, not just things but issues that he could fire himself up about, and *then* bring in grant money for support.

In the meantime he was putting together a massive historical/literary anthology of "urban affairs" demonstrating that, yes, most of the cities' troubles had been suffered by the world before the 20th Century. He moved the anthology very slowly from profound statements by ancient Assyrian kings right up to and through 19th century wisdom by Dickens, Engels, Henry James, Samuel Butler and others. He was a bit leery of entering, other than casually, the 20th century, but the omission was harmless. History's presence was being acknowledged and the Humanities were being kept alive between covers. There was just one hitch. His fine anthology couldn't find a publisher.

R had had several anthology ideas before and after that didn't find publishers as well. More than ten years earlier, for instance, he had found Elizabeth Abell at Ballantine Books encouraging enough for him to propose an anthology of protest literature. (Originally it was to be an anarchism anthology, though Protest, he wrote Abell, is "a milder and more useful literary center" than active politicking.) He included in this collection Thoreau's "On Civil Disobedience," Mark Twain's "Cooper's Literary Offenses" and selections from *The Innocents Abroad*, Melville's "Bartleby," James's "The Author of Beltraffio," Faulkner's "Red Leaves" and H.L. Mencken's "Democratic Man." These selections, he wrote in a preliminary preface, "have been chosen as intelligent and literate examples of unaggressive and even timid protestation. They have also been chosen," he added, "because I am a fairly timid protestant myself." Abell's encouragement went no further.

At least, schools and teaching were things R felt he knew about and certainly had definite opinions on, especially the way that English Departments had been managing to isolate themselves from American culture. In a letter to philosopher Peter Caws, for example, he wrote about a small attempt at a remedy in what turned out to be his last year at Carleton: "I have actually been experimenting with a psych teacher in what might be done to team-teach Rhetoric and Psych 10. Nothing has come of it yet other than an enormous journal I've been writing, plus an education for both of us. I am really quite impressed by the possibilities of getting teachers to learn a little." He had been focusing on such ideas for a while and in the fall of 1966, wrote a couple of proposals, one for high school teaching — in Montgomery County and D.C. he would employ college English majors and would introduce them, as future college teachers, to fundamental writing problems — and the second for revamping the teaching of English. In a letter to Carl Lang at the Central Atlantic Regional Education Laboratory, R wrote that he had just started work at NIPA and "among the projects to which I am now committed is a large one for setting up an institute in the Washington area dedicated to *innovation* in the teaching of English." Support came from a grant he wrote to the Carnegie Foundation.

In December, he wrote Caws that his aim was to "experimentally teach rhetoric in conjunction with other courses, like history, biology, etc."

> Such experiments have been approved, but we haven't so far found any teachers willing to go ahead. There are some other interesting possibilities floating around for expanding the dimensions of studies in a student's major field and thus, hopefully, breaking down a bit of the walls between departments.... What I have in mind is that the faults of the little magazines are akin to the faults of English Departments, and that a new principle for the teaching and promulgating of literature and good writing needs to be enunciated and backed. The principle isn't really new at all, but it's under the bushes these days, and one would have to fight the whole present establishment in our colleges and do a hell of a lot of teacher education to make the principle visible.

What is the principle, he asked rhetorically. "Is it that Literature can't be divorced from Life, which we all pay lip service to while, in the academies, constantly insisting upon the integrity of English department domains (in colleges and graduate schools) and, in the literary magazines, constantly insisting, in a similar way, upon the integrity and distinctiveness of Lit as opposed to journalism and what-all?" R then referred to a symposium he had run in *The Carleton Miscellany* on graduate training in the humanities. "In the broadest terms what I would like to see is a radical revision of what a department of literature, or a magazine of literature *is*."

At the moment [he wrote] I'm just nibbling around the edges with my proposal for interdisciplinary rhetoric courses, combination issues of little mags, etc. I think a good many writers share my feelings — I think immediately of Howard Nemerov and Karl Shapiro who are, like me, awfully fed up with English Depts., etc — but I think it will be very hard to get support from within the establishment. Even if an English teacher agrees in theory he is not anxious to trouble his life by obligating himself to be partially reeducated.

NIPA and these projects lasted only a few years — grant money vanished — though they could have been a model of sorts for carrying on with what is now repetitively known as the peace process. The high moment (if it can be called that) came during the sudden riots in April 1968 after the assassination of Martin Luther King, in most of the eight cities on NIPA's list, when a number of intelligent managerial participants directly involved in urban trouble came together, and managed to upset a little managerial officiousness. Also it educated the NIPA staff, especially the educationist himself. As for kind Carl Stover he retired, eventually, to College Park where he and R still have lunch every two weeks.

During that fall, R had been invited by the National Council of the Teachers of English to their convention in Houston — he was to be one of a dozen poets of "different ages and various dispensations" (as he later wrote) in a "Festival of Contemporary Poetry." The others included Robert Bly, Robert Creeley, Robert Duncan, Donald Hall, Galway Kinnell, Carolyn Kizer, W.S. Merwin, Josephine Miles, Gary Snyder, May Swenson and William Stafford. R and Bill Stafford had gotten to know each other in 1960 when they shared a platform in New York at the YMHA Poetry Center. (A couple of years later R was one of the judges who selected Stafford's *Traveling through the Dark* for the National Book Award.) The festival was to be a well-orchestrated affair for NCTE members, mostly public school teachers, that included a program of simultaneous readings by the ingathered poets. The opening sentences of Bill Stafford's article on the festival, "A Poetry Happening," for NCTE's *English Journal* only hints at the fireworks that got the festival going

> Robert Bly, it was, who lunged from his place in the front row among the dozen gathered poets, turned to the NCTE audience, and — quite expectedly — blew the top off.

Expectedly, that is, in the sense that everyone wanted actions, when current poets confronted teachers of poetry; but no one had planned what the reactions would be. As if one could, with such a group!

Richard Eberhart as main convener and speaker for current American poets had just finished his opening lecture on academic and non-academic poets.... The general drift had been that poetry draws on the wellsprings of life and that we should all accommodate to various kinds of poetry, and be happy to bring students into such a rich heritage.

"Not at all!" — from the front row. And — alive and kicking — the assembled ingredients went critical. Robert Bly did not accept easily some kinds of poetry. Further, he contended that poets and all others present should never blur immediate first issues that their society faced — namely, for the American people, the war in Viet Nam.

It was not the usual Convention session that followed. Once it was evident that audience and speakers matched each other in eagerness to have real encounters — the meeting swept forward to a new phase, ending with interchange among members of the audience and then a succession of sample readings from the poets. And that pattern kept on for the two days of the poetry festival, as the poets improvised a system whereby they delivered their individual readings and then converged for group readings and discussion. Teachers experienced immediate interaction with writers and underwent many kinds of readings, including the free-speech variety. And the writers enjoyed some of the liveliest and readiest audience interchanges they had ever met.

R referred to this gathering in "Poetry and the Skinner Box," a public lecture he gave soon afterwards. For him, and for the other poets, it was a significant one in which they broke out of that box as R called it where they were expected to perform as it was set up.

Some of us rose to complain about the Eberhart speech. He had maligned the sternness and integrity of poetry, we said, making it a namby-pamby all-around good thing like Wheaties and democracy. And others of us rose shouting to say that we should each be allowed to read an introductory poem to the big audience before being shipped off to smaller rooms. We were eloquent and loud. The teachers were fascinated. In half an hour our dozen, with Eberhart concurring, had formed a team to fight the Establishment.

We reorganized our own program. Then we performed in gangs for the rest of the day. We not only read poems but also talked and talked about Vietnam and dirty words and teaching...it was a breath of fresh air. English-teacher meetings are not known for their fresh air.

Though R had his disagreements with the Beats, it was they he acknowledged who had taken poetry out of its private place. "The revolution that took place [began] with Ginsberg's "Howl" at its center.... It left us with engaged poets preaching disengagement, poets with an audience, with public-speaking obligations, shouting down the public." Though the affair during those two days changed things forever, wrote R, still from his perspective it "was mixed with doubt...the uneasiness of preaching the virtues of self and the spontaneous, free shopping life, while remembering urgently the hell of self, and the hell of always asserting the self, which has been the poet's special hell in our time.... I am upset as much as pleased by Houston. I still don't know what to make of it."

In 1965 Lyndon Johnson ordered 50,000 more troops to Vietnam — monthly draft calls were increasing from 17,000 to 35,000. By 1966, 385,000 troops were there; at its peak, more than 535,000. Opposition to the war had begun inflaming campuses. In Washington, R was on the planning committee of Artists of Conscience, a group that had loosely allied itself with a national organization to gather manifestoes by artists opposing the war and to set up performances to support that opposition. R set about compiling lists of writers who he sent the manifesto to for their signature.

ARTISTS OF CONSCIENCE

I join the Artists of Conscience by subscribing to the following statement: We are opposed on moral grounds to the United States involvement in the Vietnam War.

I give Artists of Conscience permission to use my name in efforts to enlist other artists.

I understand that Artists of Conscience plan to publish the above statement with the list of signers in as many large newspapers throughout the country as possible.

I understand that Artists of Conscience plan to dedicate a week of concerts, poetry readings, drama and exhibitions to the above cause, the events to take place in the nation's capital beginning mid June for about one week.

Signed _____

Enclosed is $ _____ to help Arts of Conscience in the above listed endeavors.

In his accompanying note, he included a shorter statement that, as he said, some had signed rather than the longer one.

> We whose names appear below are opposed on moral grounds to U.S. involvement in the Vietnam War. We will support our administration only in effective measures to insure the stopping of bloodshed. On the issue of this war we discover daily that we are no longer represented by the government we helped elect.

Call that statement "B." If you want to sign, but prefer "B," simply indicate your preference for "B" on the form and return.

While he had his own list of poets, he wrote others asking for names and addresses. Robert Bly replied, "the danger of your idea is that it could become just a pale parade of celebrities across the stage — or a parade of pale celebrities — each with a couple of well-chosen words the audience has heard 1000 times before." Saying that, Bly offered his help.

Some poets like William Stafford signed on whole-heartedly, others wrote that they wouldn't or couldn't. "There can't be such a person as an artist-for-peace," Allen Tate replied. "There can be citizens for peace: I would sign that kind of manifesto...or to put it differently: As a citizen I am against the war; as an artist I am neither for nor against." Another wrote that he could not sign, though wishing the U.S. "could show more imagination about peace talks," then adding, "demonstrations and protests of minorities like yours create an impression of weakness or indecision in the pursuit of a policy that I believe represents the conscience of a great majority of Americans." Among the writers "who have signed on," R wrote Archibald McLeish in trying to get his signature, "are the following: Richard Wilbur, Louis Untermeyer, Robert Bly, Robert Duncan, Robert Creeley, Bink Noll, Louis Simpson, Louise Bogan, Donald Hall, Brendan Gill, Kay Boyle, William Stafford, William Jay Smith, Barbara Howes, Charles Bell and Louis Coxe." Duncan, who had been at the Houston Festival wrote R, "It does seem to me that a Washington, D.C., declaration-demonstration of conscience — will be — a demonstration of the honor of American poets."

Artists of Conscience was planning a weeklong program dedicated to dissent that was to include concerts, poetry readings, plays, film, dance performances, art exhibits, as well as the improvisational "happenings" that the 60s gave rise to. The *Post* article, written by Carl Bernstein, before he became the second half of Woodward, pointed out that the organizers were working with New Yorkers who had organized the Angry Arts Festival the previous month. Edward de Grazia, a Washington lawyer, was one of the spokesmen — Bernstein quoted him on the seven-day event as "an answer to the feeling that artists in this country have virtually no political power.... The protest is a chance for artists to make themselves heard."

Whether this national protest came about as it was planned R no longer remembers, nor has a friend who searched back issues of *The Washington Post* found any reference to one. What she did find was an advertisement sponsored by Artists of Conscience for a special reading by Norman Mailer, Paul Goodman, Robert Lowell, and Dwight Macdonald a couple of nights before a march on the Pentagon, October 21st. The big headlines in Washington and New York were Mailer's arrest. In *The New York Times*, James Reston wrote afterwards, "this was a sad and brooding city tonight because everybody seemed to have lost in the anti-war siege of the Pentagon this weekend." But Reston's so-called "objectivitiy" is another story — while Artists of Conscience preoccupied R's activist self, it was small stuff in the anti-war movement.

R would continue to be engaged in activities against the war, though now he still had to contend with making a living. With the NIPA position at an end, that fall he returned to teaching, this time as an English Professor at the University of Maryland. He was there just in time to participate in new colleague and poet Rod Jellema's Poetry and the National Conscience conferences, the first of three annual gatherings of poets who met in panels to speak their thoughts about poetry and political engagement and to read their poems. The conferences drew hundreds each spring.

Meanwhile, R had two books come out in 1967, *From Zero to the Absolute* and *Poems New and Selected*. The first was largely made up of lectures on modern poetry that he gave at Beloit in 1966 as well as a number of other essays, including his Library of Congress lecture, "Ways of Misunderstanding Poetry," "Poetry and the Skinner Box," the Bain-Swiggett lecture, and others, among them, "Graduate Training in English, Yet," an address to teachers of English at the Modern Language Association, a

The editors of the long-gone Furioso *got together in 1966 for a reunion in Washington at the house of Bob and Barbara Gale. Standing: Ambrose Gordon, James Angleton, Howard Nemerov and Bill Johnson; kneeling: John Pauker and R.*

Advertisement for Anti-Vietnam War program in The Washington Post, *1967. (Robert Lowell's name was misspelled.)*

talk that caused an uproar among the attending teachers. In effect, R had argued that graduate training was largely a scholastic, i.e., a medieval, enterprise. "I am just saying in loud, arrogant tones to anyone in authority or near authority in our graduate schools: Move." Were he in charge, he would issue a number of memoranda if, that is, he was charge and believed in memoranda. Regardless, here are the subjects of a few of R's proposed memoranda.

> You are directed to conduct a search for the art of persuasion or effective speech, and bring it back alive.

> You are directed to arrange a collective research project into the languages of various social groups, notably sociologists, journalists, administrators, and college sophomores. And report back. Also, you are directed to begin a course or two in the study and correlation of terms in different academic departments. For example, I would like to know the difference between a romantic and a neurotic. Please throw in a few theses on these problems as you go along.

> You are directed to arrange for at least a quarter of your candidates for the doctorate in English to conduct a team research project with fellow graduate students in one of the behavioral sciences.

> You are directed to arrange for every graduate student in English to serve as apprentice, for a short period, to an elementary school teacher and to a high school teacher, as well as to cope with the usual freshmen.

Reflecting some years later on his views of this time, R felt his "relationship to the literary community was a dangerous one."

> Serving on literary committees and writing magazine pieces, I began to look like an enemy of all that confused dissidence to which the literary community was committed, or like the unqualified enemy of self-expression, or perhaps like the unqualified enemy of just forgetting social affairs. I wasn't an enemy of that magnitude, but I was certainly becoming an enemy of the inward, isolate, Neapolitan-balcony excesses of the poetry being published around me, so much so that I even wrote a piece that [Allen] Tate himself delighted in refuting.... It was called "The Poet in the Bank" and made reference to T.S. Eliot's early position in a London bank,

one that Pound started, a one-man fund-raising campaign just to spring him from. In it I said that a bank might even be good for a poet, which aside from being heresy, was almost as bad as saying that Washington might be good for a poet. And I believed what I said, mostly.

Meanwhile, R's *Poems, New and Selected* included discursive poems that derived from the summer residencies at the McDowell Colony in New Hampshire, among them, "Dear God," "Seven Days," "The Departure," "Return, Alpheus" and the first appearance of his Shaggy poems. They were another try at a serio-comedic voice. He referred to them, maybe not satisfactorily, in "Poetry and the Skinner Box," in relation to anti-war poetry: "everything he can think of saying about Vietnam has already been said about it, but said in ordinary English.... The manner of such statements is crucial to poets; it has to be right somehow, fitting the current demands of medium, universe and audience; and yet it has also to be special, something never before heard." Here's "Sad Postscript Shaggy," the sixth of "Six Shaggy," which has this epigraph: "The thought of 'those American boys' being labeled war criminals, he [President Johnson] said, was 'deplorable and repulsive.' — News Item."

Once upon what time would loyal U.S.A. boy
Be Commie?
If boy said loyal bomb kill "peaceful citizen,"
That's when.
And if that muddle youth shd madly add then (oh fie)
That him who drop bomb crime done did, that lie
Would die
For no one else to speak it but Hanoi.

Rule 1: all U.S. soldier: boy.
Rule 2: no boy Hanoi.

But are we Red Cross knights not mucky lucky
That rules is side of always our boys plucky?
And labels like such "criminal" the thought yet
So righteous we that never have we thunk *nyet*?
For hearkened we to speakspooks we might find
Our bomber boys did but as Dad opined.
Come label then, cd Dad be far behind?

R kept at his Shaggies and had a run with them in late 1979 and early 1980, when *The Washington Post* printed one each week in its Sunday *Outlook* section.

Years before, Thom Gunn wrote of R as one of the country's "funniest living poets," a characterization that had stuck, though R had written Howard Nemerov at the time that Gunn managed to say it "in a way that has made me feel uncomplimented." Writing about the *New and Selected* in *Poetry*, Michael Benedickt may have had Gunn's label in mind when he wrote, "there is nothing particularly hilarious about the poetry of Reed Whittemore" and went on to clarify himself: "One might have grown suspicious about the critical truism about Whittemore's funniness from the phenomenon that though most of those who have written about him think Whittemore is best characterized by mirthfulness, almost nobody accuses him of writing light verse." Was R then a poet of "spiritual misery," as Benedikt claimed? "The particular kind of spiritual misery engaged in his work has to do with the utter emptiness of all the realities — but especially the American reality — around him."

<hr/>

For all the Whittemores the NIPA job had helped establish a permanent Washingtonian base — and their rented house in Cleveland Park proved to be a good place for making Washington connections. Across the street, for instance, lived the Washington Cathedral's Bishop Paul Moore and family. Next door lived Richard Dudman, Washington correspondent for the *St. Louis Dispatch* and his wife Helen, manager of a Washington radio station. A half block away lived Gilbert Harrison, who owned *The New Republic*. So the Whittemores were now effectively in residence and, sure enough, R's next job, one that overlapped his teaching at the University of Maryland, was suddenly as *The New Republic's* literary editor.

Years earlier Harrison had read and admired R's essay on Churchill in *The Yale Review* when R complained about the myths that great leaders construct for themselves. The previous *TNR* book editor, Richard Gilman, had run the back pages from New York, but had written few reviews himself. Harrison must have had mixed feelings about an anti-New York neighbor doing the review work and writing reams of the pages, usually dissenting reams; but as far as R was concerned Harrison remained one of the great hands-off editors in history. He did not complain, he relied on R to do all the day-to-day back-pages editing, and he didn't even seem to mind when R wrote learnedly about matters, such as the New York Stock Exchange, he thankfully knew little of. Only once did Harrison mention (very mildly) that he thought perhaps sometimes R could be just a little bit more complimentary to all those poor bastards he kept reviewing.

A fine job it was. R's office was quieter than most libraries, and it had no checkout desk. In its quietude R once even wrote a piece describing the career of a review copy — how it entered in a mailman's hands, was received and opened by excellent secretary Dianne, and placed by Dianne on the right upper corner of R's large desk; and how then it was flipped through by R who made important mental notes about who might review it before assigning it, rejecting it as impossible, or putting it on the lowest shelf (possibles) on the Great Wall. After a decorous period of waiting, the possibles became less possible and were moved to the middle (neutral) shelf until they became impossibles and were jumped up to the highest shelf. When the highest shelf became full, a message was sent forth — by Dianne — for proles to come and remove the impossibles so that they could be given to all sorts of worthy organizations.

So at the age of 50 R became an experienced critic of academic people who were not on his side. They were the ones over in the social sciences who would talk and talk about the Quality of Life and how to improve it. R could bristle about them day and night, and one of his early reviews, "A Prejudiced View of the Social Sciences," was of a model social-science volume. A committee of course wrote it. Or, rather, two committees. The committees were the Committee on Science and Public Policy of the National Academy of Sciences, plus the Committee on Problems and Public Policy of the Social Science Research Council. If R had had all his wits about him as he reviewed the volume he might have mentioned that the book had not been written at all in the ordinary sense of "written" but had been moved into print by sheer administrative force. He was at least able to pan it thoroughly, being particularly annoyed by the "authors'" plans to develop a "giant" quality-of-life "indicator" comparable to the measuring of economic values in dollars. It now seems clear that even in innocent middle age R — though not a religious man — knew just where the devil was hiding: in a social science, perception-management committee.

> We can already measure economic values in dollars, the committee
> tells us, but "there is no corresponding unit of value to measure the qual-
> ity of life." Well gosh all hemlock, let's get one. First, we will need a
> "national data system" and then we will need a new federal agency to pro-
> tect us from the national data system. Then we will have to expand the
> amount of social science research, and then we will need new schools to
> be called graduate schools of applied behavioral science. All these needs
> will be hard to satisfy, but, gosh, the social sciences "are our best hope, in
> the long run, for understanding our problems in depth and providing
> new means of lessening tensions and improving our common life."

During R's reading of this committee volume he also found a single
sentence that stirred him to the bone. The remark was as neutral as a
brainless committee could make it but the sense was not. The sense was
that studies of human behavior had at last become serious, so that they
now put earlier studies — such as Shakespeare's perhaps? — in the shade.
R didn't need to know anything about the studies proposed to be indignant (ignorant people are like that), but his clever editorial reaction was
to review (and pan) an equally annoying volume by a sour old English
teacher. Now there was balance.

He enjoyed the *TNR* job. Back in the 50s, R had written numbers of
articles for the magazine which he thought had been "useful" to him, he
wrote Howard Nemerov at the time. "The obligation not to be alienated
like a good poet but committed to the world's affairs has helped me to an
awareness of my own (alien) vacuums pretty fast. I don't think it's a matter of being political, but merely of being involved." Meanwhile editor R
wrote a great deal about poetry and poets — for instance, Kenneth Koch
("I like Koch but don't like the nonsense world that much of his poetry
edges toward"), New York Poets, Charles Olson, Allen Ginsberg's *Indian
Journals*, Mayakovsky, Ho Chi Minh ("What I fear is that 500,000
American high-cloud addicts will dutifully read Ho and like it, and then
solemnly think to themselves that after all Ho was only writing the sort
of thing Robert Frost might have written if he had been in prison. The
next thought to that is, 'What's wrong with us? Why is it that we cannot
have poets who are political leaders?' "), and the old guard: Eliot, Pound,
Cummings, Auden. But he also wrote about The Beatles ("In the still heart
of most of the lyrics the deep truth is revealed. Hell of a way to run a revolution.") and Cole Porter and took on books covering a range of cultural

issues that he later gathered in *The Poet as Journalist: Life at the New Republic* under "The Kulch": Black Studies, the Gallup Poll, Charles Lindberg, the problems of English departments, and of course — what had become his bête noir — the social sciences.

———

In 1968 R began to experience double vision and droopy eyelids — that was followed by muscular weakness in his hands and feet, then lung trouble. It added up to no-see, then no-write, then no-walk, then no-breathe: a thorough no-can-do syndrome. He was spread too thin and everything was becoming too much, financially, parentally, professionally. He was diagnosed as having myasthenia gravis that soon had him going to hospitals and trying futile experiments. His family and friends began to gather around him; his friend John Pauker wrote of that time in the issue of Bill Claire's *Voyages* featuring R, in 1972.

> R sick, and his illness dreadfully complicated by bronchial pneumonia. R, knowing that his recovery from the pneumonia would only restore him to the certainty of the earlier and irreversible illness. R, uncertain whether to live or die.
>
> At the moment of extremity in that tranquil autumn of 1969 I stood at the side of R's hospital bed, and clutched his hand, and wept hot tears upon his forearm, and urged him to want to live. At the other side of the bed stood the Devil, who whispered that it was no use, and that R should want to die. But God was with me at my side of the bed, and it was two to one, and R decided to live.
>
> ....
>
> Eugene McCarthy came. It was R's 50th birthday. In the cubicular lounge where Helen and her sister Ruth and Shoo Shoo [Pauker's wife] and I were peacefully tippling and relishing Shoo Shoo's homebaked tassies, the Senator sipped champagne from a paper cup and relished a tassie. Then he entered R's room, exclaiming:
>
> "We poets are tough, aren't we?"

Recovering from the pneumonia, he was blessed by an unexpected cure not for pneumonia but for the myasthenia gravis by the common hormone drug prednisone, which he still takes today. He emerged nearly whole but there were scars and they showed up in his poetry. Thus he was led away from the platform poems that the Washington experience, let alone his mock-epics, had encouraged. The long-term effect of the disease was to drive him back toward quieter, more introspective poems, such as "Inventory."

> To pass through the season of loss and emerge with a good suit
> Is to thank God
> And take inventory.
>
> The season of waiting is slow.
> The clouds hang listlessly.
>
> Where the path bends into the woods
> From the meadow
> The light is a half light,
> And one looks to the north to the hills,
> Which are blue.
> I will carry the meadow view
> Back to the city.
>
> But the woods are close.
> They crowd in officiously,
> Shutting the heavens out.
> One sits in the sullenness
> With spiders.
>
> I think that before I die I would like to live
> In my good suit
> In the meadow.

Because the myasthenia gravis had so incapacitated R and made it difficult to sit at a desk, Harrison kindly invented a new, softer, supplementary job for him, one to be handled while his mind was not in gear and he had nothing to do except watch television druggily from a hospital bed. At such moments he became the *TNR's* TV reviewer, Sedulus — constant, steady, persevering like a sedulous bee. Thus he wrote wildly in praise of old Mack Sennett comedies and even took on advertisers. Being Sedulus was much better than pills. Here is an excerpt from one of his weekly columns, this one called "Equal Brainwash Time."

> My favorite ad at the moment, for a dry-skin remedy, brings us a scholarly bespectacled geezer who takes a medical book from a five-foot shelf, sits

down at a dignified desk, recites a gentle melodious patter about both ailment and remedy (with no claims for it at all), and then launches into his key testimonial line: "X provides ephemeral relief in mild cases."

EPHEMERAL RELIEF IN MILD CASES! It could be said of dirty crankcase oil. I am reminded of P.T. Barnum's come-on under the big tent: This Way to the Egress. Ain't no court gonna find fraud here. Heavens to Betsy, some of this selling is even truthful — except that it comes at us ten times an hour. With none of it are we to be persuaded even by bad argument. We simply slowly drown in product awareness.

And here is one other:

Remember the bloated capitalist of socialist cartoons? He had knife and fork in hand, and his napkin was tied around his neck. The world and its people were spread before him on his groaning table, and he was busy, busy a-gobbling. Well, nowhere has that caricature been more truly brought to life than in TV sports. I'm fifty and have kept my cool watching the selling of individual souls to Absorbine Jr., Wheaties and the like for most of that time, but the new TV sell-scene is getting to me. The big boys are buying and selling whole games, whole sports in wholesale lots, bringing everything except maybe checkers into their sleazy, pyramidal, holding-company syndrome. I guess I'm a bad sport, for I find it unsporting.

So there was R in his early fifties. He would live for another several decades, only to discover that the bloated capitalist of cartoons, though still exceedingly present, slowly lost caricature time in the newspapers. He became a *nice* bloated capitalist and even expanded his bloat to include the writing game. R didn't try to keep up with such matters but he couldn't escape what came in the mail, such as a bloated pamphlet called *Literary Horizons* published in New York by what he had supposed to be a respectable outfit, one even with roots back in R's little magazine association. It was called "Poets and Writers," and in it the writing horizon was crammed with a glorious sunrise for a smart entrepreneurial Writer who took the right seminars (information available by writing *Literary Horizons*). These would help him/her pitch his/her verse or novel or "creative nonfiction manuscript" properly and make a pile. What did he/she want to know about what editors want? Where could he/she find an agent? What was the "key" to "successful publishing"? All such questions were to be answered in the seminars (or on tape). Perhaps the most per-suasively infuriating paragraph in the brochure was headed "Writer Beware" and began, "There's a con in any game." For pete's sake. If the old *Furioso* manifesto (1948) against New York publishing could have been brought up to date and given a supplement, it would have included a sec-tion on cons like this at the heart of the trade.

All in all this kind of creeping insistence on writing as a money pro-fession kept driving him back on his amateur status. Call it his socialism. A money cynic might say that he had that status anyway since he had no talent for writing anything saleable. But whether he was talented or not his notion of a writing career had never been really separable from some-thing low-paid — like teaching — that simply provided a steady living. Wasn't that wish serious? Whether it was or was not it did lead to a kind of writing that — in prose or poetry — took on social jobs. And for that kind the work at *The New Republic* under Gil Harrison was just right. Accordingly, in his four years at *TNR* R at least wrote, among much else, a number of fairly ferocious poems not designed to win favor among the money professionals. Two actually appeared in *TNR*, with one simply called "Money" that mostly recommended moving that substance away from the money people, and the other, "Ode to New York," that seemed to recommend simply removing New York — by way of example, here's the beginning and conclusion.

> Let me not be unfair Lord to New York that sink that sewer
> Where the best the worst and the middle
> Of our land and all others go in their days of hope to be made over
> Into granite careerists
> Let me not be unfair to that town whose residents
> Not content to subside in their own stench
> Drag down the heavens let me not be unfair because I have known
> An incorruptible New Yorker (he was a saint)
> Also NY has produced at least three books
> Two plays
> A dozen fine dresses meals shirts taxidrivers
> Not to mention Jack (Steve?) Brodie
> And Mayor LaGuardia why should it matter
> That the rest is garbage?
> ....

Oh New York let me be fair you hell town
I was born to the north of you have lived to the west of you
I have sneaked up on you by land air and sea and been robbed
     in your clip joints
I have left you hundreds of times in the dreams that I *could*
Leave you
        but always you sit there
Sinking
        my dearest my sweet
Would you buy these woids?

Then there was a third poem, "Let it Blow" that appeared in — of all
places — *The New Yorker*.

Let it blow, said the union of amalgamated winds,
And let it drip, said the cloud trust.
Where is there an end to it,
The self-interest?
Whither my feet takest me I find lobbying,
Invented by Joseph Lobby,
Who wrote a non-partisan editorial in behalf of his own candidacy for alder
    man in a tiny New England slum housing development in 1802.

Now each purple mountain majesty requires a private sunrise.
We pass individually unto grace, cutting each other on the thruway,
Singing the brotherhood of one.

Let it blow.
Let the assorted selves drop leaflets against litter,
Picket the morning.

Who will volunteer to park in a bus stop?
Foul the word supply?

The right of the people to keep and bear arms shall not be infringed
Nor other rights of the righteous
So that the pharmaceutical firms may suck forever
On the inner heart of our headache.

How can a nation of smart cookies be so dumb?
Did Jefferson do it? Hamilton? Thoreau maybe?

I look into the kindly eyes of my anarchist soul mate,
She (he) dreaming of a Greek isle with her (his) American Express card,
She (he) wanting 400 hp and a water bed
    (and a mountain, a guru, and an independent income).
Not an institution in this country is not betrayed by its souls in residence.

Who is left to pull the weeds from the Xerox machine?
Where will we find the manpower to carry this week's privateering to the
    town dump?

Let it blow,
And let the associations for the preservation of freedoms publish the
    unexpurgated results
At a profit.

A hint of R's liking for socially-responsible journalism as a literary way of life can be seen in the book title, *The Poet as Journalist: Life at The New Republic.* The New Republic Book Company took it on after his four-year tour there, with the title properly suggesting that R was an outsider to journalism who just happened to drop in. For better or worse R liked such a role. It was a fine antidote to the casualness of little quarterlies, since it was basically relentless in its weekly discipline, differing from any other writing-editing role he had ever played. He even

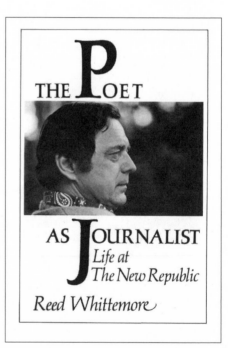

liked it as a teacher, and not having a PhD helped here. A psychiatrist with capitalistic views might well have advised him he had somehow achieved some sort of lifelong blockage that kept him from making serious (there's that word again) commitments — perhaps because he had once fallen off the wicked tricycle of his childhood. But R had a different theory and would have been happy to give the psychiatrist an early essay of his to read, "The Alienated Poet Insists," in which he "proved" (the word might be too strong) that the commitments involved in becoming a writing professional in modern America were deadly for a writer with *JOBBING* commitments like his. He had to stay away from all that, remain an outsider.

⸺

A quick look back. In 1969, while R was teaching at Maryland, Carleton invited him to give the Ward Lucas lectures, the now-annual series of college-wide talks that Karl Shapiro had inaugurated in 1963. For R it was an opportunity to look at modern poetry, his own work, and American social science.

In the first lecture he began with Erasmus, not a poet, but "a very early Humanities man, a man of letters among priests, but himself not a priest. He lived with and loathed clerical fanaticism, Catholic and Protestant. I think we prize his memory," R said, "chiefly because he was one of the great prizers of intellectual independence. As a thinker he insisted on being a loner." He then went on to include T.S. Eliot as another example of a loner, one who had "a basic preliminary mission in life escaping or at least getting beyond orthodoxy." The subject was one R felt close to. Despite his tenure in English departments — at Carleton and now at Maryland — he still saw himself as a loner: "if the poet's obligation is to see and report the world and himself with an unpropagandized eye," then said he from his podium, "one has to stand apart from it."

The days are gone when it was easy to imagine heading out for the territory and starting over, like Huck Finn (another great loner). The territory has long been occupied physically by the forces of orthodoxy, and the physical occupation has certainly contributed to our sense of spiritual occupation. If even the wild west physically is occupied by General Motors, the behaviorists and Huck Finn's aunt, we can't hope for great intellectual independence when we get there. Free enterprise used to be part of the physical side of the self-made man myth, and in a frontier economy a money man could believe in free enterprise and not be a dreamer. Not any more. The mental frontier life has closed down too.

Or so my poems keep discovering.

Speaking of his early poems, R said he worked in terms of the great American myth of the self-made man, a myth that has been recognized as simply that, myth. He then went on to reflect on how his work had developed over 25 years. "I'd say my poetry has been largely a matter of heading out for the territory and finding it doesn't exist. In one long poem I create a sort of composite self-made man busy making it in his own territory so that he can, as he must, find that he has no territory. In another I have a poet playing at being god, and busy creating the world in seven days just as god did — only to discover that god has already pretty much preempted possibility for the poet — the world is already there."

> I am complaining about the myth, saying there are no gods or self-made men among men; but I am also finding a bit of the delusion in myself, and trying to instruct myself against it, create myself smaller than my own romantic dreams....
>
> I prize my freedom and I would like to wrest it from orthodoxy and the behaviorists; but I've discovered a close limit to what I can wrest. In the long identity-creating process that poetry is, and that began with me in prep school, I discovered that I was not a wild Russian anarchist after all. It was Erasmus for me. And Eliot.

R had reached the august age of 50 when the University of Minnesota Press brought out *Fifty Poems Fifty*, mostly reflective poems, some of which derived from his bout with myasthenia gravis, several with children — "The Girl in the Next Room," "Why Do the Children Shout," "The Chair" — some with aging and decline. First, "The Chair."

> So the baby chair overturned on the soft carpet,
> And the baby herself, who had felled it, said it Fall Down.,
> Yes, yes, said I, Fall Down; and Boom, said she,
> Happily, giving our loved a bone.
>
> I sat reading the paper.
> She tiptoed off to the kitchen to implement Boom.
> When she returned she was hitched.
>   There was the story,
> And picture too: baby and groom.
>
> I put down the paper.
> I righted the chair.
> Dearest baby, wrote I in the wax weave of the carpet,
> Why did you give your dada the air?

In "The Mind" R was getting at his own:

The mind wears many hats, many different wares.
Like a bird on a spit it turns in its living sleep.
It is quick, slow, open, secret, crammed with jokes, prayers.
It knows not what it knows deep.

Yet I have known one kind of mind whose vision
Is steady as the sphinx's, and whose mold
Is rock against all sea and salt and season.
Such a mind, soul, have the old.

They traffic in fixities; they sit in corners sipping.
In the sharp declivities of the times they save their breath.
They are more put out by a misplaced tool or letter
Than birth or death.

And when they talk they talk to themselves; their rhetoric
Wanders off into privacies where a word
Cares not who hears it, and eloquence
Is a canard.

I know a mind, soul, whose time now leads it
Shoreward to silence.
Not long ago it chattered like half a school,
And bade the desert dance.

~

The 70s had barely begun and several awards landed, first from the National Council on the Arts for R's "lifelong contribution to American letters," then an Award of Merit from the American Academy of Arts and Letters. Meanwhile, Carleton College called him back the year after his Ward Lucas lectures to honorarily welcome him into the academic club as a Doctor of Letters. Former Carleton President Larry Gould, who was then at the University of Arizona, returned to help convey the honors. Thus Gould to the assembled seemed to summarize R, perhaps with editorial assistance from Wayne Carver, one of his co-editors, and then editor, of *The Carleton Miscellany*: "a poet who does not trust poetry, a professor who does not trust professors, a former chairman of the English Department who is down on English departments, a man of public affairs who suspects public affairs are the devil's handiwork, an organizer and mover who knows that life flows best between the walls of organizations and movements, a teacher and friend to students who would no more have them following at his heels than he would follow at theirs." And Gould concluded, "R has hammered from the tensions of his life both a literary life and life style that melds the music of driftwood with the lean dry agonies of skepticism. In his shortest poem, R says: 'It is not clear where we go from here,/Or, for that matter, who we're.'"

Poet as Biographer

The University of Maryland is a vast institution inhabited by more than 57 varieties of specialists, and in such a world even the announced role of the interdisciplinarian could have intellectual dangers, especially in the social sciences. Yet Maryland was kindly to R as an oddity, even neglecting to ask him to teach Creative Writing. That now-professional subject had not yet surfaced as a big entrepreneurial dream for English departments, so he was able to continue teaching traditional literary courses up to 1985, while advising a few graduate students, keeping office hours, and maintaining his anarchist gospel by helping to start a faculty union.

Naturally he found the word "union" unpopular with campus officialdom, though the same distaste of many colleagues surprised him. Still, most Maryland teachers were willing to contemplate, if casually, the possibility of their having a voice of their own in campus matters. He and a few other dangerous radicals founded a faculty coalition that had as its aims a greater voice in governance, better salaries and guaranteed pensions, the protection of tenure and not least of all academic freedom. R was one of the organizers of what became Maryland's Faculty Guild — and from this came (eventually) a regular paper, *The Faculty Voice*. A few faculty meetings were held in that time that were actually run by faculty members. As a result R even felt, occasionally, that the high managerial set was stuttering a little. A sense of not very threatening solidarity seemed to be growing amidst the university's not seriously oppressed proletariat.

But then his hopes diminished. He found that the managerial lords were more persistent than the workers, and the workers were spread out among many discrete departments. Worse, the workers could only find time for solidarity on odd Tuesdays. Soon their cause was not so much lost as forgotten, and R's amateurish hopes for the rise of downtrodden academics faded away. He had discovered that faculty folk, poor fools, didn't even think of themselves as oppressed. Worse still, they were right.

So *The Faculty Voice* was soon replaced by an official monthly run by the Alumni Office, and even a minor experiment by R in changing the teaching world — that of making the Freshman Comp course more than just "Remedial English" — expired after one term. While his co-teaching venture at Carleton some years before with a friend from Psychology had met with a tiny bit of success (or so he thought), at Maryland he and his collaborator had gotten on poorly and left the students confused. Interdisciplinarianism grew tiresome, and with that failure R's educator life seemed to be running out of steam, though for years he had been pre-occupied (obsessed?) with the failures of English departments — the evidence was there from the beginning when he wrote his letter of resignation to Arthur Mizener after his first semester at Carleton and through the years in addresses such as his MLA blast "On Graduate Training in English," and articles like those he published in *The New Republic*, "English Department Ills," and *Harper's*, "Faculty Survival." Luckily, then, eureka his writing life was given a sudden boost by a letter in the mail from Houghton-Mifflin suggesting that he take on a "life" of William Carlos Williams, with the possibility of a collection of poetry as well. It was also the kind of assignment the Guggenheim people liked, and soon Sedulus was no longer Sedulus. He was not an editor and (with Guggenheim in hand) for a year not even a teacher either. He was, as he wrote elsewhere, "an explorer in the unknown seas of a new genre."

If ever there was a genre in which a practitioner needs to display professional and personal modesty, it is biography. Its obligations are only incidentally to the forms and graces native to other literary struggles, and only minimally to the art of self-expression and salesmanship. Always there is the biographee to reckon with, and even if the biographee is Attila the Hun, he comes first. Nor is he apt to be Attila the Hun — biographees who are deserving victims of a biographer's scorn are not many. The tradition of biography is largely commemorative, and though our age is one of muckrakers looking for muck, a biographee — a literary one at least — is not usually chosen if he does not have a few qualities worth honoring. Ignorant though R was, he knew this about biography before he entered upon it, and he also knew that he would not have been approached to "do" Williams if he had looked unfriendly.

After the letter from Houghton-Mifflin, R wrote a letter to "Mrs. Williams" — Flossie — near the beginning of April 1973 asking if she would "look kindly upon a biography undertaken by me?" He told her that in 1939 WCW had given R and roommate Jim Angleton three poems for their first issue of *Furioso* and that he still had the letter they printed from him in the second issue and that there were other poems of his in *Furioso*, including his tribute to Ford Madox Ford. R was *eager* to do the biography.

Flossie gave her approval as did Wiliams' longtime publisher James Laughlin, founder of New Directions. The undertaking was made sensible by the quick Guggenheim that enabled the year's leave from Maryland. His only problem — not really a problem for a true interdisciplinarian — was how to write a biography.

R had read a good bit of Williams though not methodically and he had coped with his best-known poems over the years in his teaching. In 1966 he was on a William Carlos Williams program of the English Institute at Columbia with Muriel Rukeyser, Mark Linenthal and William Ober. (Ober, a physician, poet and essayist, had become a friend ever since R published his poems in *Furioso* and *The Carleton Miscellany*; he's probably best known for *Boswell's Clap and Other Essays*.) But best of all R had met Williams in the late 30s, and had admired him for his enthusiasm about little magazines, as well as for a semi-comic hate-Eliot letter he had written for *Furioso's* second issue. R had also reviewed *Paterson (Books I-III)* in *Furioso* shortly after it came out in 1950 and in 1955, Williams' *Selected Letters* in *The Yale Review*. But a biography of the man? Was biography something for a *poet*? I'll back up for a moment to look first at what R wrote about *Paterson*, for though he much admired Williams — especially as "a reassuring symbol of successful revolt against authority" — he had difficulties with *Paterson* the poem.

It is one thing for the poet to describe chaos to his reader, another for him to describe it chaotically, and still another for him to make his peace with it. In the first instance he is merely a witness and recorder; in the second he is a participant; and in the third he is a votary, or even a priest. This may be appropriate — for Dr. Williams has always been as much a spokesman for a kind of art as a practitioner of it — but it is also unsettling. I for one have the feeling, reading *Paterson*, of being in a murky dream factory with automobiles, textbooks, silk stockings and their salesmen all coming off the same assembly line.

Despite his difficulties, R remained in Williams's corner — and in *The Yale Review*, he wrote of him as "one of the healthiest, least eccentric literary figures of our time." But a biography had to be "complete" somehow as well as accurate and readable. And when one got down to the nitty gritty of the genre, where did one (for instance) begin?

— With the birth of the subject of course.

— But why not start with the *where* of the subject's birth?

— You mean Rutherford, New Jersey? Obviously one could start there, but why?

— Well after all one of the basic facts about Williams was that he was born in that place and stayed in that place and wrote in that place and...

— But is that fact more important than...?

So R decided that a trip to Rutherford was in order as a preliminary gesture in deciding whether to begin there. He had been there thirty-five years before while canvassing the poets recommended for *Furioso* by Pound; now he drove to the place — a place Pound had called a hole in the wall — for a second visit. He walked down the Main Street to the Erie Railroad station — which he was soon to describe as looking seedy but not slummy — and then back up to the point where Ridge Road forks off to the left. Right there, first house on the left, was the Williams house. He went to the front door and the biography had begun where it ought to, by the biographer's footing it between place and person. Amen.

Later R was to run across a memorable remark about such matters — that at its best it produces "archives of the feet." The remark was by Washington poet Myra Sklarew, who in turn attributed the notion to Simon Schama. She mentioned it in her collection of poems, *Lithuania*, having "come upon" poems by revisiting and walking about in the country of her ancestors, where with her own eyes she looked upon "massacre pits in every town and village." Luckily as a new biographer R had needed only to sit for a year on a cushion reading and reading in the old Princeton library to know the limits of *not* footing it. And right away, footing it in and around Rutherford he picked up a feeling for Williams as an old-fashioned G.P. collecting his own archives of the feet while making house calls — and also while observing the female scenery, as in "The Young Housewife." In this poem at 10 a.m. the nameless heroine comes out to the curb to call the iceman and stands "shy, uncorseted, tucking in stray ends of hair." WCW in his car compares her to a fallen leaf, and then

> The noiseless wheels of my car
> rush with a crackling sound over
> dried leaves as I bow and pass smiling.

Of course R did indeed spend time driving along the Passaic River to get a sense of the larger place, a Williams sense for the lively humanity of industrial New Jersey. He also actually footed it around the Passaic Falls in Paterson, and talked with old local friends of Williams as well as with Williams's sons Bill and Paul. In fact son Bill and R very quickly became pals and there was a good deal of letter writing between them, with Bill commenting on chapters as R began producing them. But the crucial moments of the book were with Flossie, several long comfortable sessions at 9 Ridge Road.

One session began with Flossie sitting him down beside her on the living room couch as she pointed to the obit page in *The New York Times*, on that day reporting the death of Margaret Anderson, long-term editor of *The Little Review*.

> She looks at the obit picture and is led to remark that Margaret was one year older than herself. A slight smile. The subject of Margaret is over [but R now mentions] something that Malcolm Cowley said that keeps her stirred up. "That son of a bitch," she says and the subject of Cowley seems over.

But then some months later she apologized to R saying that Cowley was a good friend and that she may have been thinking of what Robert McAlmon thought of him. She proceeded efficiently through a list she had prepared of well-known acquaintances, demolishing a few — Hemingway for instance — but being mostly kind, even sentimental. As for Bill himself, she defended him steadily, sharing his feelings about T.S. Eliot and the academics, and talking of how badly Bill was once treated at Harvard. Finally, putting acquaintances aside she arrived at Bill's own life, which was indeed — though they had traveled and lived abroad —

Rutherford and environs. There they had settled for fifty years firmly together (with a few times out).

> To bring back the past with her is to sit beside her on her couch next to her good ear, and ask questions but mostly listen, listen to and admire a strong voice and mind in a frail body. Her face is an old face and a child face. A smile shows steadily but the smile is not always smiling. She is the servant of the WCW legend and the loving widow. She is also her own woman.

So Flossie was the heroine accompanying R's hero through the wilds of the past. And R, looking back later on his labors, could not complain, though some reviewers of the biography did. The writing took him sensibly back into history and what a writer had to do with it when not sitting on a cushion and taking notes on 4″ x 7″ cards at Princeton in the old Witherspoon Library. He learned a good deal from the experience and would over the next five years become moderately scholarly about the genre itself by going back to the days when biography and history were often effectively partners. The eventual result were his two books about biography's history — *Pure Lives: The Early Biographers* and *Whole Lives: Shapers of Modern Biography.*

And in the process R became a student of Williams's own scribblings as a historian-biographer, since they pointed up Williams's sometimes healthy, sometimes fanatical annoyance with scholarship. Thus, his 1920s volume *In the American Grain* was an angry tract describing in just 233 pages a group of about twenty important figures that he tied to American greatness. Princeton scholars would not have approved the result since it lacked both balance and thoroughness. Worse, he rushed right into presenting his subjects' thoughts, and those thoughts were entirely Williamsy. For instance, in handling his first hero, Eric the Red, he had Eric head off to Greenland at a good clip with Eric raging to himself about his troubles at home but thinking favorably of the land he was about to discover. Then he — that is, Williams — gave opinions to Columbus, Cortez, DeSoto, Cotton Mather and so on that served up his own opinions well. Williams also reported that Puritans mistreated nearly all his chosen subjects. Thus, there was Daniel Boone, that "great voluptuary," who became a "native savage," loving the wilderness and hating the damned Yankees — and losing his shirt to them. And most particularly

there was Williams's Aaron Burr who was up against the wholly villain-
ous government man Alexander Hamilton, a "balloon of malice." The
Burr-Hamilton chapter was a revealing tirade, showing Williams's insistent discomfort in scholarly circles. There he let loose at the whole tyran-
nical law-and-order world of right-thinking academic historians. Sample:

> History follows governments and never men. It portrays us in generic pat-
> terns, like effigies or the carvings on sarcophagi, which say nothing, save,
> of such-and-such a man, that he is dead. That's history.... Then it fixes up
> the effigy; there that's finished. Not at all. History must stay open. It is all
> humanity. (from *In the American Grain*)

By such thinking Burr became an intelligent passionate anarchist, a live
force in a living landscape — like the Paterson Falls. And the Falls were to
be loved though they were the origin of what had become the "vilest
swillhole in Christendom — the Passaic River."

R did have trouble with Williams's raging (as the Princeton Department of History also would have) and he sympathized with Pound's well-
intended remark about him, that he was the most incoherent bloke who
ever gargled. Oddly, though, the gargling often also brought forth
Williams's most persuasive prose — where the perceptions were sharp,
the dialogue wholly convincing. R was himself too academic to share the
man's intensities about scholarship, but he did come to agree that the
writing of biography — or history — had to be at least partly served by
research in the "archives of the feet." And the writing also had to make the
author visible — a clear part of his role — as he footed it. Then too R's
lecture experiences for over twenty years had taught him that even a pul-
pit role was also best played on foot. To win audiences one shouldn't be
lordly. It was better to drop a prepared speech on the floor beside the
lectern and show proper confusion in picking it up. (Aristotle never mentioned this device.) Of course R had never liked preachers collectively anyway, so writing a biography of the man had at least a healthy sharing of
certain common views.

Yet in writing the book and staying with it, R had put himself into all
sorts of trouble and felt at times like abandoning the whole project. There
were seemingly simple questions such as how was he to refer to Williams
— the familiar Bill or the more detached Williams? He settled on WCW,
though in years to come, he wrote two extended pieces: in "William

Carlos Williams: 'The Happy Genius of the Household,'" the centenary lecture at the Library of Congress, he wrote about "Williams," while in *Six Literary Lives: The Shared Impiety of Adams, London, Sinclair, Williams, Dos Passos, and Tate*, he wrote about "Bill." Then there were the interviews and permissions. He was in touch with Allen Ginsberg over letters Williams had included in *Paterson*, needing Ginsberg's permission to reprint from them. "Shamed as I am of the stupid gaga of my local pride with Williams," Ginsberg replied, "it's what I wrote so there's no objection on my part or better herewith you have my formal permission to quote from my letters to W.C.W." He said that Williams was right to exclude the sillier passages, then added, "I'm in your hands — please pay attention with delicacy to contexts of excerpts. But anyway, anything written there, is open, in practice & on principle, for yr use."

Only in rereading Ginsberg's letter did R remember a poetry reading he gave in New York around that time and Ginsberg's remarks later on: "Ann W[aldman] had her mind blown by your conversation about Angleton & the CIA and I must admit I was bowled over a little in the Cedar Bar, that you'd helped prepare text for Rockefeller testimony, it's such a small world, I got a glimpse of that in Washington, but got a weirder glimpse next day when Ed Sanders (*Fuck You/A Magazine of the Arts*) (& Fugs & Book on Manson) walked in with a copy of the first issue of *Furioso* which we both thought looked great, it's Pound Politics and WCW tone...."

R sent copies of his manuscript to Bill, Jr., and brother Paul — he also sent a copy to James Laughlin, and the one responsible for the Houghton-Mifflin contact with R in the first place. Laughlin was complimentary, though he did not wholly agree with R's approach, proposing that R "devote another year to the book — not enough 'Billyums' in it." "Billyums"? Laughlin felt R had not interviewed enough of WCW's poet friends, especially the younger poets who looked up to him as a godfather. R wrote Bill, Jr., relaying Laughlin's remarks, saying that he decided no, he wasn't going to make any more substantial additions. He had already referred to a number of poets who had "clustered" around Williams — among them, Charles Olson, Denise Levertov, Robert Creeley, Cid Corman ("the list could be extended indefinitely") — and, as he wrote Bill, "felt from all my readings of the letters that WCW's relations with the younger poets was as a whole fairly uniform, that I had covered it, and that I didn't want to pad the book further with duplications."

So R went at it. Through it all, he and Bill were in touch regularly. And to say that he was cheered after sending him half the manuscript and receiving this from Bill, dated September 11, 1974, is an understatement:

Jesus Christ!
Holy Cow!
Formidable!
And other expletives of wonder, amazement, respect, admiration and appreciation.

> This is some kind of book. My hat is off to you. You must have put yourself through several wringers to come up with all you have done. And only half way to the goal! Your image has changed considerably in my eyes. The affable gent who came to Rutherford seeking bits and patches of information is transformed into the demon reporter who does his home-work well. This is a very impressive ms. It is not easy to read, but as I told Jim Laughlin, "I understand the need to establish Dad's 'sources,' and I think he has done it." Further, "if one is really interested and concerned about the subject as artist (WCW), it is fascinating, apparently all inclu-sive, and once into the thing, very hard to put aside." Neither mother nor I incidentally find anything objectionable in anything you have written....
>
> You can easily understand what a "Freudian" experience the reading was for me. It has done something to, for, at, around or in me. I'm not quite sure which, but for the most part I think it has been a beneficial catharsis.

All along, the title for the biography was to be *William Carlos Williams: The Happy Genius of His Household* — only at the last moment was it changed by the publisher to *William Carlos Williams: Poet from Jersey,* though R no longer remembers why. The "happy genius" line is from Williams's "Dance Russe."

> If I when my wife is sleeping
> and the baby and Kathleen
> are sleeping
> and the sun is a flame-white disc
> in silken mists

above shining trees,—
if I in my north room
dance naked, grotesquely
before my mirror
waving my shirt round my head
and singing softly to myself:
"I am lonely, lonely.
I was born to be lonely,
I am best so!"
If I admire my arms, my face,
my shoulders, flanks, buttocks
against the yellow drawn shades,—

Who shall say I am not
the happy genius of my household?

For R the poem was emblematic of Williams the man and the poet.

> This particular satyr standing before the mirror doing his dance shows the
> self-consciousness that an old-time Greek satyr would not have felt, a con-
> sciousness of his sex-being and of how that being is different from the
> daytime being who lives with the wife, Kathleen and the baby. It is in the
> contrast between dressed selves and the naked self that the specialness of
> the satyr self comes out. So the poem's self-consciousness turns out to be
> an asset for the poem helping it to emphasize that in a world as messed
> up as this one the genius is always a loner and conscious of his loneness,
> conscious of his difference. Hamlet. Manfred. Ahab. "Strange me."

Finally the book was out and the reviews soon began coming in. The
reactions were — well — divided. The literary community with a professional stake in Williams went after R, at least those like Helen Vendler in
The New York Review of Books and others in the academic research camp.
The community, R felt then and still feels, was wrong. From Allen Tate,
who had never much liked Williams, he at least learned how he had
erred, tactically. Tate wrote R a postcard with the simple, courteous intent
of praising the book. So he said he liked it, and that was good news, but
then he added that the trouble with Williams was that he had no brains.
That was, inadvertently on his part, the bad news. "The trouble with
Williams." R had not meant to describe a trouble so much as a quality.

Biographee and biographer, 1975.

He had meant to reinforce Pound's semi-comic remark, already quoted, about WCW as the most incoherent bloke, etc. R had thought that if Pound could dwell on the impressionistic urgencies of the man's writings and speech, while still respecting him, he could as well.

But R was wrong, as he later wrote in *Contemporary Authors*. "For the professionals it was clear I had not shown respect: their kind. So: lesson number one about biography came his way expensively. The book was praised but in places or by those without clout. After all, it did not make the jump into paperback." On the one hand, Christopher Lehmann-Haupt in *The New York Times* wrote, "This is a poet's biography in every sense — a biography about a poet by a poet employing the language and logic of poetry" and J. Hillis Miller in *The New Republic* said, "The story of Williams's life is told with circumstantiality, warmth and verve." On the other hand, some reviewers found the biography to be "an exasperatingly talky account" (Justin Kaplan, *New Boston Review*), "often careless and repetitive [in] style" (Katha Pollitt, *Saturday Review*), or that "The poet who emerges from Whittemore's New Jersey is either a cretin or a mental case" (Mary Geisheker, *Baltimore Sun*)!

Despite the opposing reactions, which R could suffer through, he was particularly annoyed by a purist-reviewer of some kind who thought he should have paid less attention to Williams's prose than to his remarkable innovations in poetry. R bristled, not having belittled the poetry one little bit (except for *Paterson*). Another work about Williams, *The Knack of Survival in America* by Robert Coles, appeared at about the same time and took roughly R's position though Coles, as a social psychiatrist, emphasized Williams's talent as a superior social observer rather than as a short-story writer. At any rate, Vendler panned both Coles and R at the same time. What accounts for taste? While poet Henry Taylor in *The Washingtonian* wrote of the book's style as entirely appropriate since Williams was so concerned to hear and recreate an American language," Vendler characterized R as writing "like someone trying to 'shoot the breeze....'" If there was any upside to this piece, it put R in a commiserating correspondence with Robert Coles.

When Houghton-Mifflin editor Charles Corn had first contacted R about doing the Williams biography, he also held out the prospect of H-M pub-

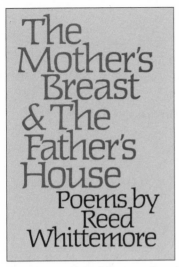

The Mother's Breast & The Father's House Poems by Reed Whittemore

lishing a book of poetry. Just what the book was to be — new poems or a new and selected — neither he nor Corn was yet sure of. Strange as it now seems at this distance, R wrote Anne Sexton asking for advice about the book itself, perhaps helping him make a selection or writing a brief introduction. He had been in touch with Sexton over the years. In 1962 he had written her about sending poems for *The Carleton Miscellany* and then later published a number of them at *The New Republic*. Though they hadn't met, they had become "telephone pals."

Sexton expressed interest in selecting poems — in sending a large manuscript he mentioned several long poems he still liked and in August 1973 Sexton wrote, "Your poems are a quarter selected." Soon after though, she was apologizing that she just couldn't complete the job — she was "desperately sick," let alone having other personal problems.

R of course did the selection himself for what became *The Mother's Breast & The Father's House*. The book was divided evenly by poems published in earlier books and those written since 1970, including "Ode to New York," "Mrs. Benedict," "Let It Blow" and "Inventory." Another was "On Looking Through a Photo Album (Of Viet Cong Prisoners)."

> These pictures show us a ragged, un-uniformed enemy,
> Many too young to shave but with trim haircuts,
> Many too old to fight but strong in defiance,
> Many frightened, hurt, dazed,
> Many despairing,
> Some squatting numb and expressionless,
> Some dead.
>
> Their captors surround them in big boots.
>
> Note that most of the faces are looking off stage;
> They see something unpleasant approaching.
> But in this one the dog is too tired to look,
> And the woman in front is done looking.

She has seen it, whatever it is, and turned off;
                                                    her eyes
Are not focused; she dreams
                                of no mortgage foreclosure,
                                of no missing relief check.

And here is one of mother and child beside stretcher,
Looking at corpse,
Presumably daddy.

And one of a tall American sergeant with scholarly glasses
Holding foe by scruff of neck.

Then there are pictures of blindfolded females,
And slim males with their heads in sandbags, their hands tied behind them,
And fierce youths plotting against us,
And graybeards with sealed lips.
All the tags on them.

I am American, middle-aged, male, with college degree.
I have been to war, I have studied war.
I know war to be part of man, death part of war,
And cruelty, deprivation, slaughter of innocents
Part,
Visited on both sides.

Yet I am sold out to this enemy; I like his small ears.
I am struck by his wide forehead, his high cheekbones.
His suppleness pleases me, and his spirit.
When I look at the gun at his chest, the knife at his bowels,
I fear for him.
When I see him hung by the heels I am sick.
The griefs that I find in his wrinkles, his patience in crossed legs,
The sullen undauntedness issuing from him
Swamp me with traitorous feeling.
Don't I know that this is war? that this is the enemy?

While his previous book *Fifty Poems Fifty* had "bombed" as he wrote
Sexton, *The Mother's Breast and the Father's House* was nominated for the
National Book Award. A number of poet-reviewers, among them Joseph
Parisi in *Poetry* and Josephine Jacobsen in *The New Republic*, focused on

his themes: "a blend of wit, warmth and fury... for the most part a sad and occasionally horrifying vision of the contemporary scene" (Jacobsen). At any rate, the NBA nomination meant R's publisher, as he wrote Howard Nemerov, had reserved a room for him at the Algonquin Hotel; it also meant his having to write an acceptance speech beforehand. "It's the way it's done," the publicity director wrote him. "If you will send your speech to me, in a sealed envelope-within-an-envelope marked 'speech,' I will hold it, unopened, until the winners are announced. If you are not a winner, I will destroy the envelope, unopened." The envelope was destroyed, unopened, and R has no recollection or copy of just what fine humble words he wrote.

Meanwhile after *The Mother's Breast and the Father's House*, after the NBA ceremony and hotel, after the WCW biography and the reviews he continued writing for newspapers and other magazines; he also returned to teaching at the University of Maryland. At that point, an unexpected trip was awaiting him: with Helen and son Ned, a literary excursion to the USSR.

Journeying Abroad

The two-week trip to the USSR was courtesy of the U.S. State Department and the Moscow Writers Union (with further funds presumably drawn from the Writers Unions in Leningrad and Tbilisi). The hidden arranger was John Pauker. Working for the Voice of America, John had also managed to arrange good will trips for others including himself and wife Pamela — 1974 was his year to facilitate the Whittemores. But first, about John himself.

Within the very small world of the *Furioso* editors only Jim Angleton and John became true Washingtonians, that is, workers in the very large world of Washington governance. Neither ever learned to be bureaucratic, but it is to the bureaucracy's credit that they were able to live within it at all. Each was a first-class eccentric. Jim's long-term solo performance inside the CIA has been described by too many (severe) critics, but John has been described little and deserves a full biography. His own accounts of himself are trickily Paukerish, as in this self summary from his last book, *Angry Candy*: "Poet, playwright, novelist, propagandist, political official, patron of the arts, playboy, political commentator, editor, critic and translator was born across the street from the National Museum in Budapest." The reader should note that JP's first-mentioned trade was poetry. Here is "Soldier Song," one of his poems published in *Furioso* under another disguise, Thomas Rowley.

> Prepare no more prepare no more
> The hero peace is at the door
> Wipe that war out of your eye
> Cross your heart and hope to die
>
> Hurrah for Peace and malt and hops
> Better to be a corpse than crops

A few of John Pauker's many disguises. Pauker held court at his More Fun House on Porter Street, NW, in Washington, DC, a museum of wild and unpredictable art.

The young Whittemores in the 70s: Ned, Jack, Daisy, Cate.

Scotch and bourbon gin and rye
Cross your heart and hope to die

The war is done you've fought your last
For want of a war the die is cast
So on your back and face the sky
Cross your heart and hope to die

Here's a pillow pound your ear
Them two bucks is for the bier
Here's a penny for you guy
Cross your heart and hope to die

So it was Pauker who had the three Whittemores flown off to Russia to improve perhaps their own Quality of Life. R had limited familiarity with Russian literature — a learned paper at Princeton years before, the few required novels by Dostoevsky and Tolstoy, fiction by Chekhov, and less than a handful of other Russian works he had written about over the years. So at this point R's brief erratic journal of the trip (and readying for it) will take over, abbreviated here, though with some interpolations from an article he later wrote for *The Nation*, "The Soviets' Problem — Or Is It Ours?"

Feb. 2, 1974 (Still in U.S.)
The prospect is intimidating. I should grow a beard at least and cultivate a cruel look while speaking of the state of contemporary culture. What will I tell them and read to them over there? I will be incoherent, drink too much, be sent home with a bad report.
So it is raining. Helen is off to the North aiming to reach Andover for Ned's birthday tomorrow. How do we spring Ned for the coming trip? Is this exciting enough for you, Diary? Saturday is a deadness and I would like to sleep but must read a dozen or so papers about J. Alfred Prufrock. Ugh.

Feb. 3
Ned's B'day. Read an M.A. thesis about C. Day Lewis's poetry. And it is raining on my window with a little ice thrown in. And Jack's classmates took his new textbook on Friday and managed to run a bus over it. Says Jack. And here is Ned, 18 today and telling me on the phone he can now inhabit a liquor store. And Daisy has just run up and down three flights of stairs five times because it is a very good way, she thinks, to practice counting. And I am

*reading a Yevtuchenko poem in which he says that during his salad days he
ate wild garlic in Siberia. I have trouble imagining wild garlic, even in
Siberia. And who might be an American wild-garlic fan now? Ginsberg, I suppose, under a bridge in Calcutta. Tomorrow I must cope with passports and
visas.*

Feb. 4

*If this is a psychosomatic cold I had best worry about the Russian trip —
for it's a ripsnorter and I've just put myself on penicillin (Doctor is skiing in
Vermont). Passport photos at 11 a.m., passport office at 12. Tomorrow is
Russian visa time. At 2 p.m. I discussed with JP[auker] an arrangement for
translating a sampling of my poems into Russian. At 6 p.m. delivered a fat
packet of poems to a translator in Rockville. At 7 p.m. had cheeseburger with
children, took shower and retired to a nice flat place where — at 8:30 —
these lines are being writ.*

*If we spend two weeks in the USSR we will have more than a week for
Gay Paree and other capitalist points. Last night at JP's I met Jim Fitzsimmons
of the* Lugano Review *(he has printed quite a bit of JP's work) who has spent
the last 15 years in Switzerland. I asked him where, given the novice condition
that Helen and I are in, he would spend our extra week. With no hesitation
he named Venice. In early March? Yes, the fog hanging over the canals is gorgeous and there are no tourists. Now there's a rationale — but there remains
the dampness to refute it. Hmmm. I think we'll hang in with the tourists in
Paree and London; the gorgeous fog will have to wait. Not JP's fault. He'd
have been glad to facilitate fog for us elsewhere with relevant authorities.*

Feb. 5

*This dubious old poet taking on Russian — and in Feb — is quietly
spooked. Will he understand a single word? What will he be able to offer in
exchange for their English other than "Nyet"? I must con my possible Rockville
translator — a sensible person named Natasha Clarkson — into translating a
greetings-paragraph for me, an all-purpose offer of hands-across-the-sea amity
that should sound like, maybe, this:*

*Oh you lovely enemy. Greetings from a Connecticut Yankee who once
wrote a learned paper on the Siberian Fur Trade but is otherwise unacquainted
with your country — may we have a vodka martini, s'il vous plait?*

Feb. 6

Penicillin is building a Chinese wall against my possible enemies. I have made it home again from the University after a commuter's day, have received passport in mail, heard from Natasha Clarkson that she is translating my poems and thinks "Ode to New York" (a dreadfully long diatribe) is good for Soviet consumption, though who knows how she will handle the New Yorkerisms, especially the last line, "my dearest my sweet/ Would you buy these woids?" She also has shorter poems – "High School Band," "Still Life," "Ladders," "On a Summer Sunday" and a few others — that JP asked me to send her.

Am reading an extraordinary Soviet lit critic of the 20s and 30s, and wonder if he is still in favor. Name of Roman Jakobsen. He has enlightened me on some of the mysteries of socialist realism that Lukacs (in my reading) omitted. In the first place there are the fallacies to dispose of etc. etc.

R had thought for example that he *knew* something about Socialist Realism. He had read his old friend Arnold Kettle's Marxist criticism and he had worked hard over George Lukacs' *Realism in Our Time*. He knew that though Lukacs had had trouble with the Soviet regime (if he had not he would never have been well-read in the U.S.), his stand against capitalism and its literary offshoot, modernism, was firm and stern. In modernism Lukacs found only Angst, chaos, uncontrolled subjectivity, and an unhealthy preoccupation with form and style that militated against the kind of literature of which he approved, an Aristotelian literature as he put it, a literature that dealt with man as "zoon politikon" (a political animal). Lukacs asserted that any modern writer with perspective was a writer with a Socialist perspective. He insisted that realism itself consisted of recognizing the Marxist "objective" historical view of society and social change. R, with all such anti-capitalism built into him, did not think that he could go far astray in his talks if he mentioned him, especially since he — R — had found himself sufficiently perceptive about modernist literature that he could be honest in praising him.

Feb. 8

Daisy with temp of 103 at 3 a.m. but the day finally dawned and by noon normalcy had arrived. At 4 p.m. took Jack to be interviewed about entering Andover. His grades not good. The man proposing that he drop back a year made Jack quite reasonably annoyed. I had three years of Andover — a great

*plenty — and Ned, just finishing three, is finding it more than plenty. What
to do? I'll have to be a good daddy on the trip with him and persuade him
that Andover is workable.*

*Returning from interview at 6 p.m., a call from Natasha Clarkson. She
has finished the "New York Ode" — had trouble with "woids" at the end! So
will the Russians.*

Feb. 9

*Snow at dawn and through day. Washington grounded. I stay home, build
fire, play with sick Daisy, meditate about my great speech to the Soviets — but
it doesn't come.*

*Yes, it comes a little. About the delusions of Americans: that our literature
of dissent has amounted to a revolutionary consensus.*

*If I were a Siberian and put wild garlic on my bread the gods might come
to me and say, "You perfect specimen, you nature man whose instinctive intellectual being is totally in accord with the tides and the seasonal growth of wild
garlic, will you be one of us? Then I would reply, "Thank you you are most
kind but you have mistaken me for someone else. I have never really liked wild
garlic."*

Feb. 10-11

*So my lecture is to be "Dissent and the American Poet" and point to the
limits of our dissent. It will move to WCW as a characteristically unpolitical
poet, a poet writing mostly of the periods between commitments. Hmph.* (And
now the journal becomes thoroughly boring as the trip is delayed —
visa problems etc — and R is largely incoherent about his fool lecture
for days and days.) Meanwhile, as he wrote in *The Nation*, the political
timing of the trip was not very good. R, Helen and Ned arrived in
Moscow "in the week that Solzhenitsyn appeared on the covers of both
Time and *Newsweek* for having been booted out of the USSR, presumably at the behest of the Writers Union."

Feb. 22

*The three of us are practically in the air — but lacking Ned's visa. By now
the U.S. Embassy in Moscow must be lined with my works, which JP has sent
on in diplomatic pouches. The question, what kind of luggage is to be taken?
Perhaps we should practice packing tonight. Yes we are babes in the woods —
and to think that during the war I was in Supply and Transportation.*

Feb. 26

 Overnight to London — jet 1/3 full — good for sleeping. Had a bad movie. Ned protecting his guitar. Helen wouldn't wake for the dawn breaking like thunder. In London, got together with Scott Elledge and wife Liane who are staying at Sonja Orwell's flat.

Feb. 28

We are at 30,000 feet on Aeroflot and Helen is alone in the seat in front of Ned and me, writing up a storm. I think we are over the Gulf of Finland, all clear, the sea shining, Helen doing Zen and lecturing her inner calm. The plane is fine but has no visible emergency oxygen equipment and the latch to the emergency door beside which I sit looks unpleasantly simple. Still, we are comfortable, the lunch was fine, Ned has beaten me at chess and is now protecting his guitar while reading a poem by Voznezhensky. A quiet orderly flight — and now we must go to work.

March 1

 Yesterday we were met by David Nalle and Will Sutter of the U.S. Embassy and two members of the Moscow Writers Union, Freda Lurie and Valentin Kotki, a mild-mannered translator who has done John Cheever and Agatha Christie and now wants to take on the next Arthur Hailey. These combined forces wrestled us through customs with dispatch and we were driven to town and the Hotel Sovietskaya without trouble — except perhaps when Helen, having mentioned her wall-papering business, asked if most Soviet women worked. Freda replied that they preferred to. He later learned Freda was a friend of John Steinbeck's, had traveled to Salinas for the 50th anniversary of *The Grapes of Wrath* and the Steinbeck festival. She was his interpreter as well for his 1963 visit to Russia.

 The hotel has 8-foot mahogany doors, w/ceilings three feet higher. Oriental rugs. French windows opening on balconies with stone railings. It is reserved — I read in a guidebook — for high gov officials. Ned has been placed in a single room at the opposite end of our hall. After a rest (during which we looked about us in vain for where the listening devices must be hid) we were taken to a restaurant for dinner with Embassy folk. Restaurant was a cross between an eating place and a barn. It had rotating lights and a very loud band using amplifiers familiar to Ned and mixing danceable songs like Oocichanya (Dark Eyes) with antiquated (in Ned's mind) rock and roll.

Ned was soon in conversation (English) with one of the guitar players. Also on deck were two writers, Dick Bridgman and Scott Momaday, both teaching American Lit at the University of Moscow. Bridgeman had written a book on Gertrude Stein and also The Colloquial Style in America, in which he argued that American literature developed as more than a sub-department of English literature largely because American writers were listening and imitating ordinary speech. It was a noisy first evening though Dave Nalle tells me that Will Sutter thought he was taking us to a quiet place to talk literary shop. We drank moderately — that is, perhaps five glasses of vodka (the vodka is milder than in U.S. but does its work) — plus some Georgian white wine and something odd fermented out of bread called Kvass that does taste like fermented bread. There were no Russians at this affair but I learned that Freda has been deep into my verses with Will, asking detailed questions — not, apparently, political.

March 2

Off to the Moscow Writers Union before noon. The Union is the nucleus of an organization of some 7,000 writers who run a network of publications and translation projects. The magnitude of the publications and projects is impressive, though the headquarters are modest — a drab one-story U-shaped building with many small offices and a dining hall. (I learned one cocktail party fact: the union headquarters was once the stables for a great mansion that figured in Tolstoy's War and Peace.) First we dealt with very businesslike administrators, who are now our hosts (partly paying our way), about our schedule and money. After a busy day and evening in Moscow we are to board the Red Arrow for Leningrad. (I am writing this on the Red Arrow.) We are then to spend four days with the Leningrad Writers Union before being flown to Georgia for four days — another Union — and then return to Moscow. As for money, well, I explained in English (being already convinced that I need not even try to speak native) that I am not a rich man, and though I am most grateful for their proposed generosity I am a little worried about my responsibility for my family's expenses. The administrators conferred, proposed that Ned share a suite with us in the future, and that all would then be well except, possibly, for 150 rubles. I didn't dispute the rubles (they have already given me 100) and we left for lunch and some sort of afternoon appearance on my part, to be followed by a puppet show before boarding the Red Arrow.

It was at the 2-1/2 hour lunch that we learned not to distinguish between lunches and "appearances." The lunch was attended by a Dr. Nikolov

Fedechenko, head of the Union's foreign translation magazine, a couple of others I can't name, our guide Freda, and Mikhail Lukonin who is Secretary of the Moscow Union and will join us again in Tbilisi next week where we will have a regular delegation. DELEGAZIO! Fedechenko himself is an economist with a wide reputation as a scholar — he has honorary degrees from Harvard and Illinois. He is ironic and witty, a man accustomed to command; he likes to bait his conversational opponents and is good at it, though he displayed no malice in my presence. He said that English was harder to learn than Chinese and that American ineptitude at languages was a national vice. I am having trouble equating these arrangements with American conferences since they are a far cry from either MLA [Modern Language Association] meetings, or, my god, little mag orgies. Is there any equivalent of all this in — or emanating from — Washington? I must try hard to comprehend Writers Unions, but at least over lunch I was enlightened to find that Lukonin is both an administrator and a poet — further, that he like all Writers Union members favors innumerable toasts. The toasts must have jokes — but from today's lunch I can only remember one.

The joke. It seems that an old man who had arthritis in his fingers found that his vodka had been poured into a small glass. That was hard for him, so to pick up the glass he circled it with a piece of bread. Period. At this point Lukonin looked at me significantly and everyone was smiling. Have I got this right? I doubt it but anyway my glass, which was not a small but a fair-sized glass, was full, so I thought fast. I took a piece of bread in hand and picked up the breaded glass. Laughter (why?). And toasts.

When the lunch tapered off my performance was due. We wandered not very far to a large room where some ten teachers of American Lit were waiting, and I performed with large-glass vigor. I read a few poems. Then two translators read me in Russky. Then Freda backed me up with a fine interpretation and I read, upon request, William Carlos Williams' "English Grandmother" poem. I also talked at random about my canned lecture subject, American dissent, and asked (cautiously) about socialist realism. We didn't go far with the latter and all seemed well. Freda even kissed me, and I suppose that meant I had picked up at least a "B."

The Writers Union quarters are very aged — an old mansion plus outbuildings that were probably once stables. It is a curious mix of a genuine revolutionary presence and ordinary seediness, of solid serious stone (they are serious people) and clapboard.

So back to the hotel exhausted. Helen and Ned to the puppet show while I rested before the train trip.

March 3

After the long night ride we were met yesterday morning about 8 a.m. by the Secretary of the Leningrad Writers Union at the Leningrad station. (I think it is the famous one — why don't I know?) During the trip Ned and I played chess and I wrote, while Helen and our very own (and very nice) translator, a young woman with a leopard coat and yellow boots named Tanya, talked in an adjoining compartment. She's been guiding us through the wilderness, reading menus and directions, translating toasts, and solving other basic survival problems. She found out why there was a delay with our transport from the station — Raoul Castro had also been on the train and mobs were greeting him. Photographers took pictures of us — mistakenly — and we went off to breakfast and our quarters at the Hotel European. There we were met by Don Sheean of the American Consulate and soon settled in for a round of touristing plus an appearance at the Univ of Leningrad. It is hard to find time for this journal but let me be a quick sightseer anyway. What a handsome city of fine old buildings and fine old-and-young well-dressed people with fine fur hats — all a tribute to Russia's past and present. There were even lovers in the freezing parks.

Now to business. At the University the audience of about 40 was again students (and teachers) of American Lit. The professor introducing me had written a book on Melville. I didn't talk Melville but read poems, then was asked questions and — upon my opening up a tiny bit about socialist realism — was politely corrected by the Melville man who said that in reading Lukacs I was behind the times; I should instead be reading Christopher Caudwell and a book called The Novel and the People *by a certain Ralph Fox. At this proposal everyone laughed — I suppose the Melville man has been selling this Fox as the latest Party Line?* Interpolation: R had skimmed through Caudwell once, and pictured him as a sort of British Stalinist of the 1930s who would hardly be an "advance" over Lukacs. He had not heard of Fox who in his short 37 years (1900-1937) — he died in Spain — wrote four books, one each on Lenin and Ghengis Khan. *Anyway we were soon away from Fox and onto Edgar Allan Poe about whom some of them were writing papers. Then there were more timely subjects and I was of course amused to be asked, for instance, how do young poets get their work published in the U.S.? And how popular is poetry? And is it common for people to gather in a concert hall and listen to readings? Do people in the U.S. distinguish between the poetry of the white and the poetry of the black? What is your attitude toward Marxism? Could you please tell us if Faulkner fits your idea of modernism? Please say what you can about Ogden Nash. How about Edgar Allan Poe's influence on contemporary American literature?*

Then there was a music question that I passed swiftly to Ned: do you consider singers such as James Taylor, Judy Collins and Carole King to be poets in their own right? Of course that was far beyond me but Ned was embarrassed also, though having quiet knowledge, said just a few words about Taylor. Not that Taylor and company would have been ready for the question either. (Ned said afterward that next time he would bring his guitar and play James Taylor. The American Way.)

But a fine session all in all. Then we were off to a ballet where we looked up at Raoul Castro in the "royal" box.

March 4-5

The last two days have somehow merged but I'll report on three events that may or may not have occurred on just one of them. (My problem is not entirely vodka.) First there was a visit to the Hermitage, once the Winter Palace of Peter the Great. The Communists have restored it, along with many other palaces, and it is a past they are far from rejecting. Big on Rembrandts, Rubens, Van Dykes — and on the third floor there is an immense early Impressionist collection moving from Monet through Picasso, etc. And who should show up while we wandered and stared but Raoul Castro. He walked by with his entourage, and our entourage was forbidden to follow him into a secret room. (I think he wanted to lie down.)

Second we visited (led by Sim Botvinnik of the Writers Union) the WWII cemetery remembering the 300,000 who died (1/3 of Leningrad) in the War. We placed mimosa beside the "eternal flame."

And third we lived through a very big Writers Union evening — the sort of event that Writers Unions seem to have been created for — at the apartment of Vladimir Somebody. There we all became blotto, especially Sheean and I. This mode of conduct is becoming familiar; one sits forever around a table covered with glasses. (JP would have liked the mode.) Vladimir read my "New York Ode" in Russian. In attendance was the enormous fiction editor of the Union's magazine Aurora *that prints much foreign work. (Circulation*

*150,000.) This man with unlimited capacity sat at the end of the table and
had little to do except fill glasses and shout his basic toast: "Let's go!" yet once
he went further and managed to call the Moscow Union people "slime."*

*So today I am hung over. Stayed in hotel room in the morning while Helen
and Ned went off to see the Pushkin (Pooshshkeen) residence. In the afternoon they stayed at the hotel while I went off to the Writers Union and sat
with more editors and bottles. A cordial but exhausting finale. I learned much,
and particularly noted (again) that the Leningrad crowd doesn't think much
of the Moscow crowd.*

March 6

*So now we are in Georgia after a three-hour flight starting at midnight.
Again met by Writers Union people (Georgia variety), then settled in
exhausted. At last we now have slept, have had a quiet day with a bit of tour-
ing, and have also had a miserable but quiet, unattended supper at a Georgia
restaurant where Ned — already starved for American food — declared a vast
longing to go home. Now, in quiet, I am looking at this journal and noting the
omission of a darker moment in Leningrad, a visit to three schools where the
world of toasts and international good feeling was replaced by the System.
Students stood up when we entered and when we left. They were uniformed,
looked healthy and devilish but were thoroughly disciplined. And clearly we
were to be disciplined too. Much English speaking mixed with patriotism, and
the high point in our education was a visit to a school "museum" where a fervent young woman told us that her particular school had been renamed
recently for Richard Sorge, a famous Russian spy executed by the Japanese. On
the museum walls were pictures and descriptive spy matter, all put together,
said the fervent one, by the students themselves. We were made to sit in the
museum for twenty minutes while Sorge and his spying and his eventual exe-
cution were explained to us by a doctrinaire female pedagogue of great earnest-
ness. As this woman concluded her address to us she brought forth her most
dramatic assertion, which she had been saving: the students themselves had
spontaneously and on their own hook decided to start the school museum in
his honor, and to name the school after him. (The school, we then learned,
had been so named, as had five other schools in the USSR.) So I spoke not a
word that morning but went away wondering if we in the United States had
any schools named after Allen Dulles or Gary Powers. Also, why had the
Leningradians programmed us to listen to the heroic-spy lecture?*

So already I am beginning to feel that Georgia will also give us a mix of Writers Union warmth and peripheral official indoctrination. So be it — there could be worse mixes and these Writers Union people are at least writers.

March 8

Morning tours. Medieval church artwork, great hammered gold and silver crosses. Trip to an aged fortress-monastery. Then to informal preliminary visitor-work: an appearance at the U of Tbilisi where I was told (but did not believe) that everyone understood me perfectly. We were serenaded by a student band playing antique rock 'n roll with its amplifiers blurry but deafening. The band's female singer was a hefty disciple of Aretha Franklin — the audience knew all the American words to her songs. And then to the real business of the day, another endless luncheon — the first in Georgia— at the magnificent apartment of the secretary (I think) of the Georgia Union. German grand piano. Walls lined with books, paintings. A groaning board, but Ned was absent, back at hotel with sore throat. Two hours of toasting, by the use of silver "horns" that were passed around. Each toaster was supposed to empty a horn (4 or 5 ounces of excellent mild white wine) at one swig but I noticed that smart old-timers dodged the duty. In one of my toastings I observed recklessly how unfortunate it was that contemporary Soviet literature in my country was best known for the work of exiles like Solzhenitsyn. I said that what I wanted to say I wanted to say in the friendliest way, that it was a tragic fact about the relations between our two countries, that for us their most celebrated living writer at the moment was a man they had exiled, and that there were others like [Joseph] Brodsky in Michigan who were hardly improving our image of the USSR. My good host listened. When I sat down he rose to say that in the friendliest way he spoke to me, a welcome guest in his house, to say that he felt it was improper for me as a guest in his house to say what I had said.

Then came another diplomatic slip, not noticed at the table generally, when Tanya, talking with Helen, did not trouble to translate one of the toasts for us, and our accompanist Lukonin from Moscow noticed it, quietly asked her why she hadn't and she replied she thought the toast merely conventional. Tanya is now in the doghouse, siding with the wrong team.

So that lunch had unpleasant undercurrents but the next feast — will they never stop? — was an improvement. Our host Rezo Tabukashvili— a playwright and film director — didn't like toasts so we did just a few, sitting down. The talk was low key, and after perhaps an hour our accompanists such as Lukanin left — this must have been part of management's plan — and we were alone with our host, his wife (a dancer) and a family including two grammas busy in the kitchen, a young playwright-son with handsome girl, and several in-laws. The Writers Union was suddenly missing. Talk was quiet. A teacher of Chaucer held forth, annoyance with Moscow crept in, and Georgia (population four million, birthplace of Stalin) emerged as a thoroughly independent place.

March 9-13

Back to Moscow and the Hotel Sovietskaya. Dark day. Ned wishes he could go home on first flight. We are not getting on with Will Sutter. Tanya is tired and unhappy. But then with a fine switch we are off to the Moscow Circus — tigers and clowns — while Tanya departs to her husband. My trouble becomes that of having to rewrite my script for Univ of Moscow performance in two days. In the meantime we go sightseeing around the Kremlin, take in the Bolshoi Ballet, and are motored out of town to a much mentioned writers colony — and to Pasternak's grave — but are not allowed out of the car! A coolness has settled in, and when we make it to the University for my evening lecture a genuine freeze seems on, since the chosen lecture room is too small. Much fussing in halls. But after 15 minutes of my chatter, with my back against the blackboard, Freda rushed in upon us to say she had found a larger room down the hall where we are moved — maybe a hundred persons converge and seem happy to hear me read poems and struggle to explain what sort of foolish anarchist rebels the little magazine editors of my country like to be. There are many questions and anarchism seems to go over just fine.

Then two more days of meetings, speeches, parties at the Nalles and Lukonins, sessions with real experts on modernism. And finally we have Ned up on stage with guitar. He does several songs but mainly "Alice's Restaurant" and a blues one. Cheers.

But the Moscow Writers Union people are tired, the Whittemores are certainly tired, and so is socialist realism. Today everyone is happy when our team drives to Moscow airport in three cars, shakes hands, exchanges gifts and winds up the orgy. Now we're in Paris. Ned leaves for Boston tomorrow.

At this point R's journal broke off and there were several scribbled pages about which I now casually speculate, guessing that a poem loomed here, then vanished. Then the scribble vanishes and the journal resumes very briefly.

DP, the Distinguished Poet, resumes his account in Paris, and wife Helen has now returned from a Paris bookstore bringing DP a copy of Hemingway's A Moveable Feast, *perhaps to improve his style. Added at this point is a complaint about Paris's rootless cosmopolitanisms where even café au lait costs a dollar and Parisian taxi drivers are driving Mercedes.*

Clearly he is back in the world of capitalism again and notes that poet Osip Mandelstam's widow's account of the Soviet tyranny is running serially in *The London Observer*. Then, perhaps to apologize to his late hosts, he adds that *there remain arguments against the West*. Next line: *Helen and I decide that we will have an expensive drink at the nearby Hotel Ritz.*

After this there is further crossing out, then a blank page, followed by silence. It now seems obvious that R, in Paris in March, wrote no more because he could not possibly give a coherent rational account of what had happened to them in their two wild weeks of the USSR. The steady feasting hadn't brought on his blockage. Nor had the complications of living with the miscellaneousness of three competing Writers Unions. (In fact hearing the Unions' differences seemed like old home week for a little magazine entrepreneur.) Perhaps the basic strangeness was simply the image of the writer in society that Russians projected to visitors, not just a Communist/Soviet image though certainly the political power of the Unions in the USSR was impressive. There remained — aside from the Communism — a thoroughly unAmerican image of the literary life, something much less separatist than was apparent at American little-magazine events. There was plenty of friction, yes, but not an acceptance of isolation of performing away from the big world of makers and shakers.

While in Paris R and Helen received a call in the middle of the night to cable permission to allow son Jack to have an emergency operation. They got directly on a plane and arrived at Dulles, going straight to the hospital where Jack had just emerged from seven hours in the operating room. The doctors found this time two ulcers or perforations in his small intestine. Three-and-a-half years before he had a perforation of the colon. He was in intensive care for four days, tubes going in and out of him, though he recovered or was out of immediate danger, until he was struck again.

In the article R wrote for *The Nation* he tried to summarize his Soviet experience and then make sense of what he felt he had learned. "There I was walking about their country as a characteristically dissenting American literary intellectual, talking glibly of the importance of the American dissent tradition, professing to be broadminded — and all the time feeling irredeemably American, incapable of breaking away for an instant from our language, money, hamburgers. If we were stupid about the limitations of our dissent," he wrote, "they were silent about theirs. I would mention Solzhenitsyn, Mandelstam, Brodsky, the forbidden names, and there would be no follow-up, the names would not be mentioned back. Even Yevtushenko wasn't mentioned back. We had a fine lunch at the poet Sergei Narovchatov's, the conversation seemed warm and open; but after the party I learned that he had spoken out publicly — and presumably officially — against Yevtushenko in a letter to the *Literary Gazette* (circulation 1.5 million) just that week. Why at the private lunch could he not have mentioned the public letter? I was learning how little I knew." So, for the purposes of what he had learned, R came away, at the time, with this — and writing these sentences now in the midst of the Iraq war, how similar are his observations in *The Nation* of the Soviet Union's view of the U.S. as devil to those of many Muslims in the Middle-East.

Never out of my mind after I had achieved ignorance was the question of how much the West, and particularly the United States by its long-term top-to-bottom denial of all things Soviet, had managed to shape and strengthen the Russian defensive postures we were constantly and uncomfortably witness to. There seemed little doubt that Socialist Realism is itself a defensive ideology in the same league as elevating espionage to the realm of the heroic. Soviet defensiveness is hard for an American to understand because we think we have been defensively holding them off for three-quarters of a century. But it is obvious that they think they will not survive if they can't keep us out — us in the form of our decadence, nihilism, immorality and anti-social individualism as much as our money and our prattling about the freedoms. Not just our soldiers and shekels but the whole capitalist "sickness" is what they fear, from modernism to Coca-Cola. Even a subtle, sophisticated thinker like Lukacs cannot refrain from polemic when contending with the "diabolic" character — he actually uses that word — of capitalism. Lukacs is generous enough to acknowledge with Gide that without the devil there would be no art, but the puritanical elements in the party cannot be expected to do so. Anyway, the big point is not what they ought to believe or acknowledge; the point is that for all shades of Soviet opinion we are the devil. Our recognition of that opinion of us may well be the first important step in our understanding them.

～

The trip concluded, R returned home to his much quieter writerly and teacherly life. Months later, he received the "confidential" embassy report that Will Sutter and Dave Nalle wrote about his "performance." On the plus side, they reported that "R did well before both large and small groups, changing his manner and presentation well to suit his audience"; on the negative, they noted that "his poetry did not make as large an impact as his lectures and question responses [because] his poetry is cool, subtle, sometimes wry and often understated. He reads it without the intensity and rhetorical flourish that Russian audiences are used to."

The USSR trip ended R's foreign sojourns until, unexpectedly, nearly a decade later, in February 1983, when another Pauker-organized poetry gala took him to Israel, this time without Helen and Ned, but with second son Jack. Though this is jumping ahead chronologically, it may be a good place to do so because of the Israeli poets he met, and would invite to the Library of Congress when he was interim Poetry Consultant, and because of traveling with 21-year old Jack.

R was scheduled to meet with poets in Jerusalem and Tel Aviv — they included Dan Pagis in Jerusalem and Yehuda Amichai, and Karen Alkalay-Gut in Tel Aviv — to participate in a literary conference (his talk would be on the "state of American poetry," Christopher Lehman-Haupt on "creative reviewing," and Raymond Federman on the novel), and conduct a poetry workshop at Hebrew University. He had begun reading Saul Bellow's *To Jerusalem and Back* on the plane and found himself wanting "to defend the American character as at the moment it surfaces in poetry. It is hard," he wrote in a journal. "I should not perhaps blame them for being soft, but I do, and will — but who am I to do so? I guess I can only say that from the vantage point of an insider, one born to the softness conditioned by it, I have at best worked toward being tougher — in verse and politics." Reflecting further, he wondered if "perhaps the hardness of Jews could be turned around, especially the American ones like Bellow, and say they would be better off if they, with their mixed backgrounds, worked toward being softer, worked toward a less patronizing view of the limits — for example, in suffering — of the American experience."

In the meantime R and Jack arrived in Israel without their luggage — it turned out that they left the U.S. on a day that was to see the heaviest snowstorm in decades. Whether this had something to do with the lost luggage, R didn't know. He did know that all he and Jack had with them for the next several days were the clothes they were wearing and whatever else they had carried on board. Not much.

In Jerusalem, poet Dan Pagis shepherded R around the ancient city. Pagis, a fine poet whose book *Points of Departure* Stephen Mitchell had translated, was also a scholar of Golden Age Hebrew poetry. "He is most pessimistic," R wrote in his journal. "Israel has done as much wrong in 25 yrs as America in 200. The militants have taken over…he's against the West Bank colonization, against the whole Lebanese thing."

While R used his journal for working out ideas or clarifying what he felt about his reading — Bellow in particular — he also recorded day-to-day events such as his get-togethers with Pagis. "Dan arrives with his book, plus clothing for both of us. We are most touched but grateful in a practical way too. He drives us through the Old City in his Fiat after dark.… We stand on top of the great Wall. We walk through the changed, rebuilt Jewish quarter. Clean, winding, the old evoked in unlimited Jerusalem stone, and without Arabs."

During his stay, the American ambassador had a garden party in R's honor at his residence in Herzliya. There R met Moshe Dor, a poet and translator of English poetry — he brought him a copy of Maariv's *Literary Supplement* with a translation he had done of one of R's poems. Dor began translating more of R's poems and in 2007 Keshev Publishing House in Israel brought out a large selection as *A Season of Waiting: Selected Poems, 1946-2006.*

～

Like his father, Jack, too, kept a journal that began once on board their TWA Flight, to be precise, at 4:50 p.m., Day I: "In the plane. Wow." For the next seven days, he was all wonder and observation. For example:

Day 2, 12 noon Jerusalem
The Bells are ringing madly. Who's to know it they are the oldest bells in the
world. Sitting on our sun porch, Dad and I are looking at the walls of the Old
City of Jerusalem. Sunny Hot 70 degrees. Shirts are off. Just got back from a
walk through the most deserted town I have ever seen. Saturday a.m. every
Jew is at the synagogue. We walked for two hours. 9:30-11:30. Did not see an
open store. Millions of shoe stores. Few pubs. Pharmacies. Nothing open. Must
have let the people out of the service early. Wonderful sight. I love it here.
Really want to rent a moped and drive around madly.

10:45 p.m.
We got hungry, since it was the Sabbath, we had to go to East Jerusalem.
Where the Muslims hang, to get something to eat. Took a long walk to get
there. Completely on the other side of the Old City of Jerusalem. Up and
down. Very Hillish of Hilly town. Went inside the walls. Wildness. Mass of
people. Every persuasion ever possible. The joint was what you could call
Jumpin. Too crowded to really walk and make any progress. Back outside the
walls we went, not before seeing soldiers with M-16's (Guns, Big Guns) walk-
ing casually down the street. The Barrel of one of these large guns bumped into
my leg, and the soldier said something in a foreign tongue. Was it "excuse me"
or "watch it Buddy, I'll shoot you next time"? Hard to say, but he did not seem
angry. Common thing. Brush your gun barrel upon some poor guy from South
Minneapolis. I reckon not. Incredible. So we walked on the outside not only to
keep moving, but also to avoid the soldiers. My knees were knocking together
like crazy every time I saw one of those Bad Boys. And I mean Bad Boys.
Never seen a gun so close to my body.

Meanwhile, Jack wrote his first poem — *"shall we give poetry a try?"* he
asked himself. *"Why not,"* he replied. *"My First Poem."* he wrote, satisfied,
after 16 lines. But then said to himself, *"told the reader too much — work on*
it." So he went on with a *"second try,"* then a third and fourth, which R
later brought into a poetry workshop in Tel Aviv.

Day 3   Midnight

A tall girl with darting eyes
    A wild animal

She smiles
  to make friends feel secure
  Her sweater
  She thinks
Will protect her
like the elephant's hide

A tall girl and very quiet
  a little mouse
trying to escape
from the ties that bind her
like a convict
in the Hennepin County Jail

  Glancing out the window
  She dreams of getting away

A house in the mountains
with the man she has dreamt of

Pa and I talked about poetry. We analyzed many poems too. I figured it was about time in my life where I started to try and write some of this poetry stuff. I have always had a block. I need a bunch of work, but me thinks that this kid can do some serious stuff.

Day 5   2 p.m. Tel Aviv
Went to creative writing seminar. Heard dad speak. Very good. Lots of clapping. I suppose I should have taped it. Next time.

Day 7   9:15 a.m. Tel Aviv University   Room 206
Pa's Poetry Workshop
He somehow convinced me that this would be the place to hang out. We'll see. It should be fun. Dad's on a roll. The class is spellbound. Wait to see what now happens. Not enough attention paid to poetry as music. In Maryland prosody is out. We're talking Rhythm. Dad is reading my poem now to this class of Intellectuals. Some of these people are real jerks. They mean well. But Woooeee. Nasty. There is a wild discussion going on about my poem.

    ....

People in Israel always have to argue. They have to speak their mind. Just gotta. It gets almost maddening. If I were dad up there, I would say if you guys want to argue, I'll just sit down. And you guys can teach this workshop… he's shut them up now. He has figured out how to captivate them. What a guy. He figured it out during coffee break.

Ah Jack.

Leave Taking & Delos
chapter thirteen

In writing the Williams biography R had of course been subjected to all the dark pits of the genre, and he had even come to know a bit about its history. He would soon advance further and produce two texts of that history that The Johns Hopkins University Press put into print: *Pure Lives: The Early Biographers* and *Whole Lives: Shapers of Modern Biography*. More about these shortly. Though his mix of roles — as poet, critic and (former) editor — now included biographer in addition to respectable teacher at the University of Maryland, one who even tried to help earnest graduate students in seminars to wisdom about biography, still with the Williams biography completed his literary life had achieved what some critics might describe as a lack of focus. He had momentarily lost a project really of his own to be intense about.

The daily commute from Cleveland Park in D.C. to teaching in College Park in Maryland had become tedious — *that* had to be changed. So Helen and R moved to a small house on the southern wooded edge of that college town — tiny beside the university's immensity — and there they watched their children move effectively out and away from them. So Cate, having received a B.A. at Connecticut College in New London, proceeded in several more directions — she graduated the School of Scenic Design in New York and did an MFA at the University of Minnesota — before marrying. Ned took two years at Maryland and two at Carleton and, though a musician at heart, moved into the graduate school world of biochemistry in Minnesota, where he took a PhD with a post-doc in California. Jack tried several schools in Washington and Fergus Falls, then had *his* educational trip abroad to Israel with his father, settling into a cook's life where he ran his own restaurant before illness took him over. As for little Daisy she became grown Daisy and went off to St. Timothy's near Baltimore before settling in at the University of Maryland.

And Helen and R? Their move to College Park was not easy. Loner R liked to think of it as one toward simplicity, but Helen took it to be a kind of social downgrading. Her hopes kept drifting back to her Lundeen family's prominent lives in Fergus Falls, and particularly to summers at nearby Otter Tail Lake. There the Whittemores eventually picked up a small cottage of their own. During all this R was dutiful about Maryland faculty meetings and reading graduate theses, though his basic trouble was that he *was* aging. As was his literary career.

In the fall of 1977 a surprising offer arrived from Texas Christian University in Forth Worth that R teach two courses during the spring term, one in literary modernism and a second in creative writing. So R went off to Texas and took son Jack with him — Jack was 17 and taking a break from high school. He worked in Fort Worth and got a dog that he later brought back to Washington.

R held the Cecil and Ida Green Honorary Chair, which also required that he give a public lecture. He titled his lecture "Why Shouldn't a Poem Mean?" — the allusion was of course to Archibald MacLeish's "Ars Poetica" and its famously quoted line, "A poem should not mean/ But be." The poem as "globed fruit" — this served as R's primary complaint about a poetry that is autotelic, "having its own organic being." According to R, this was another way of marginalizing the importance of the art, by assigning meaning to prose and focusing on the exclusiveness of a poem's being. He knew that his was an "unfashionable thesis," and that he was no doubt offending many in saying that "there have been too many globed-fruit poems in recent decades." Referring to an essay by Gerald Graff in the *American Scholar* (Fall 1977), he paraphrased Graff's assertion "that the real reason critics despair of finding the meaning of a poem, or of reaching rational agreement with any other reader about its meaning, is that they fear that what they might find or agree upon would show that the poem means precious little." R agreed. As for himself, he said, "I refuse to deny that poetry and prose are in a meaning competition out in the big world. I was brought up with a higher view of the art and will stubbornly cling to it." The classes themselves as R remembers them were pleasant enough and soon enough he and Jack were on their way home, stopping off in Nashville to see another respecter of poetry's meanings, Allen Tate, who was ailing. Jack retained a vivid image of Tate in bed and incapacitated.

———

R wore a topical poet's hat and was engaged for a while in writing weekly Shaggies for *The Washington Post's* Sunday "Outlook" section. Unlike Calvin Trillin in *The Nation* who's been writing political rhymes for some years, R's "Shaggies" proceeded for just a couple of months in 1979 and 1980 with such subjects as "The Washington Suburban Sanitary Commission Blues," "The Heterosexual Bishopric Diversion," "The GSA Strange Disposal Shaggy," "The College Park Drag" and "Xmas Shaggying."

> So now you water pippul mebbe soak us
> More cuz we use less. Don, pliz, broke us.
> You want us sprinkle lawn in rainy season?
> OK, we swamp ze grass if that you pleasum.
> But how you pleasum us? Build reservoir?
> Nah, to meters read you buy big car.
> > "The Washington Suburban Sanitary Commission Blues"

> The furniture the government in hurry
> Bury
> Must be for some big happy funeral wake,
> But if they bury chairs why don't they bury
> People in them, for taxpayers' sake? —
> Say a heap of GS Twenty
> > "The GSA Strange Disposal Shaggy"

> Shout the boys at Safeway that they sellum
> Stuff at Everyday Low Price.
> But in same ad they whisper down at bottom,
> Prices two days only. Is that nice?
> > from "Business Notes"

The Shaggies were small amusements in between essays R was writing for *Harper's* — on the teaching of English — and the *American Scholar*, while continuing to contribute brief essays to "Outlook" and reviews for the *Post's Book World*. With his post-Williams immersion in the art of biography, he reviewed such books as William Pritchard's *Lives of the Modern*

Poets and C. David Heymann's *American Aristocracy: The Lives and Times of James Russell, Amy and Robert Lowell*. Having been through the fire of writing a biography and now engaged in writing about the genre itself, he came to read such works differently. In *Lives of the Modern Poets*, for example, he pointed out how Pritchard's focus, while it kept "a reader attentive to the nuances of a poet's words rather than the journeyings of his soul," its limitation "is that it encourages the exclusion of many not unimportant poetic elements — a poet's thoughts, beliefs, themes." "His approach leaves out much elementary material about what poems are 'about' and what the poets have on their minds aside from their stances." Pritchard's approach, R concluded, was largely a "professional approach" in its "friendly arguments with other literary/academic critics" — his orientation was essentially theirs. Pritchard was the kind of professional lit critic that R found himself annoyed with — as he wrote in "Why Should a Poem Not Mean?" — because he subordinated a poet's themes to voice and tone, thus depriving "the poet the privilege of just plain saying." He added that in effect such criticism *demanded* of poetry "that it be trivial."

R *was* still writing poems and published several longer ones in *The American Poetry Review* in 1982. In that year Dryad Press, a literary publisher in Washington, brought out *The Feel of Rock: Poems of Three Decades*. So R was in print again. The book included personal lyrics as well as meditative ironies such as "The Quiet Ones":

> All the creatures of earth are commissioned
> To wander about for their term on the earth and make gestures
> That serve to keep the affairs of the earth in motion
> And please commissioners.
> But up in the trees and down in deep holes there are quiet ones
> Who offend commissioners.
> "Keep moving the earth," cry commissioners.
> The quiet ones sit there.
> The earth sits there.
> How pleasing it is
> To offend commissioners!

Among the newer pieces was "The Destruction of Washington," an exercise in coping with the city to which he had moved.

When Washington has been destroyed,
And the pollutants have been silting up for an age
Then the old town will attract the world's Schliemanns.
What, they will say, a dig! as they uncover
The L'Enfant plan in the saxifrage.

So many plaques, so many figures in marble
With large shoulders and lawman lips
Will have to be pieced together and moved to the new
Smithsonian
That the mere logistics will delight vips.

For how can one pass by a muchness? There will be fund drives
With uplifting glosses.
Teams of researchers will mass with massive machinery
At the Rayburn ruin
To outscoop Athens and Knossos.

Dusty scholars will stumble in, looking nearsightedly
At gray facades
Of pillar and portal
And at curious acres of asphalt
For clues to the mystery of that culture's gods.

Money of course they will miss,
Since money is spoke not at all on the plaques there,
Nor will they shovel up evidence
That the occupants of the chambers and cloakrooms
Were strangers in town, protecting their deities elsewhere.

But sanctums they surely will guess at,
Where the real and true pieties were once expressed.
If the Greeks had their Eleusinians,
Surely this tribe on the Potomac had mysteries too?
— Having to do, perhaps, with the "Wild West?"

Like most of us sitting here now beside the Potomac,
They will find the Potomac primitives hard to assess.
Oh, may their ignorance be, than ours,
At least less!

Now in his sixties, R found himself emulating Melville's Bartleby —
the sufferer who preferred not to — a dubious posture. And at the time of

his Maryland retirement he was at least given reason to defer it by a project dreamed up by a group of poet friends. Led by poet and teacher
Michael Collier this group ignited a fine blast for him at the Folger Library
where, after reading a few of his own poems, R sat in the middle of a large
audience and listened to the works of others, some touching on him and
some on Washington matters, but all serving to make an aging organism
think of other happier models than Bartleby. Of the writers performing
that evening the best known was Gene McCarthy who cleverly avoided
the subject of Washington and in "Courage at Sixty" talked about how to
cool down. R and McCarthy had come together on several occasions — R
had also reviewed a book of McCarthy's poems in *The Washington Post.*
And earlier, in the stormy days of 1968 when the Senator and Robert
Kennedy were contending for the Democratic nomination, R had written
"Hither and Yon: For Bobby and Gene," which the *Post*, in an article about
the two of them on the front page of the "Outlook" section, positioned
smack in its center.

> "Whither, oh Yon, whither?
> Two roads diverge in a wood.
> The chart has run off with a college boy,
> And that's not good."

> "To the right, Hither, is war,
> To the left, revolution.
> Come, Hither, unto these quicksands,
> And frame a resolution."

> RESOLVED, that Hither and Yon
> Go separate ways to election,
> But meet again in Chicago
> To sever their connection.

Then there was poet Robert Sargent, older than R, who summed up
twelve volumes of the works of Samuel Johnson in a poem of 34 lines
that he addressed to Dr. Johnson. Sargent cast himself as a Johnson
admirer, each night retiring to his bed where he read from "your books":
"He's halfway through, almost./ He's grown to love your style: the con-
structed sentence,/ The careful choice of words, not only for meaning/ But
for balance within the sentence. And frequently/ He repeats to himself a
sonorous, eloquent passage/ Before he goes to sleep." The Johnsonian
Sargent was followed by Merrill Leffler, poet and publisher of poets

(including R's *The Feel of Rock*) who took a crack at current fashions in poetry plus the merchandising evil that was "franchising itself to hell" in most of America. Linda Pastan then raced through the seven deadly sins, finding herself implicated with all of them. Myra Sklarew lamented the verbal inheritance of her generation — "broken down sentences still talking" — from Stalin and his kind. Ed Gold mocked the worldly triumphs of the Post family starting with Postum, moving unto General Foods and at last triumphing with ice cream in Brazil. Edward Weismiller worried — without mentioning any capitalist names — about monsters in peaceful pastoral places. May Miller and William Holland were content with unmalicious, certainly unWashingtonian memories of childhood. John Pauker presented well-rhymed trouble with a girl who didn't care. Coleman Rosenberger had similar trouble with poetry and publishers. Lisa Ritchie read an excerpt from a presumably fictional chronicle of a Yale man (later than '41) who was a damn fool. And Ann Darr started off with the casual mention — by an unknown at lunch — of a shoeshine in Chicago, a thought that moved her mind rapidly off to the nine ages of Troy, for each of which she found herself barefooted but trying on appropriate footwear. All these performing friends made for an evening R could gratefully not forget, including kind praise about his own work by Rod Jellema and Henry Taylor. The evening encouraged R to wander off without thinking of Bartleby as a model (often).

———

In 1983 Anthony Hecht was Consultant in Poetry at the Library of Congress and invited R to give a Centennial lecture on Willliam Carlos Williams. This time around he was able to use the title that he had wanted for the biography, "The Happy Genius of the Household" (from Williams's "Danse Russe"). He began by referring to a Williams pronouncement in a letter he sent R during his Yale *Furioso* days: "What men seldom seem to learn is that the end of a poem is a poem. I don't know a thing about the value of a poem as such or of a hunk of gold as such but I do know *that*." The flatness of this remark — the end of a poem is a poem — made it seem like the rock upon which the art has always been based. Actually Williams' own poetry had been jumping on and off the rock for years.

Later R was to note that the rock had become, for better or worse, the rock of the English departments for half a century or so. "Indeed the rock had become so orthodox that Williams, if he were here, would surely say the opposite, the end of a poem is not a poem!" R went on to say:

> I would love to hear him say that, and will take advantage of his absence and say it for him: the end of a poem is not a poem. Williams himself proved it in all his best poems, the poems I want to send off into his second century. In the best poems the Williams balance between poem and world moves toward the world. The poems are poems but are not front-and-center about poems. The reader doesn't have to worry about the poetic quantum, though it is there, because he is attracted to other quantums, which may be the war quantum, or love quantum, or life quantum, or death quantum, but is always the human quantum, that is, the plum eater quantum, the quantum that is the end — in the sense of final meaning — of poetry.

While R was now merely an occasional visitor to the Library of Congress, in the summer of 1984 he was offered — at the last minute — another stint as Poetry Consultant, replacing Robert Fitzgerald, suddenly taken ill. At the opening program, R read Fitzgerald's poems and a moving memoir Fitzgerald had written about his father. R wrote Fitzgerald the next day about the event, and continued to do so as the season went on.

Fitzgerald had been instrumental in planning three of the programs that fall, which R now introduced, They were Sir Charles Johnston reading from his translation of Pushkin's *Eugene Onegin*, Annie Dillard reading from her fiction and John Hersey reading from his novel *The Call*. In addition to these programs, R was able to add readings by Israeli poets he had met in Israel, Yehuda Amichai, Nathan Yonathan and Karen Alkalay-Gut. The three performed in the Coolidge Auditorium in the evening but were also harnessed to an afternoon discussion about the wonders and snares of cultural identity and translation. R presided there, showing his helpless monolinguality. His own consultant talk, near the end of his tenure, was entitled "Poets and Anthologists: A Look at the Current Poet-packaging Process" — he whizzed along from the Greek Anthology, c. 60 B.C., to the current Norton Anthologies with stops along the way, his aim, a description of the historic role of anthologies and a definition of the genre.

In his year-end report, R wrote that he had not intended a special project for himself, though before the year was out he had a project in mind and surprisingly for him it had to do with translation, an issue that kept appearing like a ghost in the Poetry Room. Every week or two there were foreign writers at the library, from France, Holland, Israel, East Germany, Lithuania, Norway, Yugoslavia, Bulgaria, China, Korea, India, Quebec, Mexico, Chile, Argentina, Colombia, El Salvador, Montserrat, Peru, Uruguay, and Bangladesh. The chief subject discussed with these visitors was always translation and who or what in the United States was doing anything about it. R made his own sallies into the translation jungle and, as he wrote, "I became, slowly, a sort of fanatic on the subject." He even proposed a new little magazine, this one modeled on *Delos*, an excellent venture published at the University of Texas from 1968 to 1971. He began by trying to bring together a consortium of Washington colleges and universities for support though these efforts turned out to be fruitless.

~~~

After his one year appointment at the Library of Congress, R was asked to succeed Lucille Clifton and serve as poet laureate of Maryland, a three-year term. Though the job was largely ceremonial, it did give him an opportunity to travel around the state while trying to raise support for *Delos*, which he did (though without grandeur) through private contributions, small foundation grants, the National Endowment for the Arts for one year, and various small pots at the University of Maryland.

Delos was launched in 1988. A utopian epigraph on the opening page had multilingual Delian maidens singing (according to a Homeric hymn) a melodious affair "to enchant all the nations of mankind." A most impressive 158-page issue somehow followed, dedicated to R's former co-editor of *Furioso*, the recently deceased Jim Angleton. It contained a 30-page tribute to an early backer of *Furioso*, translator, poet and teacher Dudley Fitts (1903-68) with an introduction by Jim's widow Cicely. Then came a miscellany of translations from several tongues including the French, the South Slavic and "the dialect of Cree (of the Algonquian language family)." The mildest item of transnational learning was a short conversation between three deaf Englishmen that R had heard from his father: "Is this Wembley?"/ "No, it's Thursday."/ "So am I. Let's have a drink." R also brought back Wayne Booth, editor of the Department of

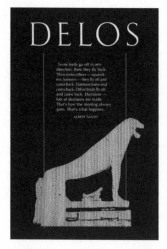

American in *The Carleton Miscellany* — reprinting his "A Humanities Profressor Translates Einstein for Us."

The *Delos* issues numbered twelve and contained translations from many languages that R's advisory board helped bring in. Poems and prose from Slovenia, Urdu, French, Austria, Greece, Hungary, Israel, Palestine, Japan, China, Bulgaria and other countries, as well as interesting novelties such as Karl Shapiro describing "Life in a Schloss" (at the Salzburg Seminar one winter) and Bill Williams, the doctor son of William Carlos, describing his father's year as a medical student in Leipzig. R himself contributed several essays — "When Freud Translated Biography into Psychoanalysis," another on William Lyon Phelps, English Professor at Yale in the Twenties and Thirties, and another on T.S. Eliot and *The Criterion*. On top of all this were interviews (one with the Russian writer Andrei Sergeiev), and fables by Scott Bates and R, plus various versions of "The Fox and the Crow," among them Milt Gross's "Nize Bay," which opens this way:

> Oohoo! Nize baby, it opp all de bolly zoop, so momma'll gonna tell you a Ferry Tale about de Fox, witt de Crow, wit de Chizze.... Wance oppon a time was seeting opp in a bench from a tree a crow. So she was kipping in de bick a piece from Swees-Chizze. So was wukking along a Fox wot he was sneefing witt de nose, so he smaltt gradually de chizze – und right away he began skimming how he coult ketch it away from de crow de chizze — Hmmm! sotch a griddy critchure wot he was!!! — (Nize baby — take anodder spook bolly zoop) —

Of course sufficient amounts of money to support a quarterly of some 160 pages remained a constant problem and soon the various sources began drying up.

But money wasn't the only problem. R had not found a job, a *mission* for a magazine to which he could be clearly dedicated. Not that little magazines were often clearly directed — muddle-headedness was normal in the "profession" — but at least most of them, starting back in about 1910, were conceived by editors seeking to resist or at least complain noisily about forces in the society around them — why, otherwise, the name *Furioso*?

Nor had many of the early little mags been served, as R's *Delos* was, by a committee. The committee was a fine one, a collection of friends and backers who were full of help as well as money, and who were mostly more knowledgeable about translation than R. The root trouble was probably just that they were a committee. For a committee is always an establishmentarian entity, and as such it has to sound like a committee. Surely therefore the *Delos* committee could have been held responsible for (a) calling itself The Center for World Literature, and (b) declaring on the magazine's title page that its "primary purpose" was to "maintain and invigorate the world's literatures by making their best works more widely available in other than their original languages." Invigorate? Hmmm. What did that mean?

In 1991 R turned the publication over to a gentlemanly physicist with college funds at the University of Florida and *Delos* disappeared shortly after. By that time, R had become much too wise to be other than amused by his own committee's grandeur. But having watched the publication's fate from the sidelines, both curious and skeptical, he wondered how, under ideal conditions and without a magazine, one might actually go about the language-invigorating business. Pretty soon, he was carrying on a dialogue with himself.

> "Did 'invigorating' a language have anything to do with *saying* any-thing?"
>
> "What do you mean?"
>
> "I wondered if one could invigorate a language merely by talking about important social matters like, for instance, communism." (At *that* time the USSR was just becoming Russia again.)
>
> "Of course you mean that *Delos* should have been political to be vigorous."
>
> "I just wonder if at the time it should have been."
>
> "But surely that wasn't what the Committee had in mind."
>
> "What *did* they have in mind?"
>
> "Plain English perhaps. Common speech."
>
> "Is language vigorous *because* it is common?"
>
> "Of course not, though it often contains swearing. What I am thinking of is the fuzziness in the Committee's statement as it announced what *Delos* should reach for."

"You are wondering how one goes about being 'vigorous'
verbalisticationally?"

"You've got it (I think). In other words the Committee didn't know
what it was talking about." R's ears were now reddening as his father's had
under stress, and he added, "I am no philosopher and am simply *trying* to
get at why the blurb about maintaining and invigorating all the bloody literatures in the world was off base."

"And why *Delos* itself was off base?"

"Yes, but let's be polite. As an English teacher staring at student themes
for a number of decades before *Delos* I naturally had to worry a lot about
plain old ordinary dull unvigorous 'meaning' in the sentences whizzing
before me, and…"

"I understand."

"…and I found that 'invigoration' often emerged in the themes as a
plain sin against, let us say, 'clarity' and 'truth.'"

"I understand."

"So in the student themes of my past I mostly pushed clarity and accu-
racy (and spelling) rather than, say, social invigoration. How does one go
about 'invigorating' meaning anyway? The committee's blurb on the title
page of *Delos* was trying to get at something bigger — I can only remain
hopeful that in the back of its committee-fied mind there was something
a bit more."

"Oho. So now you're getting down to the nitty gritty. You are saying
that a complaint against Class III was hidden away in *Delos*' blurb, which
was a Class IV blurb."

Thus the icy back and forth banter with himself went on for a few minutes until R settled in to unpack the meaning of Classes III and IV. He was
referring to the divisions of membership established by the mighty
American Academy of Arts and Sciences in Cambridge, Mass. R had been
elected to it in the mid-70s and placed in Class IV, the Humanities. The
Social Arts [sic] and Sciences were Class III. (The other two didn't matter,
being merely the Mathematical and Physical Sciences, Class I, and the
Biological Sciences, Class II.) Yes, Class III was, for R, where villainy lay. It
seemed to him that he and sensible other Humanities folk had been
working up to a blast of some kind against such a combine for decades.
What to do?

He tried a few stories but was not impressed; neither were certain publishers. He tried an ambitious series of essays *about* the conflict between
Class III and Class IV — but that made him depressed. Then, most casu-

ally, he took on modernizing a few traditional fables. In entering the fable
trade R began to think it might be made adult again. He had already
begun reworking a number of Aesop's fables and other old familiars such
as "Punch and Judy," but he soon found that revisionism for children's
contentment had been going on so long that for anyone to help fabling
grow up again (to "seriousness") was hard. Usually he fabled in a kind of
easy free verse, with the line endings present for pauses and with long
lines balanced against short lines — except when they weren't. It was all
relaxingly casual. Here is a simple beginning from "The City Mouse and
the Country Mouse."

> I have at last decided to be a guru
> said the city mouse to the country mouse
> and that is why I am here with my thoughts and baggage
> in your pleasant *merde* in the meadow
> > > Where is my suite?

> I have no sweet
> said the country mouse
> not even *a carte aux cerises*
> > or a *bombe glacée*
> > > or an etc.

R liked that sort of fooling, but tried to avoid making it all fooling by
having the tales carry political or at least suggestively adult statements. For
example, in "The Boy Who Cried Wolf" he made the real wolf a big bad
capitalist who ate a nosey agitprop lamb right in front of the wolf boy's
eyes. (He's not sure if the Soviet trip inspired that one.) And because such
writing came easy he was able to experiment with problems of tone and
voice without getting jumpy and unpleasant (his customary writing ail-
ments). In the case of "Punch and Judy" he first produced a version with
heavily rhymed stanzas, then put the piece aside for a month before going
at it again in prose, a lowdown dialect prose. Again, samples.

> rises the curtain on crib for sweet baby
> enters sweet Judy sweetly with baby
> words of love crooning
> > lullabies humming
> placing sweet baby in baby crib gently

enters the surly old Punch swearing slowly
tugging from off stage some great beast recalcitrant
preaching and swearing
swearing and preaching forth at last dragging an indolent dachshund

Now the alternative prose opening.

Well now it was Judy there in the kitchen wearing her polka dot jumper and
Indonesian galoshes who talked first and she said to Punch Punch you
watch that fool baby hear?

So Punch in his red suspenders and state college sweatshirt who was totally
tied up lighting a stogie and scratching his left foot grunted Yes Ma'am.

So Judy tracked out to shopping and fool baby went to screaming and
Punch muttered Baby shut your mouth hear?

R liked both approaches, but when he was well into the dialect version
he suddenly decided that he had a fine occasion for satirizing (seriously?)
the now tiresome diplomats' call (in the 1980s) for starting a Peace
Process. So he had Punch — after much violence — start one by grunting
"sorry" to the empty room while at the same time throwing baby out the
window.

Yet the big question for him remained — how could one make such
joking properly satirical, that is, socially relevant? And therefore vigorous?
He could try being serious again, he thought. And wary as he was with
that thought in mind he was soon back in biography. Luckily his myasthenia had long been under control by alternate-day doses of prednizone,
and he still had enough energy to do battle with a genre he had thought
he was done with.

Now to R's two books on the genre of biography itself, which I referred to
at the beginning of this chapter. In *Pure Lives: The Early Biographers*, he
became vastly historical, racing from Plutarch's descriptions of solemn
leaders such as Pericles and Antony to the witty 18th century eccentrici-
ties of Laurence Sterne. In the second, *Whole Lives: Shapers of Modern
Biographers*, R displayed those earlier biographers' limits by focusing, in
contrast, on the psychological interests of modern biographers — his chosen first author being Thomas Carlyle and his great men, then following

through with Leslie Stephens' studious *Dictionary of National Biography* (together with Stephens' daughter Virginia Woolf's complaints about it). The chapter on Freud and his disciples was an expansion of the essay in *Delos*, and then came the psychobiographies by biographers such as Richard Ellmann on Joyce and Oscar Wilde.

Johns Hopkins University Press brought his biography books out in modest hardback editions — one judgment upon them may be that they didn't make it into paperback. His longtime friend Howard Nemerov of course had nice words to put on the backs of both dust jackets. Others ranged: in *The Washington Post Book World* Richard Altick found *Pure Lives* "an example of that most extinct genre, a collection of essays in analytic appreciation," though he took R to the woodshed for using non-biographers such as Holinshed, Machiavelli, Shakespeare and Laurence Sterne. Then in *Whole Lives*, R came to the influence of Freud: while writing in an admiring tone of Freud's looking beyond the "manifest content of a life" in studies such as Leonardo da Vinci, he railed somewhat against the characteristic modern biographer-psychoanalyst who had become a bully.

> There is something about the arrogance and assertiveness of the modern, professional, analytical mind that has annoyed me throughout my readings for this book, with the annoyance being stirred about equally by the various professions I have confronted, including my English-department own. My doubtless prejudiced conclusion is (here is where my virtue becomes troublesome) that in our world the professionals have generally come to feel obliged to deal as specialists with private lives, and that while they vary widely in the range of their vision, few seem ready to admit that other professions have knowledge and talent equal to their own. Each seems fixed in his own wondrous way of "taking hold" of the genre of biography.... The taking-hold is sometimes impressive and persuasive, but it is sometimes also absurdly self-serving, dedicated to promoting the biographer's welfare within the profession. The results can be dismal.

In print the book had its supporters and detractors. *Book World* hired a different reviewer for this second volume, Marc Pachter, himself the author of *Telling Lives: The Biographer's Art*. R had some satisfaction in Pachter's characterization of the book as "quirky... and ultimately subversive."

Meanwhile, R was preparing his mind for a different writing challenge, that of taking on that lofty organization he's already written about, the American Academy of Arts and Sciences. For some years, he had been receiving promotional material from the Academy, though doubting that such an organization was supposed to promote itself. (It advised members of its past wonders, celebrated the Academy's golden accomplishments, and even mentioned many of its olden accomplishers such as George Washington and Henry Wadsworth Longfellow.) He first reread Daniel Bell's *The End of Ideology*, which had been issued in a new edition (by now the 1990s), and advised the world that there were no more ideologies, only *history*. Bell said he had originally written the work in the hope that "by dealing with sociological problems from a critical standpoint but without critical jargon, [he] might bridge the gap between the social sciences and the humanistic world." (Humph.) In the new edition he was still hoping for this miracle, but though he properly qualified the word "history" at great length he drove R back to those brief scholarly days in graduate school in Princeton when he had been trying to be historically minded — in case he had actually to teach history. But there he had also learned that there was no such thing as history (not counting old records in town-hall basements) of the kind Bell imagined. There was only history that had been written by *historians*. And historians were indeed people, thus possessed of opinions, ideologies and suchlike though many folk — like Bell and Shotwell — seemed not to think so.

Now this Princeton learning had stuck, helping R to cultivate a fine Class IV humanistic prejudice against Class III authorities like Bell (though Bell should, damn it, have known better since he seemed to be, academically, "in" history, which is listed as a Class IV occupation). Furthermore Bell was himself an important figure in the Academy that R was still, willy nilly, in. Bell was even a member of the editorial board of its quarterly *Daedalus*, which had become a dependable menace when it arrived in the mail.

Daedalus began in the mid-1950s under the editorship of Walter Muir Whitehill, an "expert" of the Middle Ages. Whitehill was, however, kept from medieval vigor by a Committee on Publication including an astronomer, a physiologist and an engraver, plus a light-verse poet David McCord who was also editor of Harvard's alumni magazine. In 1958 Whitehill's regime was replaced by Gerald Holton, a prominent physicist who was also a dedicated committeeman on international relations and came at his task with grand international subjects such as *Reading: Old & New, Health & Wealth, Past & Present, Religion and Education, Religion and Politics* and (a bit sexually) *Learning about Women: Gender, Politics and Power*. Holton's managing editor was Stephen Graubaud, whose own first issue of more than 500 pages, entitled *A New Europe*, also carried on with fine general subject matter and was said to have been three years in the making. Was all that vigor?

By the 90s *Daedalus* was a solidly Class III enterprise, which meant that it could not possibly qualify as a little mag. Worse, its steady influence, backed by all the forces of social science it served, had helped make American culture steadily more Class III-istified, so that when R and his friendly committee took on publishing *Delos* the old little-mag principle of *Furioso* rebellion seemed simply to have departed from the writing world. And this social fact — that History had come to be steadily mixed with Social Science — had bearing not only on the subject matter of *Delos* but also on the principles that it had solemnly enunciated for itself when it declared that its purpose was to maintain and invigorate literature (everywhere, yup). Alas, R still kept asking, of what did literary invigoration consist anyway? He could now see that somehow or other the Academy and its *Daedalus* stood against invigoration as apparently the *Delos* Committee·had meant. So on a gloomy fall day R simply resigned. But *Daedalus* — the very symbol of Class III tyranny — kept coming! What could he do?

His solution was to continue reading it, or at least skipping through its pages. Despite his insularity in College Park, it had become an enemy of sorts for him. And its true enemisticality became supremely evident to R in the absence of vigor. In two issues called *Early Modernities* (Summer 1998) and *Multiple Modernities* (Winter, 2000), both edited by Graubard (oddly a Class IV historian) but with much assistance from Shmuel Eisenstadt, a clearly Class III social scientist.

"What," R wondered, "are the chief signs of unvigoracity?"

"The absence," he answered, "of authors who dare to acknowledge verbalisticationally their individualisticational authoristicity."

"Aha," thought R further, having at last developed a solid conviction about the source and meaning of "vigor" in human expression, and having also located a significant area of human thought in which it was missing.

First he asked himself if he could describe briefly how he came at his discovery. Then he frowned, admitting that brevity would be difficult since he had been studying the problem in, and ever since, college. He then rose from his chair, achieved what for an old man could be called a vigorous lecturing posture, and announced that the publication *Daedalus* was a betrayal of everything vigorous to which little mags in their short 20th-century history had aspired. Yes, and this was so because its contents were firmly (incurably) grounded in Class III modes of thought and speech to which little mags had always been (inexorably) opposed.

"Hold on," he said to himself, "it seems that in your enthusiasm, you are showing a certain amount of Class IV prejudice that in its intensity verges on high rhetoric."

"That is possible," he growled, "but I have earned this intensity by being subjected for decades to a species of thought and speech that has rendered passé my once solid and dignified Class IV approach to vigor. I grant that I became critically intense about the problem slowly — and *Delos* suffered accordingly — but being subjected to the unvigorous prose of *Daedalus* broke (at last) this camel's back. Yes, the quarterly's insistent absence of authorialistic identity in its verbiage at last drove me wild. For it is one thing to be solemn, academic and impersonal when trying to achieve objectivity in a sentence. It is another to write as if it were necessary to construct each word anew as to obscure its tie to what we used to call the English language or any remotely presentable practitionification of it. Do I make myself clear?"

"I think so," said R. "I think that my many-decaded experienciality as a writing pedagoguist among freshmen — and moving with great reluctancicity toward graduate-schoolification — I have always tried to make students realizificate that their sentences are indeed theirs, hence their responsibility, and that they are *not* to be scribblicated in the spontanifical way that spring water emerges from the good earth." "Yes," R seemed to be saying to himself, he resigned from the Academy's ranks because of some mystifyingly *un*vigorous quality adhering to the sentences in its magazine *Daedalus*.

The arroganticificatory capacitance of the *Daedalus* authors, he noted further, is without limitabilic dimensions. As one of their own kind put it, the new modernities-condition has a new language for survivalisticism "utilizing totalistic, essentialistic and absolutizing terms." And that must mean, for instance, that no simple single lonely image noted by some simple single walking human being near a red wheelbarrow — on which so much depends — can be put down on a piece of paper without missing the whole meaning of the modernities world as now existifying around us.

So S.N. Eisenstadt reached this woeful conclusion way back in 2000 A.D., thus.

> The continuing salience of the tensions between pluralist and universalist programs, between multifaceted as against closed identities, and the continual ambivalence of new centers of modernity toward traditional centers of cultural hegemony attest to the fact that, while going beyond the model of the nation-state, these new movements have not gone beyond the basic problems of modernity.... [The problems these movements face] continually reconstructing their collective identities in reference to the new global context, are challenges of unprecedented proportions. The very pluralization of life spaces in the global framework endows them with highly ideological absolutizing ideas, and at the same time brings them into the central political arena. (*Daedalus* 2000, vol. 129)

"I am worn out," R now said to himself, "and must rest."

Finale, of Sorts

chapter fourteen

R felt better, briefly, after mailing his resignation to the Academy. The other 3700 members would not miss him of course but he was free now. To do what? To go on and on with his own long-conditioned daily affairs: word-processor meditations after breakfast, a Thoreauvean jogging-walk around eleven, lunch and a nap followed by more WP plus even some actual reading followed by two drinks between 6:30 and 7:15. His "working day."

In 1989 he received a letter from Miller Williams, poet and director of the University of Arkansas Press, about publishing a new and selected collection of poems that became *The Past, the Future, the Present.* He included only a handful of recent poems, among them two of the longish fables he had been writing. This is the opening of one, "The Foxes and the Grapes."

Homebody Fox was not a vixenish feminist
She didn't snap
at Fallacious Fox
but she didn't cotton to big talk
from Fallacious Fox
she boiled chicken necks
for him
she littered and dusted
for him
she ironed his coat once a week
but was not meek
for him
      so when Fallacious told her
that he hadn't been able to jump high enough to reach the grapes
but that was ok because they were sour grapes
she asked him how he could know they were sour grapes
if he couldn't reach the grapes

yes

The book was fine, it received modest notice, hardly any waves, and eventually disappeared. But that mattered little when tragedy arrived: Jack's leukemia.

More than a year of doctored misery for this game-tough doomed son followed — in and out of the University of Minnesota hospital — with a transplant, with setbacks and recoveries and then a slow sinking, a wasting away. His death took place with all the family in attendance around the bed. And nearly a year afterwards, a small birthday party was held for him out on Maryland's Eastern Shore. The youngest Daisy wrote of her brother in "Planter's Warts."

Your "ace in the hole" abandoned you.
Our mother endured.
The others danced in and out.

All of us watching
Your death.

Lost
In thoughts of recovery and its anticipated complications.

Once again, I rushed to your side
As your living will,
Only this time in its legal sense.

When I entered that familiar hospital room
Where the air miraculously replaced itself every 90 seconds,
It was your feet that first struck me.

There, trapped in some strange pink Styrofoam shells
To prevent your long, bed-bound body from turning in on itself,
Were your sweet feet.
"Can we take these off now?" I asked no one
And did.
Carefully.

Your feet felt like you, the most obvious piece that remained
Although unnaturally large attached to your now-nothing calves.
And yep, there they were.
The planter's warts,

All three of them.
A previous discussion, you and me.
Remove them or not?
"Nah," you said.
It would be a test. Your test. Our test.
Could they, would they survive
Total body radiation,
Chemotherapy and
Bone marrow transplantation?

They did.
I told you so aloud
    And laughed.
        Remembering your laughter,
        Those unforgettable giggles,
        A mine of true grit.

R , too, could not help himself in "May 22nd."

So Jack is not here for his birthday,
Not here to blow out the candles,
Cut the first piece.

Not here, not here.

Oh but if he were here he'd have taken off from the restaurant
For a week.
He'd have brought Miles along on the plane and we'd go to the beach,
And then he'd be off to play golf with Ned and Willie,
After which we'd sit down to his dinner, his birthday dinner,

And…

But Jack, Jack, Jack is not here
For his birthday,
And all of us who are here, who are still here
Can only go off to bed after the dinner
And dream of what a fine weekend the weekend of May 22nd
Could have been, would have been if Jack had been here
To blow out the candles,
Cut the first piece.

The birthday helped a little, and soon the other children were back at
their own jobbing. As for Helen and R they proceeded at their grandpar-
ently jobbing with R still at a word processor, not computer, and Helen
struggling to keep busy at her clothing business, called Lost Resort, which
had thrived until Jack's death but was now, also, aging. Unlike R she had
at least kept a journal of Jack's siege, and perhaps someday it will be
printed as a tribute, not to Jack alone but also to the many who somehow
came within his orbit. As for her own grief it was always actively with her,
a presence sometimes comforting, sometimes devastating. No wisdom
came to annoy her more than that of friends who urged her to Take Hold,
Put the Past Behind Her, Get on with Life. Her position was that of course
one had to get on, but that one had to bring the grief along too since it
was simply there and had to be there, had to be honored, bowed to, lived
with. R shared her feelings, but as a Whittemore he tended to be sullen
and withdrawn about them. (Whittemores in their New England glums
have always wished to lie down and stare at ceilings.) And so the two of
them moved forward in the year 1999 in their different ways, luckily finding that it was another year shaping up as big, but this time happy. A big
marital year.

In January 1999 Ned, aged 43, and Christi Foster married in California
with, it seemed, several hundred Whittemores, Lundeens, Fosters and
other family present and cheering. In October Daisy, aged 32, married
Mitchell Tartt in Washington, and hundreds of Mitchell's kin were added
to the Whittemore and Lundeen contingents. As this annus mirabilis
moved to a close it seemed that after the enormous bills were paid (with
help from fine Ed Lundeen, Helen's brother who died the next year) there
was only clear sailing ahead into the sunset

～

For some years after retirement from the University of Maryland, R took
on informal teaching jobs that put him at a long table in a small room
with retired folk like himself who, unlike himself, had not suffered at
"Creative Writing" for decades and thought that creation might be fun.
He didn't try consciously to be discouraging but may often have been —
decades of moping about with pen and ink can greatly reduce the trade's
romance, especially when the romance is so commercialized.

He even tried teaching a couple of informal classes about the 1930s,
reading (with retired folk) angry books and magazines of the Depression

time and noting how remote, literarily, from his 80s era it was. In that period — filled with the memory of his Republican father's anger at Roosevelt — he was also of course leftistly angry, as was most of the period's writers, simply at the money folk. Many were trying to be a part of the messy world — that is, *furioso* about it.

But so much had happened in between the Depression Thirties and Vietnam and the social sciences that managed, perhaps innocently, to drive the individualism historically practiced in the humanities toward social irrelevance. Poet Kenneth Fearing (more about him shortly) was one of the last talents in his trade to confront the new condition whereby masses rather than single minds do all the thinking, though one penetrating social-science volume of the 1950s also went at the problem, William Whyte's *The Organization Man* protested the mass, Gallup-thinking that has become accepted as a basic register of social conditions.

———

In the meantime, while he was having his two regular evening drinks (of his own chosen reliable vodka) he was now inclined to wonder if he had sufficient control to write intelligibly about life, death, poetry, anything at all for the purpose of JOBBING, that is, carrying through with his resignation from the American Academy. He had thought that JOB to be essentially a gesture against the Academy's social-scientifically non-little magazine *Daedalus'* expertorialisticality, but he was not at all sure now what the gesture meant to him.

When younger he would of course have known. In college his principles were a clear confusion of (1) Pound's make-it-new but make-it-sublime notions, and (2) his own thoroughly unPoundian proletarian dreams, picked up while trying to be a proper leftist in the Thirties. His literary ideals then had been filled with images of poets performing (sublimely but angrily) as useful social reformers, and back then he had managed to keep the dreams active in his head even as he drove to the top of East Rock Road to write little lonely verses.

Yes, but then he had graduated to being drafted and thus becoming an inefficient jobber at ordering an awkward squad to start and stop on a military training field at Fort Benning. So his Bartleby negations had always been uneven, the consolation being that Melville himself had been unsteady while creating Bartleby. Had not Bartleby been born in the mind of a lowly clerk working in "the Dead Letter Office at Washington?"

Yes, and surely Melville, if he had simply owned R's car, would have enjoyed putting the office (and Bartleby) aside in order to drive to the top of East Rock and just scribble.

A 20th or 21st century historian (and after all R had tried to be one while at Princeton) might now point out that Melville did not have R's car, that there were several big changes in American culture between Melville and R's time, and that with each change the role of the individual seemed to shrink. This historian might even be a know-it-all (though good historians know better) and declare that single struggling souls have now become mere psychiatric cases rather than JOBBERS. And after all R himself liked to mock self-centeredness, even his own — so where could a Bartleby now fit. How could one be a reformer and a Bartleby?

If Plutarch had described this non-leader he might have come right out and called him lacking in decisiveness as well as courage. Yet R's life after the army — as a writer, little magazine editor and teacher — had at least helped him to *think* modestly about reforming the world. Why should he now not deal in a small literary way with a small group of other helpless rebels with causes. He could call them, well, Impietists.

Very well, so he tried to sharpen his wits for doing this by looking at writers who seemed to fit such a description. This thought then blossomed into an idea for a book of short biographies about such writers — starting with Henry Adams. R had long wondered why the highbrow, rich, insider Adams, together with his brother Brooks, had appealed to outsider Ezra Pound. Was it merely that Pound himself wished he had been an Adams? Anyway Adams seemed to R a good place to move in on the theme.

And what of others whose work he knew? Jack London, Upton Sinclair, and John Dos Passos were erratically proletarian amid capitalists — therefore good impietists. Then there was Southerner Allen Tate who enjoyed being impious about Northerners like Adams, and William Carlos Williams who enjoyed being impious about T.S. Eliot. As for proletarian novelist Jack London, he happened to be a money-minded entrepreneur, but his most impious book, *The People of the Abyss*, was at least a noisy documentary of his personal visit to the city of London's infamous slum in the 1920s and discovering (a bit sociologically R admits) that the lot of people in general was in need of improvement. And of course London's novelist friend Upton Sinclair also liked to preach socialism, taking on the miseries of the meatpacking industry, the coal industry, the press, churches, alcohol, Ford, Carnegie, and much else (including modern poetry, which annoyed him because it didn't rhyme). As for Dos Passos, Williams and Tate, well they didn't really know what the world had come to be about.

But why *these* particular figures, R asked himself in the introduction to the heavily-titled book, *Six Literary Lives: The Shared Impiety of Adams, London, Sinclair, Williams, Dos Passos, and Tate*? Obviously it was just he the biographer who had put them together, somehow sharing their climate of thought as writers standing apart from their culture. Especially he had shared their contradictory feelings about the culture and what writers should do in it. It may be instructive — instructive for whom? R might ask at this point — to quote the paragraph that follows.

> The source of such feelings in my own case goes oddly back to Yale, an unlikely place for such conditioning now, but less so in the late thirties. That sad decade had us reading of hungry proletarians and fat capitalists; it had us thinking of literature as full of Freudians and imagists, but also of those who are now called ideologues, writers declaring that the study of mankind included the study of man's mind as well as his id; it didn't tell us that ideology was dead.... In such a climate we were apt to read literature for what it said, and some of our important literary reference points were not owned by the English department. In such a climate dialectic was not a dirty word, Freshman English was called "rhetoric," opposites lived in comfortable combat, "consensus" had not, as I recall, been invented, and we saw no harm in talking "issues" and *The Waste Land* in the same seminar. In a sense this book began in that climate. The point is important because we have no such climate now.

Adams's role in the book — particularly his third-person narration of *The Education of Henry Adams* — was crucial. He was, as R wrote, "an anti-Washington Washingtonian, an anti-capitalist capitalist and an anti-historian historian." He was not only the widest ranging mind in R's group, but he had the extra virtue of not being known as, primarily, a literary writer at all — his reputation was as a thinker — though R was pleased to dismiss that notion since Adams *had* written, under a pseudonym, *Democracy* and *Esther*, two not very good novels. He was a grand gloomy lonely disciplinarian who managed to meditate, in lifelong comfort, about human insufficiencies. And he did write well.

Though late in this narrative, a short aside about Allen Tate, whom R had been friends with since Tate came to Minnesota in 1951. On Tate's 60th birthday, in 1959, *The Sewanee Review* paid homage to its one time editor and invited a number of writers including R to contribute, among them, John Crowe Ransom, Katherine Anne Porter, T.S. Eliot, Robert Lowell, Howard Nemerov. R entitled his own piece, "Mr. Tate and Mr. Adams" and looked back to Tate's essay "Religion and the Old South," which attacked Adams for the heresy of positivism. "Let us put three persons together who soon discover that they do not agree," Tate wrote. "No matter; they quickly find a procedure, a program, an objective." Quoting this, R then identified himself with Adams:

> I confess readily that I could be one of those three persons. Politically and socially I am always on hand bright and early with a plan (though in my defense I should add that I seldom have faith in it), and I am consistently uneasy in the presence of Do-Nothingness.... I am not sure that I should blame my compulsions on my ancestry, as Mr. Tate suggests, but I do sympathize with his disapproval of the compulsions themselves. Is it not unhappy to be, like Henry Adams, constitutionally disposed to alter, reform, improve the world when one knows perfectly well that the world will not thereby be altered, reformed, improved? I think so. Thus I have been unhappy with myself all these years, and though my unhappiness has not prevented me from attending a political rally occasionally, or joining some "action" group, it has probably kept me from displaying my positivism in my own poetry. For better or worse Mr. Tate has been an influence upon me here; his words against positivism have helped to guide my literary, if not my social fortunes.

R went on to Tate and his role as a New Critic who taught that a poem should be read on its own terms, an anti-positivist position. The new critics "have insisted, as Mr. Tate put it, that poetry 'is neither religion nor social engineering.' This is the New Criticism, is it not, which is celebrated for supplying us in poetry with what Henry Adams was always looking for in society, 'a procedure, a program, an objective.... The New Criticism has, in other words, bred its own kind of positivism even while preaching against the other kinds.'" R of course then qualified his observations, saying that Tate was not a reductionist, that the Henry Adams in him did not go towards making the analysis of poetry "a process of simplification and paraphrase." Tate wrote a friendly note later on address-

ing R as "Dear Mr. Adams" and remarking on the absurdity of scientiz-
ing human enterprise, whether in the social sciences or the reading and
analysis of poetry.

R's own impieties did not enter *Six Literary Lives* directly. Nor did those
of the two writers, Pound and Eliot, who had done most to mold his own
notions of impiety. Pound had been the obsessed reformer lurking
behind *Furioso*, and Eliot was the snobbish literary genius who, as editor
of *The Criterion* for twenty years, had been oh so loftily political, that he
described future Nobel competitor Winston Churchill's prose as "a low
verbal point in a low time." Perhaps more important he had actually published politically impious literature in *The Criterion*, including work by a
fascist or two, and had kept the magazine steadily though snobbishly on
the edge of trouble by saying such things as, "politics is too important to
be left to politicians."

As a socialist of sorts, R had often wondered why both Eliot and EP
seemed largely concerned with saving civilization from the masses rather
than the politicians. (Eliot's summary of the former: "immense numbers
of men and women voting all together without using their reason and
without enquiry.") R was hardly a prole himself but he did like to imagine that the common man was a healthy phenomenon. And he did know
that both Eliot and Pound were insistently uncommon. How tiresome.
He found himself steadily glooming about the Social Sciences and their
apparent determination to take over human understanding. The presence
of the social sciences as an insistent opponent of what he imagined standing for had been with him since undergraduate days and had then constantly simmered during his early teaching life. While doing Freshman
English, for instance he was impressed by a now almost paleolithic sample of social science — an excerpt from the celebrated book, *Middletown*,
by Robert and Helen Lynd. At that time he was much too busy reading
student themes to be a serious Bartleby about Middletown's average
houses, but the Lynds did happen to write well, while the averaging procedures by which those houses were presented lingered darkly with him.
Did they have any bearing upon the writing of poetry? It seemed not, and
yet one might at least dream of their relevance.

Then somewhere down the road he picked up a poet model, Kenneth
Fearing, who had written steadily of the miseries of Middletown's social
science living, as in "Andy and Jerry and Joe."

We were staring at the bottles in the restaurant window,
We could hear the autos go by,
We were looking at the women on the boulevard,
It was cold,
No one else knew about the things we knew.

We watched the crowd, there was murder in the papers, the wind blew
    hard, it was dark,
We didn't know what to do,
There was no place to go and we had nothing to say,
We listened to the bells, and voices, and whistles, and cars,
We moved on,
We weren't dull, or wise, or afraid,
We didn't feel tired, or restless, or happy, or sad.

There were a million stars, a million miles, a million people,
    a million words,
A million places and a million years,
We knew a lot of things we could hardly understand,
There were liners at sea, and rows of houses here, and clouds that flowed
    past us away up in the sky.
We waited on the corner,
The lights were in the stores, there were women on the streets, Jerry's father
    was dead,
We didn't know what we wanted and there was nothing to say,
Andy had an auto and Joe had a girl.

And Fearing's ironies also took in the la-di-da arts culture existing above
Andy, Jerry and Joe, though R was embarrassed (a tiny bit) to find his own
(misspelled) name well JOBBED by the man.

At the Friday meeting of the Browning Writing League, Mrs. Whittamore
    Ralston-Beckett,
Traveler, lecturer, novelist, critic, poet, playwright, editor, mother, idealist,
Fascinated her audience with a brief talk, whimsical and caustic,
Appealing to the younger generation to take a brighter, happier, more
    sunny and less morbid view of life's eternal fundamentals.
                            (from Fearing's "Cultural Notes")

Yes, in the 1930s Fearing, a mere sixteen years older than R, had become
a thorough cynic about American averagings, and after WWII — having
been brought before the McCarthy Committee as a likely Communist vil-

lain — he was even rejected by his New York publishers and obliged to find a university press (Indiana) for his last book. To that he attached a thoroughly JOBBISH preface that R, for better or worse, found admirable. Here is a sample paragraph from it.

> Even the suggestion of discord between the electronic world and the satellite press seems monstrous. All time and space in every medium is merchandise, so expensive and profitable in the great treasure hunt of the day that not a moment, not a line can be wasted on matters irrelevant to communications as a flourishing commerce. What other better kind of free speech can there possibly be than news and opinion that pays dividends?

That final rhetorical question had a fine Fearing flavor, and while he had clearly needed a few corrupt dividends when he posed it (he was trying to make a living by his writing and did produce one successful mystery story, *The Big Clock*), R's own Bartleby heart was warmed. To think that Fearing (playing Bartleby) could write — and so effectively —about what he preferred not to live. So, thirty-five years after Fearing's last volume's appearance, R found himself in Maryland's McKeldin Library looking him up once more. And right away he was further warmed by finding a graduate thesis about Fearing that he himself had personally directed.

Patricia Santora was the author and she had done well — her thesis was the only work about Fearing in that large library though there were scores and scores about Pound and Eliot. Fearing had been no admirer of either, and among the quotations in the Santora volume was this one from Fearing himself back in 1949 as he thought of the postwar academic rush into the New Criticism: "The poetry of the colleges — or may we call it the finishing school of verse? — is, first, incoherent, secondly, saturated with a pointless erudition and, finally, when it is at all intelligible, argues for social, political and economic reaction."

Fearing's last years had been full of sour grapes — as well as clumsy sentences — as his reputation sadly declined, but R was at least happy to find the grapes well-represented in Santora's work. He signed her thesis out, went home with it (along with a ten-year old edition of Fearing's selected poems that seemed to have helped little in reviving him) and found in the mail a new issue of the *Yale Alumni Magazine* containing a finishing-school-of-verse remark that would have made Fearing snicker.

One of the things to be said about poetry is that it is valuable precisely because it resists being reduced to the criterion of usefulness, which governs the economy. You can be concerned, in and through poetry, with things that most of us don't get concerned with in our jobs. You can consider, reflect on, and enjoy non-useful uses of language; you take time to think and feel, and to think and feel at the same time.

This kindly "finishing-school" statement was by Yale's Director of Undergraduate Studies in English, Langdon Hammer. R was tempted to write Mr. H and suggest that he read a bit of Fearing. But there was the difficulty that finishing-school authorities such as Hammer were not the crucial managerial authorities in contemporary American thought that the aging reformer R kept having bad dreams about.

———

Then suddenly a fine anti-climax arrived: R was asked to serve on a committee. It was an innocent offer composed of a dozen members of a small non-profit organization, The International Society of Panetics (ISP). R belonged because it had been started by Ralph Siu with the help of Carl Stover, R's friend who had in the mid-1960s hired him at The National Institute of Public Affairs. According to the ISP literature, panetics was a "pan-ethical search for ways to reduce human suffering inflicted by individuals acting through governments, institutions, professions and social groups." There was a journal *Panetics*, which R's friends Stover and Peter Caws had written for.

As a member R only had to place suggestions for particular projects into the daily pot — until a meeting with other members in a large hotel for two long days produced a few clear objectives. Then a self-professed "systems engineer" took over — he went around the table eighty times with eighty yes-or-no questions for each member of the committee to answer and then turned the results over to his computer.

Of course R had experienced Gallup poll statistics and complex election results. He had also experienced a handbook produced by Gallup's organization called *The Quality of Life in America*, statistics for which had been produced by polling 2164 Americans about their (individual uncomplex) "sense of well-being." The pollsters explored this sense by the complex use of words like "happiness," "well being" and even "the good," though the latter was only mentioned with regard to uncomplex matters like neighborhood police protection. Happiness was hard for pollsters, but near the end of their question-quest they mastered it by proposing the following complex masterpiece: "Taking all things together, how would you say things are these days? Would you say you're *very* happy, *pretty* happy or *not too* happy?"

So at the end of the IPS meeting R would have liked to supply his own response — unhappy — to all such questions. And in the back of his mind he found himself also concocting a project by which old popular tales would be converted to contemporary pollster standards. For instance, how about "Robin Hood and His Not Too Happy Men." He went home from the IPS meeting more complexly than the systems engineer would have wished him to, and after two days of meditation sent in his resignation from the ISP to the organizations' president. His second resignation! So he was jobbing in Bartleby fashion against *two* fine established organizations. What next?

In old age, one can live a simplistically caged condition, with or without television. The condition is magnified, however, by the helplessness one feels when the outside comes crashing in because it is deemed to be a wicked outside by the gallupized forces of freedom inside, forces like those that flew American bombers to Iraq in 2003. Once more R was a peacenik, this time against the U.S. invasion of Iraq, though as before he did little beyond writing and even reading against this war. "The Weapons of Mass Destruction" he wrote before the invasion, and then later read in small Takoma Park, Maryland, at an anti-war reading in the city's council chambers.

Oh!
You should know
That Weapons M.D., Weapons M.D.,
Threatening all mortal beings with instant catastrophe,
Are now being made in more than one evil foreign country,
Foreign country,

But oh! oh!
Lucky we are to be making our very own Weapons M.D.
That are bigger and better and much more democratic
Weapons M.D.

Than any weapons M.D.
Made by an evil foreign country,

And oh! oh! oh!
We have our morality,
Our lovely sweet American morality
To fight off catastrophe
Brought on by any bad evil arrogant foreign country
With their weapons M.D.,
Weapons M.D.

Unlike his younger years with *Furioso*, he has no angry I-told-you-so editorial to present about the national condition but was depressed by how
far the "free" world as a whole had moved away from Thoreau's (and
archaic little mag editors') complaints about the world. The archaic condition known as individualism — by which one can at least profess to be,
if not alone, at least an entity living quietly outside the monstrous human
age — no longer existed even when living quietly next to a quiet woods
in College Park (owned by the Washington Metro).

So R lies awake at night listening to the distant rumbling and tooting
of old-fashioned earthy CSX trains but knowing more than Thoreau
seems to have.

⁓

Now it is 2007 and R is on his way to 88. All his old literary comrades are
long gone. Arthur Mizener (1977), Allen Tate (1979), Jim Angleton
(1987), John Pauker (1991), Howard Nemerov (1992), Bill Johnson
(2004). At the moment he's not looking for a grand exit but simply for a
way to end this memoir. One idea had been to wind down with 24
improvisational poems he wrote by taking alphabetically each volume of
the *Encyclopedia Britannica* 11th edition that he's been carrying around all
these years, turning to a page randomly and starting from there. But a few
weeks later as he reread the poems, he was not much taken by them,
except for one, "Jazz," which found its way into a chapbook of his poems
that Dryad Press published this year, *Ten from Ten & One More*.

Jazz is of course missing from Enc Brit Eleven
Though it crops up, bold child of progress, in later editions
Where its origins among blacks are deeply discussed

And Benny Goodman, a hero of mine, is mentioned,
Along with dozens of others that experts like me
Once lived with.
Many styles are even described
Such as blues, ragtime and swing,
And many deep books are listed though most were composed
As late as the Sixties when of course I
Might have written better ones. .
I grant that my skill with the art remains, even now,
Immense,
And surely no true expert would ever doubt
(Were he to hear me play just one giant chord
Of "In My Solitude")
That I have been pounding the keys ever since childhood.
Alas, I have not been doing so, and now must admit
That I've learned only words, words, words in my eighty-seven years.
My piano sits in the living room waiting.

He also thought about a grand serious summing up, though after all these pages it seemed to him it would be anti-climactic. Anyway, the mind was no longer up to much seriousness he discovered as he and Cicely Angleton exchanged rueful comments on the toll of aging.

my mind she go
so me no know
where now i go
but that's no woe
like stubbing toe
so let me grow
as old and slow
as methusalow

He then thought to bow out with his "Ode to Walt Whitman" but it is quite long, though at 150 lines not as long as some of Walt's meanderings. In writing that poem, he started with the trouble he had with Walt "Ever since I became critical/ He babbled, ran on at the mouth" but found that by the end he was "grateful to him now...for just being Walt," though the writing (he also added) had not cured his headache. So finally, he's decided on a decidedly shorter exit, with a poem that is not

wordy but of words — "The Word Man" — which he's been, and more he
hopes, all these many years.

    the busy word man is tired
    he is lying down
    he is lying down with his pad
    he is lying down with his pad and writing these words
    but lowly
    slowly
    wanting to slow the flow
    the flow
    thinking slowly
    thinking that if he could slow the flow
    the flow of the words
    if he could sleep on the words
    the words
    before writing the words
    the right words
    then the crisis at Babel
    at Babel
    the sadly towering critical crisis at Babel
    could be —

    — what?
    what could the right words be
    or perhaps the right single word
    that would hasten the slowing
    or even the stopping
    of words flowing
    flowing
    and making the crisis ever more critically critical
    at babbling Babel?

    a noun like Jahweh possibly?
    or two legal verbs like cease and desist mayhap?
    or even something commanding and simple like no?
    no?

no none of these words seems quite right and the word man is dozing
dozing
his pad is falling
falling
floorward
floorward
and Babel is still
still
and the stars are wordlessly shining
shining
over Babel
Babel

spirit pleads feebly with him
to stop chattering
he generously does
he sleeps

A Literary Chronology

1939-53 *Furioso*, co-founder and editor
1941-45 U.S. Army Air Force
1946 *Heroes & Heroines* (Reynal & Hitchcock)
1947-66 Professor, Carleton College
1954 Harriet Monroe Memorial Prize, *Poetry* magazine
1956 *An American Takes a Walk* (University of Minnesota Press)
1959 *The Self-Made Man and Other Poems* (Macmillan)
1960-64 *The Carleton Miscellany*, founder and editor
1960 *Robert Browning*, Editor (Dell)
1962 *The Boy from Iowa: Poems and Essays* (Macmillan)
     Emily Clark Balch Prize, *Virginia Quarterly Review*
1963 *The Fascination of the Abomination: Poems, Stories, and Essays* (Macmillan)
1963 *Little Magazines* (University of Minnesota Pamphlets on American Writers)
1964-65 Consultant in Poetry to Library of Congress
1965 *Ways of Misunderstanding Poetry* (Library of Congress)
1965 *Return Alpheus: A Poem for the Literary Editors of Phi Beta Kappa* (King & Queen Press)
1966-68 National Institute of Public Affairs, Program Associate
1966 *The Little Magazine and Contemporary Literature: A Symposium Held at the Library of Congress, 2nd and 3rd April, 1965* (Modern Language Association)
1967 Bain-Swiggert Lecturer, Princeton University
1967 *From Zero to the Absolute* (Crown Publishers)
1967-84 Professor, University of Maryland
1967 *Poems: New and Selected* (University of Minnesota Press)
1969 National Council on the Arts Award for lifelong contribution to American letters
1969-73 Literary Editor, *The New Republic*
1970 *Fifty Poems Fifty* (University of Minnesota Press)
     American Academy of Arts and Letters: Award of Merit Medal
1971 Litt. D. Honorary Doctorate from Carleton College
1974 *The Mother's Breast & The Father's House* (Houghton-Mifflin)

1975   *William Carlos Williams: Poet from Jersey* (Houghton-Mifflin)
1975   *The Poet as Journalist: Life at the New Republic* (The New
            Republic Book Company)
1976   Travel to USSR (sponsored by USAID)
1977   *A Whittemore Miscellany,* sound recording (Watershed
            Intermedia)
1982   *The Feel of Rock: Poems New & Selected* (Dryad Press)
1983   Travel to Israel (sponsored by USAID)
1984   *William Carlos Williams: "The Happy Genius of the Household"*
            (Library of Congress)
1985-86 Interim Consultant in Poetry to Library of Congress
1985-88 Poet Laureate of Maryland
1986   *Poets and Anthologists: A Look at the Current Poet-packaging
            Process* (Library of Congress)
1988   *Pure Lives: The Early Biographers* (John Hopkins University
            Press)
1989   *Whole Lives: Shapers of Modern Biography* (Johns Hopkins
            University Press)
1988-92 *Delos,* Editor
1988   *The Past, the Future, the Present: Poems Selected and New*
            (University of Arkansas Press)
1993   *Six Literary Lives: The Shared Impiety of Adams, London, Sinclair,
            Williams, Dos Passos, and Tate* (University of Missouri Press)
2006   Author of Year Award from Maryland Library Association
2007   *Ten from Ten & One More* (chapbook; Dryad Press)
2007   *A Season of Waiting: Selected Poems, 1946-2006,* trans. into
            Hebrew by Moshe Dor (Keshev Publishing House, Israel)

Publisher's Afterword

I first read Reed Whittemore's work in the early 60s in *The Fascination of the Abomination*, his Conradian-titled collection of poetry and prose. I've been reading him ever since. I have long been compelled by his singular voice, a voice that can be comic and grave simultaneously, dead-on serious, satiric as most of his readers know, self-deprecating, witty and funny, sometimes angry, and lurking underneath it all, skeptically romantic. Romantic in that poetry *means* and is of the utmost importance — while I can imagine Reed quoting Auden's line, "Poetry makes nothing happen," I can also see him nodding imperceptibly to William Carlos Williams's often-quoted lines, "it is difficult/ to get the news from poems/ yet men die miserably every day/ for lack/ of what is found there." Both pertain.

In 1982, Dryad Press published *The Feel of Rock: Poems of Three Decades* and this year a chapbook, *Ten from Ten & One More*. I have written about his work on several occasions, most recently in the introduction to *A Season of Waiting: Poems 1946-2006* that Moshe Dor translated into Hebrew. Even before reading the draft of Reed's memoir, I knew that if given the opportunity, I would publish it.

Here he now was in his memoir, looking back over a long literary life that began even earlier than his founding of *Furioso* with Jim Angleton in the late Thirties. I took the manuscript home excitedly — I loved the narration right off, that first-person I telling the story of R. It seemed perfect for Reed, a point of view that gave him distance but also the latitude to speak personally and impersonally without having to resort constantly to the ego-driven I. I looked forward to hearing him speak on the page — his prose is engagingly conversational — about *Furioso*, his literary friendships, his year as Poetry Consultant at the Library of Congress, his editing the literary pages of *The New Republic*, the Williams biography, which I have some vague memories of having helped out on, and more.

By the time I was halfway through the manuscript, I was surprised — not by what I had learned about his literary life but by all that I had not and wanted to. One example. In two chapters, Reed wrote about his four

325

wartime years as a transportation and supply officer in England, North Africa, and Italy. When the war was over — he was discharged, a Major, in 1945 — he went home to his father's apartment in New Haven. Then, in 1946, Reynal & Hitchcock, a commercial publisher, brought out his first book of poetry, *Heroes & Heroines*. How did that happen? Where did the poems come from? When did he write them? It must have been during the war, at least many of them, but in the original draft, he glossed over all of these details as if not wanting to make a fuss. His New England reserve?

When I asked about the poems, he spoke off-handedly of the many books his father was sending to him overseas, about his sitting on a balcony in Naples writing sonnets about Tess of the D'Urbervilles, Moll Flanders, Conrad's Lord Jim, Sherlock Holmes and other literary figures — poems that accounted for a large number in that first book.

A second example. Reed wrote warmly of his friendship with Arthur Mizener and alluded to their correspondence during the war; however, there were no excerpts from the letters — some of them, if they existed, should be in the memoir, I thought. Other details were also lacking. Reed of course wrote of Pound's role in *Furioso* and of Pound spending the night in his parents' apartment, but I had lots of questions. For instance, how did the connection with Pound come about? How did the post-war *Furioso* get started? What about *The Carleton Miscellany*? There were a few paragraphs but many of what Delmore Schwartz called the "priceless particulars" were not there.

Reed could be quite scholarly with other people's lives — there is the Williams biography for one, *Poet from Jersey*, and *Six Literary Lives: The Shared Impiety of Adams, London, Sinclair, Williams, Dos Passos and Tate*. But he had not been up to scouring the past for details of his own literary development. One reason maybe was temperament — again, that Yankee reserve. Another reason was that he had begun to notice problems he was having with memory as he was completing the first draft of his memoir.

I offered to help by looking in archives for correspondence and other material. Reed agreed. I began at the University of Maryland's Hornbake Library, which has Reed's papers, starting with Mizener. I was amazed, though not yet overwhelmed: there was folder after folder of both sides of letters that went back to the late 30s and continued into the 50s. I went through as much as I could over several long days, excerpting passages that I thought anyone interested in poetry, let alone Reed's literary life, would love to read and think about. I then went knocking on Reed and Helen's door — over these last couple of years, I have kept knocking and they have kept opening the door.

What about the *Furioso* papers? They were at the Beinecke Library at Yale where he and Jim had donated them, maybe in the 50s sometime. All that pre-war correspondence was there with Pound, Williams, Cummings, Marianne Moore, Eliot, Richard Eberhart, and others — many others. There was also the post-war *Furioso* and the enormous correspondence among Reed, Howard Nemerov, John Pauker, Bill Johnson, Ambrose Gordon. The University of Washington at St. Louis had another large trove of correspondence with Nemerov — both sides of letters sent back and forth for forty years. What had I gotten myself into! Meanwhile, I would continue to appear at the house in College Park with handfuls of folders. I could imagine Reed saying to himself as I drove up, uh oh, M's here again. What is it now?

But the correspondence wasn't all. There were the essays and lectures in which Reed was taking on issues that were also reflected in his poetry and that I believed were important for poets a generation and two removed. There should be, I felt, at least a few excerpts from those. Then there were the poems: Reed originally thought to use one in each chapter. I felt the book needed more, many more — this was the literary memoir of a poet after all. And one whose books weren't in print. Thus the memoir went through several revisions over more than two years, expanding as we went along.

So here it is, the memoir that Reed Whittemore has fashioned, grafting to his original manuscript material I kept bringing over and helped find places for. As he writes in the Preface, no biography or autobiography, let alone a literary memoir such as this one, gives us a person whole — rather, if the writer is honest and doesn't fudge, we will have glimpses that enable us to get a sense of the whole person himself. I believe this memoir does that — I feel privileged to have had a small role in its making.

MERRILL LEFFLER

Acknowledgments

I began this memoir of R's literary life a number of years ago. Over this time it has gone through several revisions, mostly additions from R's books of poetry and essays but especially from correspondence that goes back to the pre-war and post-war days of *Furioso*. These additions were in part at the instigation of Merrill Leffler, publisher of Dryad Press, who kept showing up with material that I had either not considered or had forgotten about — he braved reading and commenting on each of the successive versions, then editing and proofreading the whole. Along the way, several former students, colleagues and friends have offered comments, for which I am most grateful. First and foremost is Saundra Rose Maley, author of *Solitary Apprenticeship: James Wright and German Poetry* and co-editor of *A Wild Perfection: The Selected Letters of James Wright*. She started early and stayed till the finale. Early readers were Ann Slayton, Joyce Kornblatt, Jack Greer and daughter Cate Whittemore. More recent comments came from Mel Raff and Judith Harris, a former student of R's at the University of Maryland, whose newest book of poetry is *The Bad Secret*.

I am also grateful to numbers of libraries and librarians who have been most courteous in sending material that R had long ago put away or didn't know even existed. These include the University of Maryland Libraries where his papers are housed and Beth (Ruth M.) Alvarez, the indefatigable Curator of Literary Manuscripts; the Yale Collection of American Literature, Beinecke Rare Book and Manuscript Library for the *Furioso* papers that R and James Angleton had long ago deposited there, and especially Leigh Golden, Public Services Assistant; Harry Ransom Humanities Research Center at The University of Texas at Austin; and Molly Schwartzburg, Curator of British and American Literature, Washington University Libraries, Saint Louis; Upper Midwest Literary Archives; University of Minnesota Libraries; Department of Special Collections; and Stanford University Libraries

With regard to correspondence, I want to thank the following: Rosemary Mizener Colt for permission to quote from letters by Arthur Mizener to R and Margaret Nemerov for quotations from correspondence with Howard Nemerov. Letters and excerpts from the work of Ezra Pound and William Carlos Williams are used by permission of New Directions Publishing Corporation. The letters to James Angleton are copyright © 2007 by Mary de Rachewiltz and Omar S. Pound. Letters from William Carlos Williams to Reed Whittemore are copyright ©2007 by the Estates of William Eric Williams and Paul H. Williams.

For the poems and prose I've published over more than sixty years and that are included in this memoir, I'd like to make a blanket thank-you and acknowledgment to all my publishers, which included the following: Reynal and Hitchcock: *Heroes & Heroines*; University of Minnesota Press: *An American Takes a Walk, Poems: New and Selected*, and *Fifty Poems Fifty*; Macmillan Company: *The Self-Made Man, The Boy From Iowa*, and *The Fascination of the Abomination*; Crown: *From Zero to the Absolute*; Dryad Press: *The Feel of Rock* and *Ten from Ten & One More*; Houghton-Mifflin Company: *The Mother's Breast and the Father's House* and *William Carlos Williams: Poet from Jersey*; Johns Hopkins University Press: *Pure Lives: The Early Biographers* and *Whole Lives: Shapers of Modern Biography*; University of Missouri Press: *Six Literary Lives: The Shared Impiety of Adams, London, Sinclair, Williams, Dos Passos and Tate*; University of Arkansas Press: *The Past, The Present, The Future*; New Republic Books: *The Poet as Journalist: Life at The New Republic*; Gale Publishing House: "Reed Whittemore," *Contemporary Authors* (vol. 219). If I have missed acknowledging any publishers or authors I have quoted from, it is of course inadvertent and I extend my apologies.

Index

331

About the Author

Reed Whittemore is the author of 20 books of poetry, criticism, biography and literary journalism. A former Consultant in Poetry to the Library of Congress (now U.S. Poet Laureate), his book *The Mother's Breast and the Father's House* was a nominee for the National Book Award for poetry. With James Angleton in the late 30s, he founded *Furioso*, which he then reconstituted after four wartime years in England, North Africa and Italy. "It was the *ne plus ultra* of little magazines," says Victor Navasky. In 1947, Mr. Whittemore began teaching at Carleton College, where he started *The Carleton Miscellany*. Returning to the east, he taught at the University of Maryland, served as literary editor of *The New Republic* in the 70s, and authored *William Carlos Williams: Poet from Jersey*. He is the recipient of the National Council on the Arts Award for his life-long contribution to American Letters and the Award of Merit Medal from the American Academy of Arts and Letters. In 2006 the Maryland Library Association selected him as Author of the Year. A collection of his poetry in Hebrew was published in Israel this year: *Season of Waiting: Selected Poems 1946-2006*. He lives in College Park, Maryland, with his wife Helen.